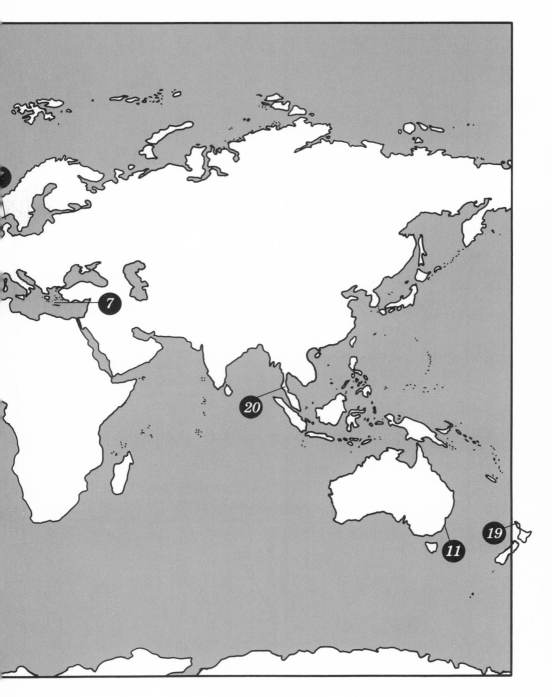

BEST SAILING SPOTS WORLDWIDE

▶▶▶▶▶▶▶▶▶▶▶▶▶▶▶

BEST SAILING SPOTS WORLDWIDE

BILL ROBINSON

HEARST MARINE BOOKS

New York

Library of Congress Cataloging-in-Publication Data

Robinson, Bill, 1918–
Best sailing spots worldwide / Bill Robinson.
p.   cm.
ISBN 0-688-10214-X
1. Yachts and yachting—Guide-books.   2. Sailing—Guide-books.
I. Title.
GV813.R565   1991
796.1'246—dc20   91-9446
                                                          CIP

Printed in the United States of America

First Edition

1 2 3 4 5 6 7 8 9 10

Book design and maps by ARLENE SCHLEIFER GOLDBERG

ACKNOWLEDGMENTS

The following have been helpful in various ways in making this book possible, and I thank them very much.

Messrs. Sohei Horii and Joseph Jackson of the New York Yacht Club Library gave valuable assistance and guidance in research. Sam Hinckley provided proofreading assistance based on personal experience as crew aboard my boats. Henry Bayard Clark, Finn Ferner, Arne Brun-Lie, Carl and Shirley Boll, William Lapworth, Severin Lovenskiold, Ray Pedersen, and Vasos Papagapitos cooperated in providing boats used. Assistance in arranging charters was provided by Robert Van Ost, CSY (BVI) Ltd., P.O. Box 152379, Tampa, Florida 33684-2379; Simon Scott, The Moorings, 1305 US 19 South, Clearwater, Florida 34624; Graham and Judy Millar, South Seas Yachts, Inc., Box 160, Volcano, Hawaii 96705; Tony and Tulimah Cozad, Asia Islands Yacht Charters Pte. Ltd., 78 Shenton Way #16-01, Singapore 0207; Vincent Tabuteau, Asia Voyages Phuket, 64/1 Pansea Boutique, Rasda Road, Rasda Centre, Phuket 83000, Thailand; the staffs of Floating Through Europe, 271 Madison Avenue, New York, N.Y. 10016 and Rainbow Yacht Charters New Zealand, 3471 Via Lido STE 206, Newport Beach, California, 92663.

The Armchair Sailor Bookstore, Lee's Wharf, Newport, Rhode Island 02840, provided checklists of reference reading for all cruising areas. Books still in print are available through them, as are charts, chart lists, and lists of guidebooks and other nautical titles. Of my books listed, all but *Caribbean Cruising Handbook* are out of print and are available only through libraries or dealers specializing in out-of-print books.

PREFACE

When Captain Joshua Slocum sailed alone around the world at the end of the nineteenth century, his feat had something of the public impact of Lindbergh's flight across the Atlantic a quarter century later: Slocum's voyage was a remarkable first, and he became a national hero. He had conquered an awesome world of long, lonely ocean passages (covering 4,000–6,000 miles) and some of the places he touched were virtually unheard-of in the civilized world.

Now, almost a century later, it is a vastly different world for the sailor, shrunk especially by developments in Lindbergh's field and made more familiar by countless long-voyagers emulating Slocum. They do it either alone, with a small crew, as married couples, or even as families with children (and they mostly use the Panama Canal instead of fighting their way through Tierra del Fuego). Long-voyagers today are to Slocum what transatlantic jet travelers are to Lindbergh.

The distant glamor ports, which evoke the mystique of the early long voyages, such as Antigua, Tahiti, Bali, Rhodes, the Canaries, and many more, are now routine havens for sailors and bases for local activity. And, though the long-voyagers continue to proliferate, not everyone needs

to make the four-thousand-mile passage to taste the joys
of exotic cruising grounds throughout the world. In this
age of the jet plane, fiberglass boat construction, and multiple charter companies worldwide, it is possible, within
the time span of a normal vacation, to experience Tonga,
Phuket, the Aegean, the Swedish skerries, or the multiple
attractions of the Caribbean, to name but a few far away
paradises. Also, owners who are not by any means full-
time, get-away-from-it-all long-voyagers, can now make one
passage to take their boat to distant waters and then com-
mute to her by air as the occasion presents.

In a cruising career that began when I was a wide-eyed
and completely hooked thirteen-year-old in 1932, I have
been fortunate enough to have been able to take in most
of the world's top cruising areas, both in my own boats in
an area bounded by the Great Lakes, Maine, and Grenada;
and in flying visits to the more distant waters of North
America, Europe, the Far East, and the Pacific. These
cruises have resulted in magazine articles and books in
varying forms, but I have never before put the experience
of a lifetime together in one book. This, then, is my personal "encyclopedia" of the world's cruising grounds, presented so that planners can know what to expect when
choosing an area, or along the route of a long voyage, and
armchair sailors can dream of "someday." To evoke the feel
of each area, I give at least one firsthand account of a cruise
that has not been included in any of my previous books
(most are from recent experience), followed by the practical information required for that area. (Reading material
is suggested for several chapters; complete entries for all
books appear in the Bibliography on page 297.) I have
grouped the cruises according to the Northern Hemisphere
season during which it is best to visit areas.

Because areas like Fiji, Tonga, Australia's Great Barrier Reef, the Caicos, the Adriatic, and a few others that I
have visited only once have been written up in *Over the
Horizon, The Sailing Life, South to the Caribbean,* and
Where to Cruise, they are missing from the personal experience accounts here, though they are covered in the area
background information. Instead of giving the name and

English Harbour, Antigua, a favorite stopover of long voyagers

address and rates of charter companies, which are often subject to change, I recommend the classified charter ads in the boating magazines as the best way to get the latest information.

Our world is a smaller and much more accessible one than Slocum's, and there is a wealth of marvelous opportunities for sailors to choose from, whether for a normal vacation or a lifetime of long-voyaging. Enjoy it!

CONTENTS

Acknowledgments   **5**

Preface   **7**

PART I: Summer

1 Splendid Desolation: *The Best of the Pacific
   Northwest*   **17**
      Additional Information: The Pacific
      Northwest   **26**
2 Balmy Newfoundland: *Easy Cruising on
   Its East Coast*   **29**
3 A Good "Invention": *Southern New England
   Waters*   **39**
      Additional Information: The Northeast **49**
4 The West Coast of New England: *What
   Vermonters Call Their Lake Champlain Shore*   **52**
      Additional Information: Inland   **60**
5 The Skagerrak's Shores of Norway and Sweden   **63**
      Additional Information: Scandinavia   **73**
6 A Dutch Treat: *Canal Barging in Holland*   **76**
      Additional Information: British Isles and
      the Continent   **85**

PART II: Spring and Fall

7   Not Really Wine Dark: *The Aegean of
    Many Legends*   *91*
        Additional Information: The Aegean and
        Mediterranean   *99*
8   Never in Summer, But Otherwise "Yes"
    for the Chesapeake   *103*
9   A Civilized Cruise: *Florida's West Coast*   *113*
        Additional Information: The Intracoastal
        Waterway and Florida   *121*
10 Making the Most of the Coast: *Northern and
    Southern California*   *125*
        Additional Information: California and
        Mexico   *134*
11 One-City Cruise: *Sydney, Australia, Has
    the Makings*   *136*

PART III: Winter

12 Hub of the Bahamas: *Fanning Out from
    Nassau's Central Location*   *147*
        Additional Information: The Bahamas
        and Caicos   *157*
13 Learning from Children: *A New Look at the
    British Virgins*   *161*
14 Three-Nation Cruise: *In the St. Martin Area*   *175*
15 The High Islands: *The Mountainous Lesser
    Antilles*   *186*
16 The Low Islands: *The Well-Situated Grenadines*   *198*
        Additional Information: The Caribbean   *209*
17 Tall Ship in the Trades: *From Easter Island
    to the Galapagos*   *214*
18 To Leeward of Tahiti: *The Raiatea–Bora Bora
    Area*   *227*

19 In Captain Cook's Wake: *New Zealand's Bay
    of Islands*   *239*
        Additional Information: The South Pacific   *253*
20 The Mysterious (South) East: *Cruising Out of
    Phuket, Thailand*   *256*
        Additional Information: Southeast Asia
        and the Islands   *269*

PART IV: Afterthoughts

21 Long-Voyage Routes   *273*
22 How to Arrange Charters   *283*
23 Personal Opinions: *Boats and Rigs*   *289*

    Bibliography   *297*

    Index   *300*

PART I

SUMMER

The cruising grounds discussed in this section are those that are available, either near at hand or with some travel, in a North American summer. Although, with a bit of luck, the season may be extended at both ends in some areas, they all are at their best at the height of the season in July and August. Though their geographic spread is wide, general conditions are basically the same.

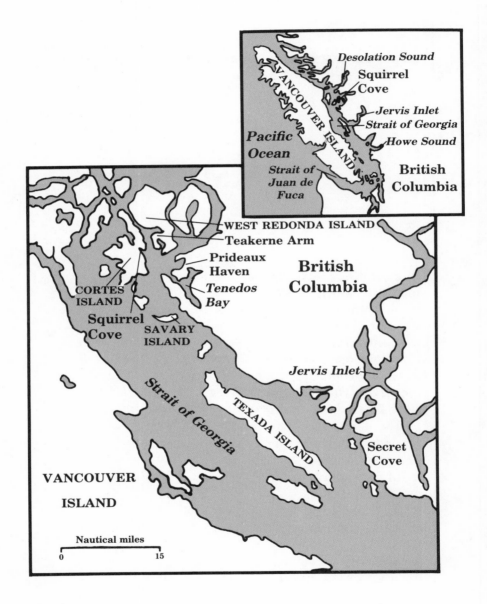

Desolation Sound
Squirrel Cove
Jervis Inlet
Strait of Georgia
Howe Sound
VANCOUVER ISLAND
Pacific Ocean
Strait of Juan de Fuca
British Columbia

WEST REDONDA ISLAND
Teakerne Arm
Prideaux Haven
Tenedos Bay
British Columbia
CORTES ISLAND
Squirrel Cove
SAVARY ISLAND
Jervis Inlet
Strait of Georgia
TEXADA ISLAND
Secret Cove
VANCOUVER ISLAND

Nautical miles
0   15

1

▶ ▶ ▶ ▶ ▶ ▶ ▶ ▶ ▶ ▶ ▶ ▶ ▶ ▶

SPLENDID DESOLATION
The Best of the Pacific Northwest

The seaplane skittered across the sheen of the harbor, leaped into flight, and circled up to the north with a fine view of Vancouver's waterfront. Canada Place, the great white building with a shiplike profile, stood out along the shore, and Stanley Park, a restful area of green set right against the city, soon slid out of sight. At three thousand feet, we leveled off and flew northwestward along the eastern coast of the Strait of Georgia. To our right, we could see the Coast Mountains ranging off into the blue distance with the deep indentations of Howe Sound and Jervis Inlet, wonderful cruising grounds in themselves, but we were bound one hundred miles onward to Desolation Sound. This was all new country to us, and we looked forward to a different kind of cruising under snowcapped peaks. Already, we could see snow on some of the heights of the Coast Mountains, and it was an exciting prospect of a new adventure.

My musings on venturing into new cruising grounds were broken into by a question from the pilot, a casual bearded young fellow.

"Now just where are these boats you're meeting up with?" he asked.

"Haven't you been told?" was my surprised reply. Arrangements had been made for us by the West Coast office of *Cruising World* magazine, and I assumed that all that information had been passed along.

"No. I thought you knew," said the pilot.

"Well, I think it's Tenedos Bay," I said. "Do you know it?"

"I've heard of it, but I'm not sure."

Fortunately, I had studied the charts a bit in advance, and I found Tenedos on the pilot's aerial chart. Together we eyeballed our way into the area, and it was a relief to see two cruising sloops rafted together in the middle of the bay, obviously the boats we were looking for.

We curved down to a smooth landing and an inflatable headed for us. Seaplanes are the "taxis" of this part of the world; to the pilot, ferrying passengers was as routine as a cabbie taking someone to Penn Station in New York. As we waved good-bye, he spun the plane, gunned it, and curved off around the hills heading back to Vancouver.

The boats were two steel-hulled sloops, an Amazon 37 and a 44, built by the SP Metalcraft Company in Surrey, British Columbia, near Vancouver; they were ruggedly handsome and as smoothly finished as any fiberglass, aluminum, or wooden yacht. Unfortunately, SP went out of business soon after our visit, but not because of the quality of their boats—perhaps because of too much quality. The 37 was *Invictus IV*, which my wife Jane and I and our friends Debbie and Jack Haight were to operate, along with Jim Gray from *Cruising World*. Cruising in company was the 44, *Mara Maru* from Friday Harbor, Washington, in the San Juan Islands of Puget Sound, with owner Ray Pedersen and Severin Lovenskiold of SP aboard.

As a contrast to our most recent cruising grounds in the Caribbean, Desolation Sound was literally an eye-opener with its north woods atmosphere of fir trees and rocky shoreline, backed by mountains topped with patches of white. Its inappropriate name was given by the explorer George Vancouver, in 1792. Captain James Cook had ranged this coast in his explorations earlier in the century, but Vancouver was responsible for its detailed exploration, harbor by harbor. He was searching for a Pacific entrance to the Northwest Passage. He was discouraged in this and in finding anything else of economic value in a wilderness area inhabited only by Indians using fishing canoes, and very little wildlife beyond eagles, bears, and whales. In a depressed mood, he gave the area the name it still carries; but it is anything but desolate for the cruising sailor. Tucked in at the northeast end of the Strait of Georgia at about latitude 50° north, it is an area of a bit over two hundred squares miles, cut through with channels, arms, and bays that make a marvelous cruising complex. There is no exposed open water, and, even though the tidal range is twelve to eighteen feet, the currents through it are not like the wild races nearby in the Inside Passage to Alaska. In summer (we were there in early July), the weather is pleasantly warm; breezes tend toward the light side; and there can be rain and overcast, but storms are unlikely. At that latitude, daylight hours are long, ending in a lingering twilight that provides extra time for cruising pleasures.

By the time we had lunch and organized our gear in our cabins, an overcast had settled in over the mirrorlike calm, and moving out seemed a waste of effort. Instead, we explored the shoreline by dinghy, did some hiking in the woods, and felt thoroughly at home by dinnertime. Seafood of the region is a special treat, with oysters, clams, and mussels for the picking, and salmon often the "catch of the day"; we enjoyed all of them in varying combinations. On into the evening twilight, there was enough chill in the air for sweaters, as we sat in the cockpit and got to know our new cruising companions. Severin is Norwegian, and he became nostalgic as we compared notes on our Scandinavian cruising.

In the morning it was still overcast without wind, but, to change the scenery, we powered a couple of miles out into the sound and around a point or two to one of the most popular spots in the area, Prideaux Haven. Shaped like a long and narrow T inside the entrance, with many offshoots and steep-to shores, it is a perfect example of Desolation's charms. There were several other boats in-

side, but we were a bit ahead of the midsummer crowd.
Pacific Northwest sailors are generally proud of their area,
careful of its ecology, and cooperative and seamanlike in
their actions. This relaxed, friendly atmosphere seems to
pervade the anchorages but Prideaux, reportedly, can get
too crowded at the height of the season.

It was here Severin had his first chance to set up a Scandinavian moor, that standard procedure in his home waters
of anchoring near shore and then tying a line to a tree
from the stern. It provides a good feeling of security, a rap-
port with the land, and, in high season, is a space saver
when the crowds arrive. With a steep, tree-clad rise just
off the stern, and a view across the water to distant peaks,
as high as six thousand feet, this is an anchorage of
breathtaking beauty. It also provides plenty of entertainment. Severin and Jim did some oyster gathering, Debbie
and Jack went exploring in the other dink, poking into
hidden coves and creeks, and I hiked the steep rise astern
of us, with its great view of the anchorage spread below,
and on to a deserted lake on the far side of the hill. As
long as we had no wind for sailing, it was as good a way
as could be imagined to pass a day.

Finally the breeze did come in with bright sunshine, the
next day, and we took off down the sound and around the
bottom of West Redonda Island, headed for almost the only
"civilization" within reach at Refuge Cove. As the boats
heeled gratefully to the new breeze, the mountains inland
made a spectacular backdrop, with the sun glittering off
the snow, and there was a vibrant sparkle to the atmosphere. "Civilization" at Refuge Cove consists of a general
store with a marina and fuel dock on long floats in front
of it. The store is remarkably well stocked with food and
liquor, all brought in by sea and air, and quite a few boats
were in for shopping. *Invictus* has the name of its home
port, Mountain Home, Arkansas, on its transom and someone from another boat came over to us.

"Mountain Home!" the woman said. "Do you know the
So-and-sos?"

I had to explain that it was a borrowed boat and we were
from New Jersey, much to her disappointment. Evidently,
Arkansans do get around in nautical circles.

Sailing among Desolation Sound's peaks

Stocked up with the few replacements we needed, we took off in the still-lively breeze for a reach across Lewis Channel to quite a different anchorage, Squirrel Cove on Cortes Island. While Tenedos and Prideaux are hemmed in by cliffs and hills, Squirrel is much more open; it is also much shallower, with no need to do a Scandinavian moor. It harbored a goodly collection of boats, but there remained plenty of room. Later in the season, that might not be so, as this is another extremely popular anchorage. There is some civilization here, as well, in the form of a small Indian village, general store, and post office.

Again we rafted and had communal happy hour, with a chance to visit aboard *Mara Maru* and to see how much difference seven feet of space can make in a cruising auxiliary. As well as an ample cockpit, which *Invictus* also has, *Mara Maru* has a roomy pilothouse and a sizable main cabin. Despite the size difference, the two boats had been quite even in sailing ability as we moved along in company. It was a clear, peaceful evening, with the glow of twilight lingering over the trees to the northwest until almost 2300. Severin, with a faraway look in his eyes, said it reminded him of an Oslofjord anchorage.

A special attraction at Squirrel Cove is a narrow tideway between the main harbor and an inner lagoon, and it is virtually a must to "shoot the rapids" in the dink. Depending on tide direction, there is a free, fast ride either into the lagoon or out of it; the Haights, and Severin and Jim, both took it. There are quite a few similar setups throughout Desolation Sound because of the considerable range of tide.

The next morning was bright and clear, with a fresh northwester blowing down Lewis Channel. Our mornings were always a fairly leisurely affair over breakfast, but on this day the breeze called and we were soon beating into it. Lewis Channel, with the low hills of Cortes to port and West Redonda's higher ones to starboard, is about a mile wide, and a good funnel for a northwester, and the boats heeled to it in a series of brisk tacks. Off to starboard, above the cliffs of West Redonda, the five-thousand-foot snowcaps of the Unwin Range glistened in the sun, and ahead, far inland, centered over the channel and framed by the island cliffs, another white-topped cone thrust into the clear northern sky. The air was windbreaker-fresh, with a hint of distant snowfields, and the dark blue of the water, laced with small whitecaps, sparkled in the light. There couldn't be a more impressive setting for cruising.

We were headed for Teakerne Arm, a fjordlike slit cutting deep into west Redonda and another "must-see" of the area, but the sailing was so great as we arrived off its entrance in late morning that we tacked on past into a narrower part of Lewis Channel, drawn on by the lure of the distant peak. At noon, though, the wind began to drop off as a fair-weather land breeze is wont to do. Whitecaps flattened down to an all-blue mirror, and we decided to turn around and drift in the light air back to Teakerne. Soon we were gliding along in Caribbeanlike warmth, windbreakers and sweaters came off, and we turned to port between Teakerne's cliffs. Great rafts of logs, waiting for a tow to a mill down the Strait of Georgia, lined the shores, and here and there a yacht was moored alongside one. This is an accepted practice as long as the yacht is ready to leave at a moment's notice when a tug arrives to tow the raft away, which could be any time of day or night.

Mara Maru had gone ahead of us, and by the time we reached the inner end of Teakerne Arm, Severin had managed a double Scandinavian moor, with both bow and stern lines made fast to the shore and the boat cattycornered across a small cove. We rafted up in time for a late lunch and an afternoon of exploring ashore.

Evidently most of Teakerne is too deep for easy anchoring, and the trick is to get into a cove such as ours, or to tie to a log raft. Around the little point that formed the southeast side of our cove was another one, the prime spot at the inner end of Teakerne. Just wide enough for a couple of rafted boats, this little cove is at the base of a waterfall, a tumble of white sweeping down from the cliffs for over ninety feet. This dramatic setting was occupied by two rafted boats we had seen in some of the other harbors, training vessels from an outfit called SALTS from Victoria, British Columbia. One was a Nova Scotia schooner

Hiking inland leads to scenery like this

called *Robertson II,* and the other a trim little brigantine named *Spirit of Chemainus.* With their traditional, shippy looks, they seemed to complement the scene perfectly. We were told that *Robertson* was supposed to be the last-built Lunenberg (Nova Scotia) schooner.

The teenage boys and girls of their complements were splashing around in the water next to the boats, with their cries giving a good idea of how cold it was, but Jim and Severin told us that Cassel Lake, not far inland and the source of the waterfall, was much warmer for swimming.

I decided to do some exploring ashore while the others went off on dinghy expeditions. The path led steeply up beside the waterfall whose tumble and splash close at hand lent an unwonted sense of urgency to the peaceful scene. At the top, there was a creek jammed with reminders from some forgotten logging operation. An up-and-down path through woods next to it eventually led to an open, rocky slope several hundred yards inland beside a blue gem of a lake with shores heavily wooded above rocky cliffs. Far across the other end of it, in the clear distance of northern sky, the inevitable white-clad peaks framed a scene of breathtaking loveliness.

On the sunny slope, youngsters from the training ships were lolling like contented seals and some were still in the water. Warm from the climb, I decided to be brave and join them, but, if this was warm swimming, I wondered what the water down below must be like. I didn't linger long, but it was delightfully bracing and refreshing. I chatted with some of the young sailors, who seemed to be thoroughly enjoying their sail-training experience; they were impressed that we had come all the way from New Jersey to try out these waters. I must admit that the East Coast seemed awfully far away.

Later, instead of the usual seafood dinner of the kind we had been enjoying, Jim had set up a good old-fashioned hot dog and potato salad cookout in a rough barbecue pit someone had fashioned on top of the point that separated our boats from the training vessels. The view in all directions was great as we munched on our dogs and topped off the feast with indecent concoctions called smores, a mess of toasted marshmallows, chocolate, and Graham crackers. Evidently this juvenile favorite gets its name from kids always asking for "s'more" and they are enough to send an adult quickly to strong drink.

Although there were many more corners of Desolation Sound to be seen, our time was about up; Jim assured us we had taken in the highlights, so the next day saw us off down the Strait of Georgia attempting to make as much progress along the one-hundred-mile passage back to Vancouver as we could, stopping when daylight ran out. It turned out to be a day of complete calm, with nary a ripple breaking the surface of the strait and we purred along under diesel at 7.5 knots, enjoying the constant scenic panorama. To starboard across the strait, the long central spine of Vancouver Island, which separates the strait from the open Pacific, was continuously snowcapped, and to port, the even higher peaks of the Coast Mountains, had their complement of white. The western shore of the strait is known as the Sunshine Coast, as it has the most open weather in the whole area, and it lived up to its name for us as we skinned along the inside of the big islands like Savary, Texada, and Thormanby. The afternoon wore on, and up ahead we could see the brownish haze of the Vancouver area with its population of two million. Then, suddenly, the majestic 10,778-foot cone of Mount Baker, one hundred miles away in the state of Washington, loomed into view, disembodied above the haze and glowing a delicate salmon pink, a final symbol of this unique area.

By nightfall, we made the ninety miles to the fishing and resort town of Gibsons at the entrance to Howe Sound, still visible in the lingering twilight, giving us a very short run before we turned the boats in the next day. The sounds of a summer night, of car tires on hot pavement, dogs barking and children shrieking at play, reminded us that we had left the special charms of Desolation Sound far astern.

Additional Information

The Pacific Northwest

In the long stretch of the Pacific Coast from Central America to Canada, the waters between Puget Sound in Washington State and Desolation Sound in British Columbia offer the only area that can truly be called cruising grounds, and that are worth a special visit. Desolation Sound is one of the highlights, but there are many more places that also provide delightful cruising. It is a relatively northern area, about 47° to 50° north, with long twilights well into the evening in summer, but the climate is deceptively mild because of the Japan Current offshore. In a latitude that corresponds with northern Newfoundland on the Atlantic side, the winters remain relatively mild, and there are many enthusiasts who keep their boats in commission, and use them, all year long.

There are drawbacks—especially a steady climate of rain and fog and a relative lack of wind in summer—but they do not keep the area from having one of the highest boats-per-capita (especially cruising boats) ratios in North America. This might suggest that the harbors are crowded, and some of the popular ones are, but there is such a wide choice of anchorages tucked away in hundreds of islands and deeply indented bays and coves that, with a little research and effort, it is possible to achieve that much desired goal of privacy.

Tidal currents are strong throughout much of the region, as there is a good range of rise and fall, and there are many islands close together with narrow passes between them, that act as funnels. A memorable spot for me, from a previous powerboat cruise, is Deception Pass between Whidbey and Fidalgo islands in northern Puget Sound. Here the current swirls in eddies, whirlpools with depressed centers, overfalls, and skittering patterns of foam. In an auxiliary, we could not have made it against a foul tide, and it took full power in the motorboat to push through. It was also a windless day in July, and an auxiliary would have had to be under power.

Nowhere else in North American cruising is there scenery to match the panoramas that are a constant accompaniment of Pacific Northwest passages when the weather is clear. Snowcapped monsters like Mount Rainier and Mount Hood, the Olympic Mountains on the south side of the Strait of Juan de Fuca, the central spine of Vancouver Island, and the mountains of British Columbia's mainland provide a perpetual backdrop of scenic grandeur. Perhaps the natives have become used to it, but, to an easterner making a visit, it is a breathtaking feast for the eyes, ever changing in its magnificent perspectives.

The seacoasts of Washington and Oregon are exposed and

inhospitable, but there is cruising activity on the Columbia River in Oregon.

Here is some additional information about cruising in the Pacific Northwest:

Yachting centers Centers that include marinas, yards, and shopping and shore facilities can be found, in Washington State, at Tacoma, Seattle, Bremerton, Port Townsend, Anacortes, Bellingham, Roche and Friday harbors and, in British Columbia, at Victoria, South Pender, Vancouver, Campbell River, Powell River, Sidney, and Comox.

Chartering Bareboat and crewed charters are available in many locations, including most of those mentioned above.

Weather The region offers a long season, with some operations possible twelve months a year. Light winds prevail in summer, rain and fog are to be expected, and there is a moderate range of temperatures all year, seldom any heat waves.

Cruising grounds The best of these are the southern Puget Sound around Vashon Island and Commencement Bay, Tacoma; the San Juan Islands in the northern Puget Sound; Gulf Islands in southern Strait of Georgia; Howe Sound; Jervis Sound; both shores of Strait of Georgia; Desolation Sound; Inside Passage to Alaska (for the brave and specially equipped); the Columbia River; the west coast of Vancouver Island (again for the well prepared).

Special attractions Prime cruising areas are the San Juans (especially at Orcas Island, Roche Harbor, and the Penders) and nearby Port Townsend; Desolation Sound (see Chapter 1); and the west coast of Vancouver, where a cruising boat is on its own in rugged, primitive surroundings exposed to the open Pacific. These all offer a real challenge.

References Robinson, *Where to Cruise*, from p. 133; West, *Cruising the Pacific Coast*; *Pacific Boating Almanac 1989: Pacific Northwest and Alaska*.

2

▶▶▶▶▶▶▶▶▶▶▶▶▶▶▶

BALMY NEWFOUNDLAND
Easy Cruising on Its East Coast

During the night, the rigging began to moan and rattle, announcing the arrival of a northeaster blowing in from the open Atlantic. We were snug at a fish pier in the tight little harbor of Bonavista on Newfoundland's east coast, but we were due out of there in the morning. It was a gray one, with spits of rain, and we got ready by donning boots, foul-weather gear, heavy sweaters, and gloves, glad that we had had the foresight to bring them with us. These were the conditions we had expected from a Newfoundland cruise. Atlantic graybeards, topped by whitecaps, greeted us as *Fidelity,* a Valiant 40, poked her bow out of the breakwaters for the four-mile beat around Cape Bonavista.

With reefed mainsail and staysail, she slugged it out in a welter of spray, handling it well as the breeze built to around 30 knots, and an hour saw us easing off around the lighthouse on the cape for a run south to Trinity Bay, the next in the succession of deep indentations that break up the island's Atlantic coast. The nearest land to port at 48° north was Brittany in France as we scudded along on an exhilarating sleigh ride. To starboard, the rather barren hills, undulating above rocky cliffs, seemed to fit the dour weather.

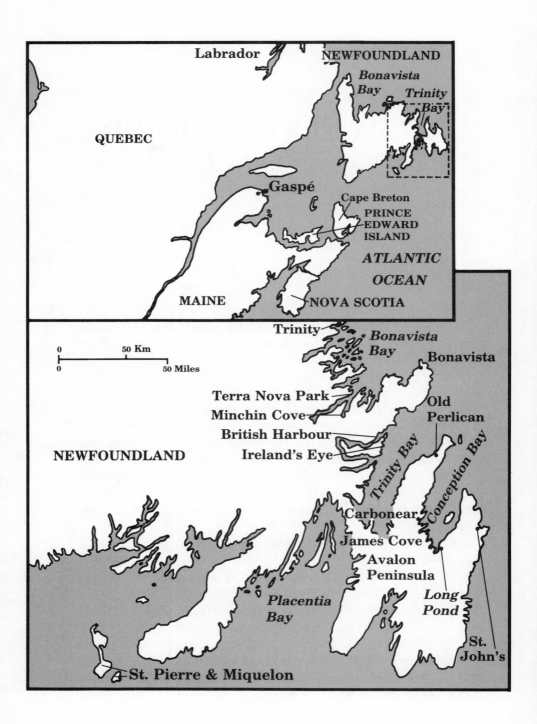

Gradually, the rain let up, the breeze eased, and, when we rounded into Trinity, the clouds began to show breaks. From the mid-50s, the temperature moderated into the 60s, and by the time we slipped into British Harbour at the end of a forty-mile passage, the late-afternoon sun was slanting through a brilliantly clear sky.

And so ended the conditions we had been expecting. We had warm, sunny weather, with pleasant sailing breezes for the rest of our eight-day mid-July cruise. The Newfies, as the inhabitants are called, part in jest and part affectionately, made a great fuss over us and kept saying, "Come back, Yanks. You've brought us our best summer weather in years."

We were there taking part in a joint cruise of thirty-one boats from the Cruising Club of America, sponsored by its Boston Station, in company with twenty-six boats from the Royal Newfoundland Yacht Club. *Fidelity* had been brought up from New Jersey in eight fog-bound, calm-plagued days by her owners, Carl and Shirley Boll, and we had flown in to join them. In one of those weird itineraries that are the product of today's hub-style air travel, our cheapest route had been Newark–Syracuse–Montreal–St. John's, instead of a more direct one via Boston and Halifax. The flight was followed by a three-hour bus ride from bustling St. John's halfway up the island's east coast to Terra Nova National Park, where the cruise was forming. On the plane, I sat next to a friendly Catholic priest, who informed me that Newfoundland scanned with "understand" if we wanted to pronounce it correctly.

The inaugural CCA-RNYA rendezvous at Terra Nova was rained on rather heavily, which turned out to be the only real rain of the week except for our dusting off Bonavista. Despite the weather, it was a happy, anticipatory gathering with Americans and Newfies getting to know each other. Local knowledge was handed out along with the drinks as plans for the rest of the cruise were discussed. Following the rendezvous, we passed a solitary night in a hideaway called Minchin Cove down Newman Sound from the Terra Nova marina, as the boats spread out on their own for three days before the next rendezvous. Under a misty overcast,

Minchin, ringed by pine-covered hills, was completely still, with only the occasional splash of a fish to break the silence, and Jane and I tried to remember when we had last had a cruising anchorage all to ourselves. Figuring back, we decided that it was probably eight years ago in the Caicos Islands. From Minchin we had a powered passage over the sheen of Bonavista Bay and a night in Bonavista Harbour, one of the oldest settlements in North America and the original landfall of John Cabot on his 1497 voyage of exploration. The fishing village there predates Jamestown and Plymouth. Cabot was really an Italian named Caboto, which accounts for the Latinate name of the landfall. It is still a very utilitarian fishing village, with square, no-nonsense houses widely spaced over treeless hills above the harbor. The piers were jammed with fishing vessels and clouds of gulls wheeled and squawked overhead, as in every Newfoundland fishing port. Several yachts from the cruise had rafted up in a section of one pier. And so, that evening, with the gray Atlantic day behind us, we were peacefully anchored in British Harbour, a fjordlike cut off Smith Sound, one of Trinity Bay's many tributaries. Two other CCA boats were rafted at anchor near the entrance, but our only other company was a few horses grazing over the open fields rising from the harbor. The evening had turned crystal clear, with a moon waxing gibbous above the sound outside, and there was a pleasant nip in the air as the sun settled behind the hills. On the open fields around the harbor, there were a few houses, but it could soon be seen that they were all deserted, testament to an odd chapter in Newfoundland history. Some twenty years before, the government of Canada's newest province (it had been a British colony until 1949) decided to relocate the inhabitants of a series of small fishing villages in isolated harbors along the coast. The problems of providing them with communication, mail, and medical services had become too difficult, and a program was set up to move them to more populous centers. The houses left behind at British Harbour were in varying stages of collapse. Some looked fairly solid, and one even had a curtain fluttering across an open window; some had a list, and one or two were just a heap of boards, with one wall standing. It was a ghostly sight. We wondered about the grazing horses, learning later that they were used for winter logging operations and had been put out to pasture for the summer.

In the morning, after the quietest of nights at anchor, we had a look at another ghost town. This was Ireland's Eye at the end of a narrow, winding harbor on a small island across the mouth of Smith Sound. There was one local fishing boat at anchor in the inner harbor, but the only life we saw was in an eagle's aerie on a cliff above the harbor entrance, where two dark gray eaglets were waggling their wings preliminary to flight tests. One of them finally fluttered and flopped down about ten feet onto a branch as we cheered it on. This place seemed even more isolated and deserted than British Harbour, and it was something of a shock to read several months later that it was being used as a drug transfer site. It was certainly lonely and isolated enough, but this reminder of modern-day doings was a jarring contrast to the peace we felt sliding through the silence of its harbor.

By noon, there was a pleasant southerly riffling up Trinity Bay, and we were due that evening at the town of Trinity a few miles to the north for the next rendezvous. Carl broke out the spinnaker, and we had a delightful run amid the other boats converging on the rendezvous. The designated anchorage was in God's Cove which was soon crowded with the more than fifty boats of our group. It was an impressive sight in this lightly populated area, and the locals

The deserted village at British Harbour

later told us that it was the greatest number of boats they had ever seen in the cove at one time.

Trinity is a trim, well-kept town. A local launch service employing powerboats taxied us to the town dock, a short walk from the Anglican church, where supper was to be served. Many of us ambled around the town's couple of streets taking in the atmosphere in the glowing twilight and then gathered for the supper, served by the ladies of the church at long tables in the parish-house meeting hall. It was a hearty affair of ham, cabbage, potatoes, rolls, salad, cake, and ice cream, and there was a great amount of what could only be called good fellowship. A bar had been set up in an open field outside, with the featured libation a Newfie specialty called Screech. This is a Jamaica rum dating back to colonial times when the triangular traffic of fish, slaves, and rum provided the province's main commerce; it had no formal name, having been served in un-labeled bottles for generations. It got its name during World War II, when an American naval officer, responding to a toast from a local official at a ceremonial dinner, downed his tot in one gulp, then followed with a strangled screech. The name is now on the label, and the rum, if taken with proper discretion, is perfectly serviceable.

God's Cove was gray and misty in the morning, and it looked as though we might have our first taste of the oft-predicted fog. As the fleet dispersed for three more days of individual operations, the gray stuff gradually lifted to above mast height, and by the time we, as one of the last boats to leave, made it out to the bay, the sun was burning it off, and a pleasant, smoky sou'wester was building. It provided a hull-speed reach across the wide mouth of Trinity Bay for about twenty-five miles to a fishing village called Old Perlican. By early afternoon, we were anchored in about eight feet of water inside a breakwater. The harbor was jammed with blue-hulled trawlers at piers under the usual wheeling cloud of gulls. A couple of yachts from the cruise, near us at anchor, were the only noncommercial craft in sight. Again, the hills around the harbor were gently rolling and almost treeless, with square, utilitarian houses well spaced out. The sun was now shining brightly, with the only reminder of the morning's fog a smokiness on the horizon, and it was warm enough to take off our sweaters.

Fidelity has a bright orange inflatable tender with a 15-horsepower outboard that can lift it up on a zippy plane with one or two people in it, and we spent some time exploring the harbor. Taking a closer look at the great rafting of trawlers at the pier, we discovered most of them had men's names; it was an amusing eye-catcher to find one with *William Shawn* on the transom. Somehow, though, I don't think a Newfie trawler was named for the longtime editor of *The New Yorker* magazine.

Back aboard *Fidelity* we found we had visitors alongside. Three teenage boys in a dory with small outboard were hanging on the rail chatting with Jane and Shirley. Shirley asked where the best place to buy fish was, and, almost without answering, the boat shot away toward the shore. In no time it was back, and she was handed a freshly cleaned cod.

"Oh, my goodness," she said in surprise. "That was quick. How much do we owe you?"

There was a shy ducking of heads and muttering, with the eventual message, "Nothing."

"Oh come on. Are you sure?"

They nodded again.

"Well how about a Coke, or something, then?"

"No thanks, ma'am" came polite murmurs, but they still hung on to the rail, with no sign of leaving. Finally, one of them spoke up softly.

"Could we maybe have a ride in the orange boat?"

Carl laughed, then took each one in turn for a spin around the harbor at full speed. When they had all had a ride, wreathed in smiles, they shouted, "Thanks a lot. Thank you," and shoved off for shore. The fish, incidentally, made a fine dinner that night.

The natural friendliness of Newfies had been very much in evidence at all points, and it continued at our next stop. We took another jaunt out into the open Atlantic to round a peninsula into Conception Bay. The ocean was a millpond as we rounded Grates Point and ducked behind Baccalieu Island into Conception, and it was diesel work all day. Some of the CCA boats had talked of going into Job's Cove, just around the point, but that was too short a run and we continued on in warm sun to a town called Carbonear, thirty miles into the bay. The name is evidently a corruption of the French name for charcoal pot. The mix of names is a reminder that the French and British fought over this area continually during the seventeenth and eighteenth centuries.

Carbonear had a sturdy concrete town dock, and the spirit of hospitality was shown immediately as the local fishermen moved their boats so that two other CCA yachts could come alongside near us. Carbonear also had that open, barren look with very few trees around the plain, neat houses, and probably seemed much more cheerful in July sunshine than during a winter northeaster. It had a good-sized supermarket and other stores along a wide main street.

We were an object of some curiosity, and a steady stream of townspeople came down to the pier to check us out and strike up conversations. I asked one man where it was possible to buy a newspaper, and he drove home quickly and came back with copies of the St. John's paper for the last three days, as well as some cod's tongues and squid, local delicacies. With the addition of cod and salmon, Shirley cooked all this up in a special seafood feast for dinner.

Most of the visiting CCA yachts were from New England ports and had cruised over via Nova Scotia in easy stages. *Fidelity* had come much farther, and one of the boats moored astern of us was a Florida-based one whose crew had been properly impressed with the contrast between home waters and Newfoundland. Many of the boats would later be left for winter storage at Baddeck, on the Bras d'Or lakes on Cape Breton Island, the northern part of Nova Scotia. There is a major boatyard there with all services and good facilities for taking care of visiting boats. The local RNYC yachts on the cruise were half sail and half power and based at the club, which has its own marina and yard at Long Pond at the bottom of Conception Bay.

In the morning, instead of being stared at from the pier, we did some staring of our own. The pier was a high one, and the tide was low, so people on it were well above us,

and there, in the early sun, was a whole group of Newfoundland dogs on leashes held by their owners. As we tried
to strike up conversations, it soon became obvious that
neither the dogs nor their owners spoke English, though
we did manage enough communication to find out that they
were all from Germany. Gradually we learned that they
were all members of a club of owners of the breed and had
come over in a chartered plane for a special show, with
forty dogs and their owners all crowded into the plane's
cabin. The show was at Harbour Grace, the next port south,
but some of the owners were staying in Carbonear. As the
dogs stood and drooled down at us, we wondered what it
must have been like in the plane. Evidently, Harbour Grace
(a corruption of Havre de Grace) was where the breed originated, and this was a pilgrimage to the source. It was also
the departure point of early transatlantic airplane flights
by such aviators as the team of Alcock and Brown and
Amelia Earhart, as it was the only airstrip in Newfoundland and the closest one in North America to Europe. Just
down the bay from here is Brigus, home of the famous sailor
Captain Bob Bartlett, who explored the Arctic in the 1920s
and 1930s in the schooner *Effie Morrisey.*

For our penultimate sail, we had a good reach south in
Conception Bay between gradually narrowing and hillier
shores and landed in a spot called James Cove for the night.
It had good protection behind a small point, forming a fish-
hook-shaped anchorage, and we had it to ourselves except
for local small craft along the beach. It had steep shores,
but the inner end was an open meadow, gradually sloping
inland, that contained one cottage. Sitting on the beach a
few hundred feet away from the house was what looked
very much like a brand-new outhouse; and that it proved
to be. At first there was no sign of life, but gradually, as
the afternoon waned, more and more people of all different
ages began to appear at the house and along the beach.
There was a party going on at the cottage, but kids were
playing along the beach, and finally, a big flat wagon, drawn
by a team of horses, appeared from inland and stopped by
the outhouse. Now the entire group assembled, and, with
a great show of manpower, the privy was wrestled onto the
wagon, and the horses pulled it up a rutted road past the

Royal Newfoundland Yacht Club marina at Long Pond

house to a small rise behind it. Here the manpower was applied again, the outhouse was lowered to the turf and then straightened up, and everyone repaired to the cottage to continue the party. The next morning, a steady stream of visitors to it confirmed that it was in business.

This "floor show" had given us great happy-hour entertainment. We followed it with a final seafood feast, and, with the moon now approaching full, it was a lovely night in which to sit in the cockpit and revel in the peaceful scene. Somehow we had expected the going to be much more rugged, and we were almost glad that we had had the rounding of Cape Bonavista as a contrast to the rest of the cruise.

As a finale, there was a gentle spinnaker run across the bay to Long Pond and the trim RNYC clubhouse, perfectly protected at the end of a narrow inlet. There, at a farewell dinner for the cruise group, everyone agreed that it had been a special experience, and the Newfies kept saying that we had to come back to bring them more great cruising weather. For our part, we said they had done very well by us.

3

▶ ▶ ▶ ▶ ▶ ▶ ▶ ▶ ▶ ▶ ▶ ▶ ▶ ▶

A GOOD "INVENTION"
Southern New England Waters

Southern New England is where it all began for me, and for many sailors. It is such a beautiful area, and so typical of what most people seek when they go cruising, that I once titled a magazine article about it "Where Cruising Was Invented." That, of course, is a slight exaggeration, but it is the area that sets the standard for many cruising sailors.

From June through September, or even a bit earlier and later if luck holds, it has all the elements that make for an ideal cruising ground. Despite the possibility of fog and northeasters, the weather is generally reliable, with the smoky sou'westers of a warm summer afternoon a trademark. The choice of well-protected anchorages is almost unlimited, and the towns, with their reminders of whaling days and display of Colonial architecture, have a unique charm that makes coming into their harbors at the end of a fine sail especially rewarding. Despite the pressures of development and tourism, that charm is still very strong, and the sandy cliffs, the rolling, bayberry-scented moors and hills, and the miles and miles of beaches create a unique atmosphere.

My first experience was in 1932, as I mentioned earlier, when I was thirteen and a camper at Camp Viking at South

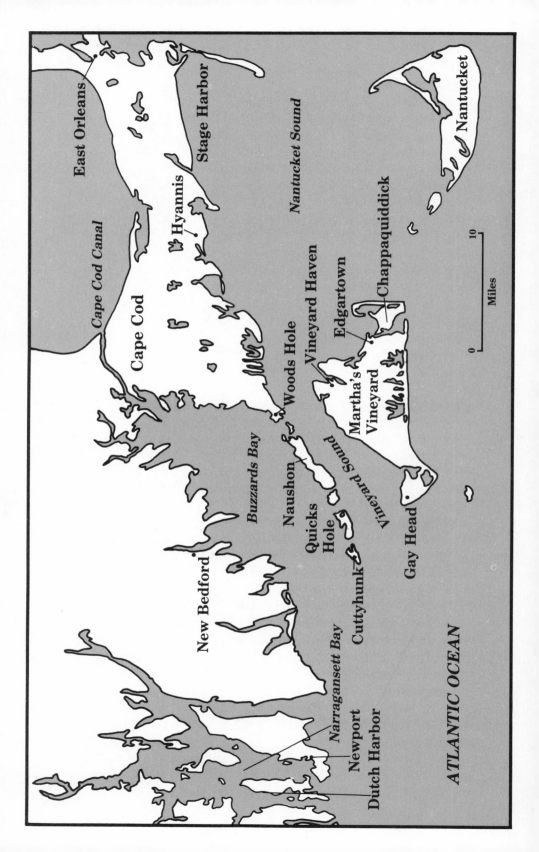

Orleans on Cape Cod. The flagship of the camp's fleet was a thirty-six-foot motorsailer ketch converted from a Navy liberty boat, and a highlight of the summer was the cruise. We started at East Orleans, on the Massachusetts Bay side of the cape and went through the Cape Cod Canal to Oak Bluffs on Martha's Vineyard. From there we went on to Nantucket, finishing up back on the south side of the cape at Stage Harbor, Chatham. The sights and scents of that cruise have remained with me ever since, and the experience was a milestone in my developing interest in sailing. From that time on, I have always thought of cruising as the ultimate escape and adventure. And because it occurred in those very special waters of southern New England, they will always stand as a shining example of all that a cruising area should be.

We had the full gamut of weather on that memorable cruise: a flat calm on Massachusetts Bay while we powered to the canal entrance; an afternoon sou'wester as we plunged out into Buzzards Bay; a foggy morning at Lake Anthony, the tiny, snug harbor at Oak Bluffs, with commercial fishing boats chugging out through the murk at dawn; a smoky sou'wester on the way to Nantucket; and a fresh, damp nor'easter as we headed back to Stage Harbor. A special touch on that passage was that it was rough enough for some of the boys to get seasick, but I didn't, and my pride in this was another clincher in my desire to be a cruising sailor.

It was also in these waters that I had my first "command" of a cruising sailboat. In the summer between junior and senior years at college, 1938, after previous summers of working as a messenger boy in New York, I decided that this was going to be the last full summer I would ever have off, the last chance to do a lot of sailing (not being prescient about my future as an editor of sailing magazines) and I decided not to get a job. Instead, much to the disgust of my father, who had been thoroughly conditioned by the Depression about how real, earnest, and unforgiving life was, I used money saved from a student employment job at college to charter a twenty-six-foot sloop for the month of August. The fee was all of $105, and I

enlisted two classmates to share the month with me, one
for ten days and the other for twenty. The boat was a
wooden gaff sloop named *Bona,* based in Mamaroneck, New
York, and, after a shakedown session with the owner, who
sort of gave the impression that I was a rapist abducting
his daughter, we immediately headed east in Long Island
Sound, eager to get to southern New England. So eager
were we in fact that we didn't bother to stow gear, just
threw clothes and stores in a heap on the bunks. When
evening came after a wonderful day's run and we rounded
up into a good chop to douse sail, the cabin became an
epic mishmash of wet clothing, smashed eggs, and other
disasters.

The whole month was a succession of lessons like this,
in which the responsibilities of operating a cruising boat
were gradually impressed on me. There were no major disasters, just a few embarrassments amid a wonderful month
of enjoying Cape Cod, Martha's Vineyard, and Nantucket.
Girls were suitably impressed by our command of a yacht,
and the fun and parties easily made up for the occasional
red faces. Perhaps the classic booboo was when I forgot to
change course at Vineyard Lightship for the leg to Point
Judith on the way back. We had to sail at night because
we had overstayed our time in paradise (and the engine
wouldn't start). I therefore mistook Block Island for Point
Judith and dawn found us on the ocean side of Montauk
Point. But, all in all, it fully confirmed my enthusiasm for
cruising.

Now, on our most recent cruise, we were in *Sabrina II,*
a Sabre 38, swooping up Vineyard Sound in a good old
smoky sou'wester that was a carbon copy of the one that
had greeted *Viking* in Buzzards Bay more than fifty years
before, and probably has been blowing the same way on
summer afternoons since the icecap retreated.

Jane, my daughter Alice, and I picked up *Sabrina* at
Newport the afternoon before, for a "test" cruise for a magazine article, and the day had developed into one of those
delightfully traditional ones. We had an easy jaunt around
the southern tip of Jamestown, leaving Newport's hustle
and bustle for a quiet evening in Dutch Harbor, one of

Narragansett Bay's better anchorages on the west side of Jamestown Island. From there in the morning, we made thirty-eight miles in six hours. For a while we had one of those sudden visitations of fog that blow in unannounced in this area. They are especially frequent early in the season (and this was early July) when the water is still quite cold but heat waves have begun on the mainland. A blanket of fog had overtaken us as we were approaching the entrance to Vineyard Sound after a fast broad reach across Block Island Sound and its deep-sea swells.

It became quite important to know just where we were as we surged toward Buzzards Tower and the threatening rocks of Sow and Pigs Reef off Cuttyhunk. We steered a very careful compass course and kept exact check of times between buoys. Then just as precipitously as it had arrived, the fog swept on by and we found ourselves in the golden glow of late afternoon. The Elizabeth Islands, uneven lumps of green, were off to port, and the multicolored cliffs of Gay Head at the southwest tip of the Vineyard stood out boldly in the slanting light.

The sou'wester had reached its late-afternoon zenith, and Alice and I had been having a little contest on the wheel to see who could get the best register on the steam gauge. As she handed the wheel over to me, she had just hit 8.6.

"Let's see you beat that," she challenged, and soon, as the breeze continued to build, I managed to meet it. In the perfect combination of surfing in sync with a wave and a fresh gust from the sou'wester, we surged along between wings of white, and the gauge hit 10.4.

This was sailing at its most exhilarating, as the sun picked up the yellow bluffs of the Vineyard. The whitecaps kept pace with us, and the big buoy on Middle Ground danced in the chop when it slid by to port. Soon we were hardening up to round West Chop for a final beat into Vineyard Haven in the bayberry-scented breeze. As the Sabre dug into the windward work gracefully, I was reminded of a similar beat into Vineyard Haven some twenty years before when we were cruising in *Mar Claro,* our Amphibi-Ette 24, and Alice had been a subteen.

Mar Claro liked windward work, and the same good old

sou'wester was blowing out from the shore as we hardened up for the final approach to the harbor. It was not long after a Tigercat catamaran had won *Yachting* magazine's One-of-a-Kind Regatta, which I had helped to run. Catamarans were a comparative novelty then, and the Tigercat's performance had opened a lot of eyes. As we tacked shoreward, a Tigercat appeared out of nowhere and shot across our stern at a great rate of speed. We kept on close-hauled as she went off inshore on the same tack. Soon after we flipped over to port tack, we heard the rapid slap-slap-slap of a bow wave off our starboard quarter, and here came the cat again, going like blazes, but still crossing our stern. The same performance continued until we got to the jetties at the entrance to the inner harbor. It was an interesting demonstration of catamaran speed versus monohull close-windedness.

The conditions were so similar that I half expected to see the Tigercat, but the Sabre had no such challenge, just a good, slashing finish to a great day of sailing. We doused sail at the jetties and poked in under power, looking for a berth of some sort in a very crowded harbor. One reason I like Vineyard Haven in comparison with more glamorous Edgartown is that we have always been greeted cheerfully and courteously there, in contrast to the launch boys and dock attendants at Edgartown, who tend to treat transients like trespassers. This held true again, as the young harbormaster managed to find us a berth at the Town Dock, the last available one. He made us feel welcome, as did the dockmaster, and we noticed that they treated everyone with the same relaxed courtesy.

Vineyard Haven had another memory for me, all the way back to 1924, when my parents and I were aboard the old paddlewheel steamer *Uncatena* headed for Nantucket, and we were caught in a storm that was called a nor'easter, but was probably a tropical hurricane. Crossing Buzzards Bay from New Bedford to Woods Hole, she took three hours instead of one, as each sea she hit seemed to stop her dead, and great sheets of spray swept across her low bow. As a five-year-old, I was at a very impressionable age, and it was one of the most exciting episodes of my young life.

Crowded but hospitable Vineyard Haven

When she left Woods Hole for Oak Bluffs, on the eastern side of the Vineyard, the sea was even rougher, and the decision was made not to try to round East Chop into the open waters of Nantucket Sound. Instead we made an un-scheduled stop at Vineyard Haven and spent the day at the pier there as the storm raged. I still vividly remember the scene of yachts in the harbor dragging anchor and smashing up on the shore, and a freighter that had run aground outside the harbor. We watched the waves break-ing over her, and it is the only time I have ever seen res-cue by breeches buoy, which was how her crew was removed to the shore.

We had no such excitement this time; just a pleasant dinner ashore in the neatly atmospheric village and a visit with the crew of the next boat at the pier, one of the casual pleasures of cruising, and it was time to head back west the next morning. It was a bit frustrating to come this far and not have time to go on to Nantucket or to sample the harbors on the south side of the cape, like Falmouth, Wianno, or Harwichport, all favorites in past cruises. I spent my boyhood summers in Nantucket, and it has always been my favorite of favorites for its happy memories and its at-mosphere of being a very special place off by itself at sea. The town is quaint and colorful, with the best-preserved collection of eighteenth- and nineteenth-century houses anywhere, and the harbor is a fine one, barring a nor'eas-ter, which can raise quite a fuss blowing down the six-mile stretch from Wauwinet. However, its big marina and rental moorings are so popular and so crowded now that it is mandatory to make advance reservations when cruis-ing there.

We had sailed *Mar Claro* there after our Vineyard Haven stop, taking the straight course across the shoals from Chappaquiddick past the lonely islands of Musketget and Tuckernuck, which we were able to do with her two-foot-four draft, and it had been an exciting venture into un-charted (literally) waters. In a memory going all the way back to the *Viking* cruise, I still chuckle over the answer a camper gave when I relieved him at the wheel on the leg to Nantucket. We were doing everything in proper Navy style, and we were supposed to give the course when being relieved. I took over from this guy and, as standard operating procedure, asked him the course; he gulped and hesitated and then blurted out, "Northeast by south a quarter west," not missing a quadrant.

Sabrina's course was only in the westerly sector down Vineyard Sound, and the sou'wester was still brisk as we rounded West Chop and headed for Rhode Island. There is a special tunnel effect between the Chops, adding heft to the breeze, and I figured a reefed main and number three jib were enough for the beat ahead. When we got out into the open in Vineyard Sound, the wind had eased a bit, away from the funnel effect, but lunch hour was approaching, so we kept the reef in for a level ride while eating. Then, before we got around to shaking it out, the normal afternoon thermal built up well, so we left the combination in and had a fast, easy sail, passing several boats laboring under full sail. We charged by Tarpaulin Cove, a pleasant anchorage on Naushon Island, largest of the privately owned Elizabeths. Then we shot with the racing tide through Quicks Hole between Pasque and Nashawena islands, and headed for Cuttyhunk. We had a last good beat down the bay as the smoke of the sou'wester almost turned into fog but never did. Joining the parade of boats heading past the stark, lonely Penikese Island, a leper colony years ago, we sailed into Cuttyhunk's landlocked pond.

Cuttyhunk used to be a secret hideaway when I first cruised these waters before World War II, but it is now an amazingly crowded place. Even on a Thursday in early July, it was jammed with boats by 1500, and it takes nerve and brass to force a spot to anchor. We managed to find one and then watched in amazement as additional boats continued to pile in and somehow find a place. It is a picturesque spot in its lonely isolation, with gray-shingled cottages on its rolling, bare hills, and one can't help wondering what Bartholomew Gosnold was thinking when he tried to establish a colony here in 1607 during his voyage of exploration. Probably in those days an island location meant security. A monument to him stands in a little pond at the western end of the island.

The busy harbor scene was subdued the next morning in heavy mist, not quite fog, and a flat calm, and we headed for Newport under power over an oily sea. The sea breeze piped in shortly before noon giving us a couple of hours of good sailing into the Newport Yachting Center, where Alice left us and son Robby and grandson Will joined us the next morning. Newport was its usual nautical version of Times Square at rush hour, a colorful scene to experience once in a while.

We managed a dinner ashore of the expected seafood variety, and the next day had a swooping spinnaker run up Narragansett Bay in steady traffic to Wickford, Rhode Island, and *Sabrina*'s home marina. There was one minor contretemps when the dockmaster tried to put us in a slip that had less water than *Sabrina*'s draft, but the final leg was a pleasant coda to the kind of sailing that can be ex-

The Sabre 38 *off Newport*

pected south of Cape Cod, and, as ever, an exercise in nostalgia for someone who has had many wonderful cruises in these waters.

Additional Information

The Northeast

The two preceding chapters offer but a small sample of the cruising possibilities in northeastern North America between New York City and the Canadian Maritimes. There is a profusion of fine cruising grounds, which is perhaps fortunate, because they border on a densely populated area. The pressures generated by the great number of people who want to get afloat are fairly well absorbed by an abundance of islands, sounds, bays, coves, inlets, and harbors. In contrast with the Pacific coast, with its great stretches of unbroken beach and cliffs, New England and eastern Canada are lined with protected anchorages. There are numerous good harbors filled with marinas, mooring areas, boatyards, and yacht clubs. Most of them double as home base for a big resident population of boats and as an attraction for cruising transients. Sometimes the crush is almost overwhelming, as on any summer weekend on western Long Island Sound, but seekers of seclusion can find what they want, if they really work at it, in some of the more remote regions.

The seasons, of course, determine operations. July and August are the peak months, and really the only reliable ones in the more northerly sections, but May into October can also provide pleasant conditions farther south. The Atlantic governs the weather, so afternoon thermals are the expected norm of summer sailing and southerlies and southwesters as the prevailing breeze. Continental cold fronts, however, can bring clearing northwesters, coastal storms, and sometimes a hurricane though they are usually well predicted. Fog, in varying degrees, is always a constant possibility. In most areas, tides have a good range, which means that the currents they generate, especially through narrow passes between larger bodies of water, can be anywhere from respectable to boisterous. Some prime examples are The Race at the eastern end of Long Island Sound, Woods Hole between Buzzards Bay and Vineyard Sound, many of Maine's coastal passages such as the Sasanoa River, and the St. John River in New Brunswick.

So much of the region is rich in history and atmosphere, dating back to early discoveries and Colonial times, and many of the harbor towns are an architectural treasure house, as for example, Nantucket, Edgartown, Newport, Stonington (Connecticut), and many of the towns of the Maine coast. The heritage of seafaring, whaling, and fishing is still in evidence throughout the area. It is an interesting contrast to see the utilitarian aspects of most Newfoundland villages and the more decorative ones of the New England seaports. There are, of course, commercial harbors too. Some combine yachting and commerce, such as Halifax, Boston, or Portland, but others are better left completely to commerce. St. John's, Newfoundland, has almost no yacht facilities, and ports like New Haven, Providence, and New Bedford have smaller outlying harbors that are much better as yachting bases.

Such is the variety here that there is a wealth of opportunities for a lifetime of cruising. I have been at it in the area for about sixty years, and there are still new places left for me to explore.

Here is some additional information about cruising in the Northeast:

Yachting centers There are so many of these that only the major ones can be included here. They can be found in the following places: all of western Long Island Sound, from City Island to Port Jefferson; Essex, New London, and Stonington, in Connecticut; Greenport and Montauk, in New York; Block Island, Point Judith, Newport, and all of Narragansett Bay, Rhode Island; all of Buzzards Bay, Woods Hole, Falmouth, Hyannis, and Harwichport on Cape Cod, as well as Vineyard Haven and Edgartown on Martha's Vineyard; Nantucket, and Massachusetts Bay from Plymouth to Cape Ann; many Maine harbors, with South Freeport, Boothbay Harbor, Camden, and all those on Mount Desert Island as the major ones; St. John, Halifax, and Baddeck, Nova Scotia; and Long Pond (St. John's), Newfoundland.

Chartering Mostly individual boats, either bareboat or crewed, are available via yacht brokers. There is some fleet and "dude cruise" chartering out of Camden, Maine.

Weather There is a short season, July and August, in the north; a longer one, May to October, in southern areas. Southwest summer breezes prevail, but coastal storms and hurricanes are to be monitored; fog is a major factor, especially early in the season, and perpetually along the Maine coast.

Cruising grounds Western Long Island Sound is recommended only for midweek, and spring and fall; eastern Long Island Sound also has many good harbors. Also recommended are Narrangansett Bay and Block Island; Buzzards Bay and Vineyard and Nantucket sounds (urban sections of Massachusetts Bay not recommended); all of the Maine coast (there is less crowding east of Mount Desert); St. John River inland from Reversing Falls; Bras d'Or Lake, Nova Scotia; all of Newfoundland for those prepared to be on their own, but the East Coast provides the best choice of harbors.

Special attractions There are excellent beaches and fishing, swimming and historic towns and museums, south of Cape Cod; scenery and more chance for isolation in Maine; isolation and scenery in Bras d'Or; and primitive surroundings, isolated fishing villages, scenery, and local people in Newfoundland.

References Robinson, *Over the Horizon,* Chapters II, III, IV, and *Where to Cruise,* pp. 13–42; Duncan and Ware, *Cruising Guide to the New England Coast;* Johnson, *Cruising Guide to Maine,* Vols. I and II; *Spray* magazine, *Cruising Cape Breton.*

For Newfoundland, write to Government of Newfoundland and Labrador, Department of Development and Tourism, Box 2016, St. John's, Newfoundland, Canada, A1C 5R8.

4

▶ ▶ ▶ ▶ ▶ ▶ ▶ ▶ ▶ ▶ ▶ ▶

THE WEST COAST OF NEW ENGLAND

What Vermonters Call Their Lake Champlain Shore

The term "lake sailing" usually evokes an image of shining, calm water and gentle breezes playing games as they waft down from the hills and do unpredictable things. It is not true, however, of Lake Champlain, the country's largest lake excluding the Great Lakes, shared by New York, Vermont and Quebec, which empties 118 miles northward into Canada.

We had a very good example of Champlain sailing on our first day out. We had been loaned a Tartan 30, *Elizabeth*[3], by a lifelong acquaintance whom I had known since we'd both lived in Elizabeth, New Jersey—Henry Clark, who had given up New Jersey's Barnegat Bay for Vermont several years before. He wanted to introduce us to the lake's special attractions and features, so Jane and I and daughter Martha and her husband, Dan Bliss, accepted the chance for a late-August week. It was 90 degrees and flat calm when we arrived at Point Bay Marina in Charlotte, Vermont, near the head of the lake. Overnight the wind began to whistle from the south, heralding a front and by morning it was blowing close to 30 miles per hour (in freshwater country) under lowering skies.

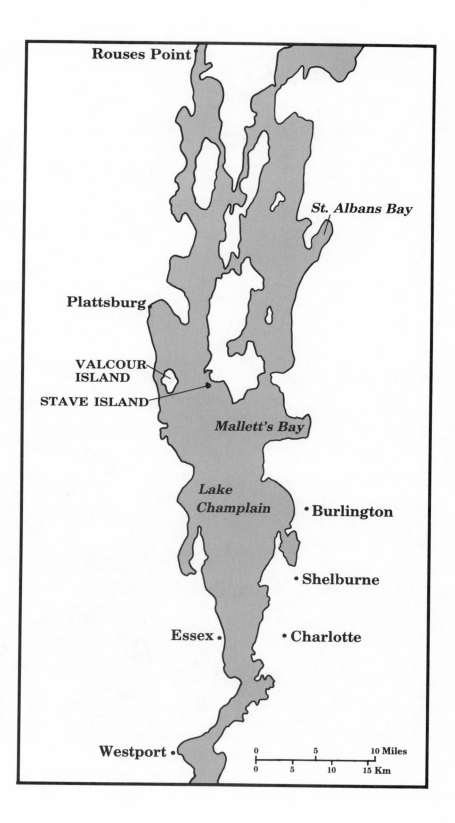

Rouses Point

St. Albans Bay

Plattsburg

VALCOUR
ISLAND

STAVE ISLAND

Mallett's Bay

Lake
Champlain

• Burlington

• Shelburne

Essex •

• Charlotte

Westport •

0   5   10 Miles

0   5   10   15 Km

Point Bay Marina, Charlotte, Vermont

Henry had arranged for us to visit Stave Island, a private one twenty-one miles down the lake (north, remember), but I was a bit leery of taking a strange boat on a strange body of water in marginal conditions, with a front approaching. A phone call to Bill Hazelett, owner of the island, telling him of our doubts, brought a positive response.

"Never mind that," he said. "Come ahead. You'll get here in no time with this wind, and, unfortunately, this is the only day we'll be here for a while to come. You'll be okay."

Encouraged by this, we girded ourselves and took off shortly after lunch under mainsail alone for the direct downwind run. The lake's north-south stretch allows a wind in either of those directions a good run, building up seas quickly. With the Adirondacks to the west and the Green Mountains to the east, it is subject to the quick weather changes brewed in their heights, and most of its harbors are open on one bearing, which can be tricky with the sudden wind shifts. We knew a front was on the way from beyond the Adirondacks from radio reports and, even more clearly, from the look of the weather.

So there we were, in a strange boat in strange waters, a front on the way, and flying along at hull-speed-plus under main alone. Once out in the open, we had a good introduction to the kind of seas that build when a wind is funneling directly along the lake's axis. They were short and steep, with typical quick-breaking fresh water whitecaps, and *Elizabeth*[3] took off like a bird. (The third power of Elizabeth comes from her being named for Henry Clark's hometown, wife, and mother). A Sparkman & Stephens design, she was guaranteed to be a good sailor, and that she was, handling nicely as she flew along, letting the steep walls of water rushing up astern slide neatly under the transom. The dinghy was not so happy, charging around its painter like a worried dog and taking some water. Fortunately, Dan is big and strong, and he would bring it up on the quarter and manhandle it up far enough to spill the water.

On we flew in the widest part of the lake, passing Essex on the New York side, with its cross-lake ferry throwing spray over its blunt bow, and Vermont's Shelburne and

The seaplane harbor, Stave Island

then Burlington, the lake's major port and metropolis. As we neared Stave Island, set well out in the lake south of South Hero Island where the lake narrows considerably on its way north, the approaching front was more obvious, with flashes of lightning over the Adirondacks. We continued to scud along before the southerly, however, which was gaining heft. At 1730, just under three hours for the twenty-one statute miles, we rounded the north end of Stave into a little cove protected by a seawall, with two seaplanes at moorings. The Hazeletts were on the wall to welcome us and help us tie up, and they invited us to come up to the house when we were snugged down. Three minutes later, the southerly suddenly stopped, and rain, thunder, and lightning engulfed us, followed by a building northwester: Not bad timing, we thought.

The heavy rain was short-lived as the front brought cool, clearing weather behind it, and Stave proved a fascinating introduction to Champlain cruising. It is privately owned by the Hazeletts, whose winter home is in Colchester on nearby Mallett's Bay, just to the east of Stave. They have a rustic main house, and there is a caretaker's cottage across the island. Trails for exploring by walking or golf cart wind along the shores and up to a watchtower on the highest point of the island.

We had dinner at the main house, and in the morning, with a sparkling clear, blustery northwester now in charge, we had a tour of the island, including the marvelous 360-degree view from the tower. The bright blue of the lake was lined with windstreaks and whitecaps, with only a few boats out sailing, and the mountain chains to the west and east made an impressive backdrop against the bright blue of the sky. There was a good hint of autumn in the breeze.

When we got back to the harbor, spray was flying across the seawall, and we were ready to do some exploring afloat. Because of poor holding ground and the presence of the seaplanes, which Bill uses regularly, he does not like visitors anchoring in the harbor, but, to make up for this, he has put three moorings out on the east side of the island for general use on a first-come basis. They are special moorings that he has designed and manufactured at his strip-casting plant in Colchester. They consist of a plastic tube and an elastic compensator that makes up for a shortened scope. The mooring is designed to stay in for twenty-five years without hauling, and to cut down on swinging room in crowded harbors. It will bob out of the way if hit by a passing boat, and its design allows it to stay in ice in the winter as the tube conducts enough heat from the water to free the ice as it thaws. There are over six hundred such moorings in use on the lake.

One of them was free as we rounded the point after saying good-bye, and we picked it up for a lunch stop before heading into Mallett's. Once again, the main was all the sail needed for the run into Mallett's, which is a landlocked two-part body of water with outer and inner bays and lots of coves and offshoots. It is the yachting "capital"

of the lake and of what Vermonters whimsically call the
"west coast of New England," teeming with yachts at
moorings and in marinas, with sail outnumbering power
by a wide margin.

The entrance from the main lake is via a narrow cut in
what used to be a railroad embankment enclosing the outer
bay, and the chart must be followed carefully to avoid some
shoal spots. We swept through and on across the four and
one-half miles of the outer bay to the entrance of the inner
bay around Marble Island. The anchorage in the southwest corner here is completely taken up with local moorings off the marinas and the handsome Mallett's Bay Boat
Club, set amid rolling lawns. There is not much room for
transients, but we had a guest mooring arranged, and relaxed at a quiet, peaceful anchorage, as a north woods
coolness settled over us. We were well protected from the
still-blustery northwester.

Martha and Dan explored ashore and did minor shopping in the morning, while I visited with the operators of
U-Sail-It, the lake's major bareboat charter company, who
said they had had a busy season. We made a stop at a
marina with pumpout facilities, a mandatory procedure.
The rest of the day was spent in a leisurely sail along the
shores of Mallett's until we found a cove on the north side
that looked like a good anchorage with wooded cliffs and a
summer cottage here and there among the trees. All was
serene at bedtime, but during the night I felt a change of
motion, and, looking out, saw that the wind was now from
the south, with a fetch of more than two miles across the
bay. There was a small chop providing some motion, but
all seemed secure on the same bearings. The morning
showed a dark overcast and an increasing southerly as we
had breakfast. As we prepared to get under way, I could
tell that we were beginning to drag anchor, and saw clearly
how a good anchorage can change character on Champlain. The hook came up with a great swatch of a weed
called Eurasian Milfoil, which is a scourge on the lake.
Evidently, that was all that had been holding the Dan-
forth after the wind came in from the south.

On our way out, we took a side trip into the marina at

Marble Island to see *Intrepid,* the two-time America's Cup-winning 12-meter, at the pier there, looking a bit out of place with her mast towering over the other boats. She had been brought here to do day-sailing excursions, but, after her arrival, the lake level had lowered seasonally and she could not negotiate the channel to the main lake, leaving her a prisoner, at least temporarily.

We began a fast reach across the outer bay toward the railroad cut in the still-strong southerly, only to have it stop halfway across as though a fan had been switched off. We wallowed for a few minutes, and soon were hit by a renewed northwester that quickly blew the southerly's clouds back into the Green Mountains. We picked up one of the Stave moorings for a peaceful lunch and then set out for the New York shore into the teeth of the northwester that had built to about 20 miles per hour. *Elizabeth*[3] took it well, and the waves, though short and steep, did not have room to build to their full height as they had in the south winds of our first day.

Valcour Lodge, a restaurant on a bluff, had moorings, and we picked one up, mindful of advice that this, typical of so many Champlain anchorages, was no place to be in a southerly. We were hoping the northwester would last, and it did, diminishing in the evening, as we enjoyed a pleasant dinner at the lodge. The anchorage here is inside Valcour Island, a prominent spot in the crowded history of Champlain. Strange as it may seem, the U.S. Navy was founded on the lake, and the town of Whitehall, on a creek at the headwaters, heralds that fact with a sign at its outskirts. Benedict Arnold (when he was still loyal to the Revolution) supervised the building of several small ships at Whitehall, and in October 1776 met a British fleet in the Battle of Valcour Island. He anchored his crude little ships in a line between the mainland, where we were, across to the island, less than a mile away. The British eventually won the battle, but it delayed them long enough, and did enough damage, that they did not gain control of the lake, which contributed to their defeat at Saratoga in 1777.

It was interesting to try to visualize that historic battle and then to turn the other way and watch a succession of military jet planes roaring in on the approach path to Plattsburgh Air Base just up the lake.

It was a cool clear evening as we came back aboard and started a prebedtime Scrabble game, only to notice out the hatch a strange green glow in the sky. It was an impressive aurora borealis that filled the northern sky almost to the zenith with flickering shafts and waves of greenish gold for an hour.

"Are you sure that's not a supermarket opening?" was Dan's wry comment as it started, but it was Mother Nature putting on her own show, a fitting reminder of our north woods location.

The nippy atmosphere melted into full summer once again, as we started sailing in the morning, rounding Valcour and exploring its eastern side. Sloop Cove, a roomy harbor that is very popular, was well filled with boats. We went on a bit and poked into tiny Smuggler's Harbor, sharing it with just one boat, and enjoyed some shoreside exploring trails through the woods.

The lake was calm under a warm westerly as we drifted south through the afternoon for *Elizabeth*[3]'s return home to Point Bay. Drifting along in sunbathing weather over a flat lake, it was hard to remember our wild sleigh ride in the other direction on our first day, and the sparkling northwesters seemed a dream as the mountains to east and west, so sharp in the clear weather, receded into haze. We had not seen all that Champlain had to offer, but we had had a good sampling of the challenges and attractions of a very special cruising area.

Additional Information

Inland

North America's thousands of lakes and waterways support a tremendous amount of boating, but most of it is in small boats on relatively small bodies of water; the system of rivers and canals is not as well adapted to cruising as the amazing network of inland waters in Europe. Europe's systems of canals and locks was developed before man had mechanical propulsion, and the water, with the help of mules or horses for motive power, was the best way to get around. North America, developed later, was not so dependent on waterways for its interior communications, and those that did serve were mostly natural rivers.

There are exceptions of course; the Erie Canal was one of the first and most notable. In recent years there have also been developments in the Tennessee Valley Authority system. While Europe has maintained its canal systems and uses them well, some of the early American canals, such as the Delaware-and-Raritan and Delaware-and-Hudson, could not compete with railroads and highways when they came along, and they fell into disuse. In Canada, the Trent Severn system has continued in use and is a popular cruising area.

North America, though, has the great plus of Lake Champlain and the Great Lakes, the largest system of interconnected inland lakes in the world and a marvelous area for cruising. All five offer endless opportunities for exploring and each has at least one prime area. Lake Huron, though, takes the prize with its magnificent North Channel, one of the premium cruising areas worldwide with its intricate network of waterways and islands and plethora of gunkholing opportunities.

The shortness of the season is a problem, as summer comes in late, with a very short transition from cool, windy spring weather to the heat waves of July and August, and fall comes early.

There are other inland lakes, many of them man-made, that are large enough to offer cruising, though they are not so likely to attract visitors and are mostly used by local sailors. Lake Texoma, on the Texas-Oklahoma border, has twelve hundred miles of shoreline, with all sorts of anchorages, and large cabin cruisers and cruising auxiliaries up to the forty-foot range make good use of it. The Highland Lakes, formed by a series of dams on the Colorado River northwest of Austin, provide a lot more water for exploration. Around Dallas, a chain of lakes with each no longer than five miles, supports an amazing population

of large power yachts and auxiliaries. While there is nowhere to cruise, the boats serve as "cottages" on weekends.
Lake of the Ozarks and Lake Lanier near Atlanta are big
enough to support cruising activity.

The major river systems are mostly commercialized and
are nautical highways to somewhere, but not attractive
as cruising grounds in themselves, although there are exceptions.

Yachting centers Great Lakes: All major cities on each
lake, plus resort centers like Chaumont, New York; Little
Current, Kingston, and Picton, Ontario; Port Clinton and
Put-in-Bay, Ohio; Menominee, Holland, Macatawa Bay,
Traverse Bay, and Mackinac Island, Michigan; Ashland and
Marinette, Wisconsin; and many more.

Chartering Chartering is mostly on an individual basis
through yacht brokers. Crewed charters are a rarity on
inland waters. Lake Champlain has commercial bareboating out of Mallett's Bay.

Weather Over such a vast area, weather naturally varies by latitude and altitude, but the norm is short seasons,
quick changes and extremes, heat waves in summer, and
frequent thunderstorms.

Cruising grounds The best of these are: on Lake On-
tario, the Bay of Quinte; Lake Erie, the Put-in-Bay area;
Lake Huron, North Channel and Georgian Bay; Lake
Michigan, the Upper Peninsula, eastern shore, and Green
Bay area on the western shore; Lake Superior, Apostle Is-
lands; Lake Champlain, the entire lake; Hudson River and
Erie Canal; TVA lakes; Sacramento River Delta.

Special attractions Scenery and atmosphere of North
Channel and Georgian Bay and Lake Champlain.

References Robinson, *Over the Horizon,* Chapters VII
and VIII, and *Where to Cruise,* from p. 60; McKibben,
Cruising Guide to Lake Champlain; Brazer, *Waterway
Guide:* Great Lakes Edition and *Cruising Guide to the Great
Lakes and their Connecting Waterways.*

5

▶ ▶ ▶ ▶ ▶ ▶ ▶ ▶ ▶ ▶ ▶ ▶ ▶ ▶ ▶

THE SKAGERRAK'S SHORES
of Norway and Sweden

It was after 1700, a time when most cruising boats head for port for the beginning of happy hour ceremonies. We had just had a quick look at the summer station of the Royal Norwegian Yacht Club in Hankø, and the two boats of our cruise-in-company were right there in slips; but this was July at 59°10′ north, the sun, still high in the sky, was glinting on the Oslofjord, and, instead of settling into cockpit rituals, we started cruising.

We—Jane, Marcia Wiley (my editorial colleague at *Yachting* magazine), and I—had been invited on a Skagerrak cruise as a turnabout of a Caribbean cruise when our hosts of the moment, Finn Ferner, commodore of RNYC, and his American wife, Monk, had been with us. Their boat is *Skarv VII,* a Gambling 34 racer-cruiser designed by Jan Linge, best known for the Olympic Soling Class. To provide more room and some variety, they had invited their old friend Arne Brun-Lie and his American wife, Ellen, to come along in *Tresbelle,* their thirty-seven-foot sloop, a veteran of a round-trip transatlantic passage.

There was a light southerly blowing up the Oslofjord as we set out on the nine miles to Misingen, a group of rocky islets at the entrance to the fjord. We powered into it while

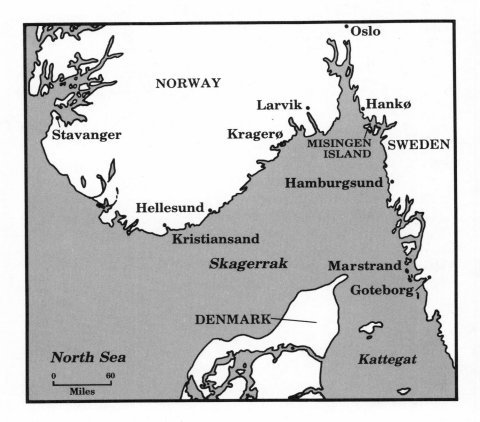

NORWAY

Oslo

Larvik

Hankø

Kragerø

MISINGEN
ISLAND

SWEDEN

Stavanger

Hamburgsund

Hellesund

Kristiansand

Skagerrak

Marstrand

DENMARK

Goteborg

North Sea

Kattegat

0   60
Miles

a bank of clouds built over the sun; it had been warm when the sun was out, but there was now a Scandinavian nip in the air, and windbreakers were unpacked and donned. Misingen has perfect protection in its coves, and we made the typical Scandinavian moor by rafting with a line to one of the ever-present iron spikes stuck in the rocks, and anchors over the stern. A couple of boats were in other coves, but there was a sense of far-north isolation amid the barren rocks, as gray as the clouds over the sun. There still was light until almost 2300, and we seemed a million miles away from the airport bustle that had started the day. It was a late but very relaxed happy hour, and Monk followed it with a special Norwegian dish, almost a stew, of ham and cabbage, that she had introduced us to in the Caribbean.

I explored ashore in the morning, clambering over the granite slopes and annoying sea gulls, who soared up in raucous protest. Though the rocks seemed barren, I found seven different kinds of wildflowers tucked away in crannies and hollows and examined the mooring spikes. They are ubiquitous throughout Scandinavian waterways, put there over the years by fishermen and yachtsmen with a lot of hard pounding with sledgehammers. Sometimes there will be a sturdy enough tree to use as a mooring post, or an anchor can be wedged in a crack, but the spikes are a great help.

The morning brought a fresh northwester with a parade of close-order cumulus, and we headed southeast along the Swedish side of the Skagerrak into a maze of islands, called skerries, and winding waterways. Everyone in Scandinavia vacations in July to take advantage of the long daylight hours. The per capita boat ownership is very high, and the traffic, as we jibed around bends in the waterways, was of I-95 density, composed of mostly small cruising sailboats, with a few powerboats as well. Everyone was observing right-of-way courtesy, and it was a jolly, friendly atmosphere. Boats were tucked up against the shore in cove after cove, and small summer cottages dotted the skerries, with a fishing village and its huddled cluster of little houses popping into view now and then.

Evening twilight, west coast of Sweden

By late afternoon we came to a spacious cove called Havstenssund that seemed to be an especially popular meeting place, with room for us to anchor out, as the entire shoreline was taken up with moored boats. From many of them, groups had spread out onto the grassy banks for picnics and games. This was one of the few times when we anchored away from shore. We had plenty of company including a Halberg-Rassey ketch from Oslo, owned by friends of the Ferners', who came for a cocktail visit while their early-teen grandsons explored the harbor by outboard dinghy. Misingen was the least crowded of all the harbors we visited, and in all of them there was very active socializing among boats. The different nationalities did tend to stick with their own, but, despite the stories about rivalries and even animosities among Scandinavians, general courtesy seemed to prevail. In these waters, there were mostly Swedish and Norwegian ensigns flying, but there were occasional Danish ones as well, and a smattering of British, Dutch, and Germans. The Germans tend to be present in greater numbers in August.

In the morning, the Ferners, Lies, and Marcia braved a quick dip while the Robinsons shivered just watching them. Swimming tends to be quick and invigorating, but there is a great amount of sunbathing on deck and on the shoreside rocks in costumes ranging down to total lack of one. We had more of the same northwester for another jibe-filled run south, during which we stopped for lunch in a tiny harbor jam-packed with boats, with little dollhouse shacks clustered on the shore. It was back to a rafted Scandinavian moor for the evening just off the channel in a narrow stretch of waterway called Hamburgsund. We worried about passing wakes, but they subsided in the evening.

It was an early start the next day, as we were heading across the Skagerrak for Norway. I had cruised this Swedish coast twice before, just barely overlapping with the Hamburgsund anchorage, marveling at the way boats shoehorned into popular harbors like Marstrand, Smögen, and Fjallbacka, but the Norwegian coast would be a new experience. Norway usually evokes images of steep-walled fjords backed by snow peaks, and that is true of the western coast from Stavanger to Bergen and north to the Arctic Circle along the North Sea. Cruising is difficult there, with erratic winds, bottomless anchorages, and rough conditions offshore, though the spectacular scenery is worth the effort for the truly adventurous.

The southeast coast along the Skagerrak is quite different. The countryside is hilly and graceful, but the mountains are well inland, and the waterways and sounds wind behind protective islands from the mouth of the Oslofjord one hundred miles southwestward to Kristiansand. Here, too, there is a steady flow of small-boat traffic, and the coastline has many summer cottages, each with a long pennant of national colors streaming from a flagpole. There is an endless choice of mooring spots, and a few towns make shopping and resupply easy when needed.

An early start here at this time of year could mean any time after 0230, but 0600 was early enough for us as we began the sixty-mile crossing. We threaded our way out through smaller and smaller and more barren skerries, dodging fish pots, as the still-fresh breeze, now in the north, promised a good reach. The wind held and the atmosphere was so clear that we never were out of sight of land. While the Swedish coast was still a line of low lumps astern, mountains inland of Larvik to the northwest on the Norwegian coast popped over the horizon as tiny cones.

With noonday warmth, the norther began to fade. The boats had been fairly even when the breeze was fresh, but now *Skarv* began to pull slightly ahead. There were no other boats in sight, not even fishing boats or freighters, a strange contrast to the crowded waterways, and we wallowed to a stop on a glassy, slightly heaving surface. To make schedule, power came on, but in less than an hour, a dark line of wind approached from the south and we were soon reaching fast in a fresh sea breeze. The low coastline loomed up quickly, and a good chop was building whitecaps when we swept by a tall lighthouse that had been our landfall into an atmosphere of evergreen trees and rocky banks along twisting waterways. The sun was bright and warm, and the long pennants on the cottage flagpoles

A Scandinavian moor in the Swedish skerries

streamed gaily in the new breeze. There was boat traffic
all around us, not quite as crowded as in Sweden, but a
great many small auxiliaries of the Folkboat type, and
varnished double-ended motor launches. There were modern outboards and fiberglass cabin cruisers too.

Wandering through narrow waterways and small sounds,
with graceful vistas up side coves and inlets, we came to
the town of Kragerø, its houses set in tiers on steep hillsides, and a swarm of boats along its waterfront. We side-
tracked to a landlocked harbor across the way called
Venneviken, whose numerous cottages were set among the
trees on its steep shores, and anchored out for the second
time on the cruise. It was a peaceful evening scene except
for the fact that a narrow canal at the head of the harbor
led on to some other waterway, and a steady stream of
outboards poured through it in a noisy hurry, subsiding
thankfully as the twilight deepened. Monk was, as ever,
producing wonderful things out of the galley, and the Lies
pitched in with a share of the feast. Marinated-on-the-spot
fresh herring was a special treat this time, along with
freshly caught mackerel. Arne once produced a heaping
bowl of finger-food shrimp. Wine and beer were good and
plentiful, but hard liquor is so prohibitively expensive that
our hosts were grateful for what duty-free liquor we had
been able to bring in.

Hopping across to Kragerø in the morning, we had a
glimpse of the local tourist influx, as the streets and shops
were jammed with vacationers wandering along in a happy
jumble. Resupply of food, fuel, and water was easy, and
the waterfront was a colorful sight, with the star attraction a 1930s 12-Meter, a far cry from the America's Cup
type in her teak decks, varnished brightwork, cockpit
benches, and cabin skylights. Kragerø provided a good example of the almost frantic approach to Scandinavian vacationing in the few days of summer.

From Kragerø, there was one stretch of coast where we
were out in the open Skagerrak for a few miles. It provided a dramatic contrast to the evergreen-lined waterways in a stiff beat to windward into a whitecapped chop
of open water. Both boats were good sailers, and it was a

stimulating interlude, before we were back into calm water again and a tiny private harbor where we were to visit the summer house of friends. The house was inexplicably deserted, and Finn finally heard from a neighbor that the couple had been injured and hospitalized when their small launch was run over by a drunk in a fast outboard who misjudged their running lights in a narrow waterway. Civilization had come to this peaceful area too.

We had no more open water to negotiate, but the next day there was a fresh breeze blowing straight up a fairly confined waterway. We guests had been alternating boats each day, mixing around with no set pattern, and this day I was on *Skarv*. Arne had gone ahead under power, making sail, so we challenged him to a brush, and the quick-tacking duel in confined waters was good for action and laughs. Nobody won.

This area was well populated with summer cottages of friends of the Ferners' and Lies', and we had a pleasant evening raft-up in front of an attractive converted fisherman's house. Until now, our weather had been beautiful, with good breezes, warm days, and a pleasant tang in the evening air, but our luck didn't hold for the last couple of days, and it was mostly powering through the winding channels. The sightseeing was ever pleasant, with attractive houses and picturesque old towns; we wound our way out through the islands to an outer ring, where we found the most isolated anchorage since Misingen. Near Hellesund, there was a long narrow cut in an island, lined by high, rocky cliffs, barren at the seaward entrance and more wooded as we headed inland. It took careful navigating to find the way in, and it was a wonderful, peaceful haven when we rafted and tied to a tree on the bank, with the stern anchors in fifteen feet of crystal-clear water that showed every detail of the bottom. Only one other boat was there, and there were no houses.

Climbing the cliffs gave wonderful views down on the boats and out the cut, but on the seaward side of the island, which was right on the Skagerrak, there were the remains of a German coastal defense battery from the World War II occupation. Arne had been a prisoner of war in a

Nazi concentration camp, and this reminder suddenly brought back sickening memories for him, but the anchorage was a peaceful antidote. As the long twilight settled over us, the cliffs took on a soft glow, turning the rocks to gold and easing old wounds.

Even the hardiest of our swimmers admitted that the water here, fed directly from the Skagerrak, was the coldest they had experienced. And in the morning, the Skagerrak sent in a damp drizzle as another reminder of its proximity. We spent the day powering through the soggy scenery back toward Kristiansand, where we were to make air connections. On our way, there was a final touch of fun and hospitality in another family summer cottage, also a converted fisherman's house on its own tiny cove. Our two boats barely squeezed up to the little pier between the rocky banks, and we were immediately inundated with a visitation of young, blond children, freshly scrubbed and in clean white clothes, grandchildren of the house. They giggled and squealed as they explored the boats, and one of them, an engaging, self-confident lad, surprised us with his colloquial English. It turned out his father was a visiting professor at the University of Pennsylvania, they lived in Bryn Mawr, and he went to the Shipley School, which was Jane's alma mater, so they had a Shipley minireunion right there in the cockpit.

We were entertained at a gala evening of Norwegian food and drink, with the youngsters rather unpredictable servers to the two older generations. Our Shipley lad capped the festivities by playing "My Country 'Tis of Thee" in our honor, slightly off key, on the flute.

All this had been a wonderful climax to the special charm of cruising in this lively, vibrant area, with its multitude of anchorages, its ever-graceful scenery, and its special contrast of the open sea stretches of the Skagerrak and the north woods atmosphere of its waterways. There is nothing quite like the peace of a Scandinavian moor in the serenity of one of its harbors as the slow twilight of northern latitudes spreads across the scene.

Additional Information

Scandinavia

Since the time of the Vikings and their voyages to North America long before Columbus, plus their forays through most of Europe's waterways, Scandinavians have been seamen. The tradition lives on today in their active merchant marine services, and small-boat cruising is a national pastime. In Norway and Sweden, almost every family has some sort of boat, and Denmark and Finland are not far behind. For example, Sweden's population of eight million supports eight hundred thousand pleasure boats. On a sunny midsummer day, one gets the impression that all of them are out at once, and that is not far from the truth. Whole countries take a full month off for summer vacation: July in Norway and Sweden. In that month, with the best chance for sunny weather in the rugged northern climate, and the long hours of daylight, almost everyone takes to the water. In these latitudes, comparable to Labrador in North America, there is daylight from about 0300 until almost midnight at the height of summer.

The geography of Scandinavia lends itself perfectly to cruising. There are thousands of miles of protected waterways among countless islands, plus many mainland bays and coves. Not only do the four native nationalities flock afloat, but visitors also abound, as these are the best cruising waters in all of northern Europe. German, Dutch, French, and English flags are a common sight, and it is not rare to see American ensigns as well.

The weather is always a consideration. Scandinavians love to pull their favorite weather joke on visitors, saying "Summer was very nice last year. It was on a Friday." There can be rough, cold, rainy conditions, and Scandinavians are prepared for them with excellent domestic foul-weather gear and weather cloths around their cockpits, but it is not rare to have days on end of balmy sunshine. I have had that luck on several July cruises, but a late-August cruise saw a cold front bring a brisk norther with winds in the high 20s and temperatures in the 50s; real windbreaker weather. The water is always cold. Spray on deck has frigid authority, and I have never tried an overboard swim. Many towns, though, have public swimming pools, and several times we took our swimming that way.

The North Sea, off to the west in the direction from which the weather comes, has a strong effect on Scandinavian climate, but its famous tidal ranges do not penetrate into the Skagerrak, Kattegat, Oresund, and Baltic, the main cruising areas. There are areas of strong tidal current, as in the Oresund off Copenhagen, but very little rise and fall.

Yachting centers All four national capitals have major yachting facilities, with marinas, yacht clubs, boatyards, and mooring areas, and every waterfront town in Scandinavia has boat facilities. The resort centers with major yachting activity are Hankø in Norway, Skoshoved in Denmark, Marstrand on Sweden's west coast and Saltsjöbaden on Sweden's east coast. Cities like Bergen, Goteborg, and Helsinki, while important commercial ports, also support a great amount of local yachting.

Chartering Because of the short season, the chartering opportunities in Scandinavia are mainly in individually owned private boats, not commercial fleets, and there is a minimum of crewed chartering. What chartering there is should be arranged through yacht brokers, who can be located in the brokerage sections of boating magazines.

Weather The season is short: early June to early September, with July generally the most reliable month for sunshine and pleasant sailing breezes. The nearby North Sea can generate heavy storms and rain, and forecasts should be carefully monitored. Fog is relatively rare in summer, but a factor at the beginning and end of season.

Cruising grounds The only areas that are more for "expeditions" than normal, routine cruising, and require special preparations, are the west coast of Norway and the northern Baltic owing to lack of facilities, isolation, and weather uncertainties. Because of political considerations, the Gulf of Finland beyond the Helsinki area has not been recommended for visiting yachts, but that could change.

The lower Baltic and the multi-island archipelago between Stockholm and Helsinki is a prime area, with the main problem one of keeping navigational track of the lookalike islands. In the Oresund and around the entire coast of Zealand, there are many good harbors, but all are crowded, with much commercial activity, and are mainly for weekending. The Fyn Archipelago between Zealand and Jutland is a fine area, with "skipper towns" (old seafaring ports) a special attraction. The Skagerrak, both on Sweden's west coast and Norway's southeast coast, is tops in Scandinavia, with many protected waterways along its shores and hundreds (or more) of choices of anchorages.

Special attractions The scenery rates high in most of the region, plus the special northern weather features of long daylight and aurora borealis. Nautical traditions evident in the "skipper towns," the Viking and *Kon-Tiki* museums in Oslo, the square-rigged sail-training vessels, and the local fishing boats all add color and atmosphere. The four Scandinavian capitals are all attractive and sophisticated metropolises, with many cultural features and opportunities for sightseeing of museums, shrines (such as the house of Sibelius), and statuary. Eating ashore, to sample the renowned Scandinavian smorgasbjord and other local dishes; and meeting the very friendly, outgoing, and nautically experienced local sailors also add much to the fun of cruising here.

References Robinson, *Where to Cruise,* pp. 69–88.

6

▶ ▶ ▶ ▶ ▶ ▶ ▶ ▶ ▶ ▶ ▶ ▶ ▶ ▶ ▶

A DUTCH TREAT
Canal Barging in Holland

The canal from Amsterdam led southward to a small lake, Weistender Plassen; this Monday in May we had to go out on it instead of continuing in the canal, because it was a church holiday. Although everyone in Holland seemed to be out in their boats on a day of thin sunshine, making the best of the holiday, the bridge tenders were also taking the day off, and our way south was blocked by a low bridge that would not open until the morrow. If we wanted to keep cruising, Weistender Plassen was it.

And Weistender Plassen, with the town of Aalsmeer on its shore, was quite a sight. It was so full of pleasure boats of every description that it was difficult to see the water; and what a floating boat show it was. There were Windsurfers and canoes; kayaks and rowboats; small outboards; modern fiberglass cabin cruisers; gaff-rigged, wooden day-sailing sloops; Solings; Flying Juniors; fiberglass cruising auxiliaries; and, dotted in among the modern boats, traditional *botters,* the sabot-shaped bluff-ended sloops with huge leeboards. And we no doubt added something to the spectacle, aboard our twenty-four-passenger hotel barge *Juliana,* a conversion from a 126-foot freight barge operated by the New York company, Floating Through Europe.

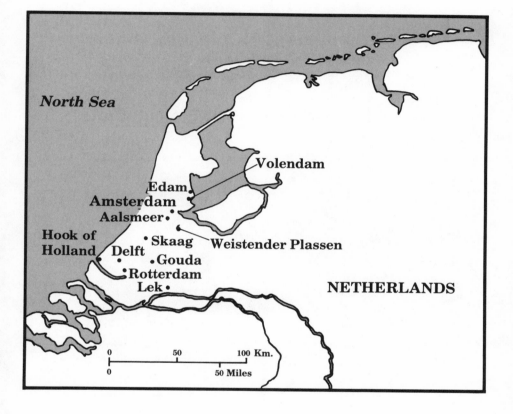

North Sea

Volendam

Edam

Amsterdam

Aalsmeer

Skaag

Weistender Plassen

Hook of
Holland

Delft

Gouda

Rotterdam

Lek

NETHERLANDS

0   50   100 Km.

0   50 Miles

Almost every house has a boat moored in front

This is certainly a contrast in cruising from reaching through the Grenadines or gliding past the snow peaks of Desolation Sound; but, in canal cruises here, in France's Loire Valley, and in the Thames River system in England, we have found it a very special way to see the countryside, and one not devoid of nautical interest and pleasures. Holland is particularly interesting. Not only is the boat population per capita very high, as evidenced by such scenes as the armada on Weistender Plassen, but there are waterways all through the country so that almost every town has its own waterfront; and Dutch history and lifestyle are closely tied to the water. Holland is also where the sport of yachting originated and got its name. In premechanical-propulsion days, most of the country's commerce, communications, and transportation was carried on by sail on its network of canals, rivers, and *zees*. Boats did the duty of buses, trains, freighters, and the family car, and the Dutch became able sailors negotiating the winding lacework of waterways.

Their boats were fast and fun to sail, and by the sixteenth century a tradition had become established to use sailboats for recreation. There were joint cruises, rendezvous, and mock marine battles, all in the name of fun and picnics, and, because of the swiftness of the boats, they became known as *jaghts* or *jachts*, which came from the word for hunter, implying swiftness. Charles II of England was in exile in Breda in southern Holland during the Cromwell era, and he spent much of his time sailing *jaghts*. When he was recalled to the throne in 1660, his Dutch friends presented him with a luxuriously outfitted jaght named *Mary*. She was a single-sticker, for which the Dutch word was *sloepe,* and the sport, with its terms Anglicized, spread to the English-speaking world.

Some of the *botters* on the lake, as we cruised slowly through the fleet, looked as though they could have been there since Charles's day, but there were sparkling new ones too, with their brightwork shining in the sun. The breeze was very light, the water was calm, and everyone was drifting along in lazy euphoria. Eventually we found a small inlet next to a marina where we could tie alongside the bank for the night, while the activity on the lake continued through the long May twilight.

As it turned out, it was almost the only sunlight we were to see in a week. The weather was pleasantly warm that first day, but, overnight, the North Sea sent in one of its cold gray northeasters, which dominated from then on, and it was time for windbreakers and foul-weather gear. We had just come from a two-week ship cruise in Greece and along the Dalmatian Coast of the Adriatic in idyllic, cloud-free warmth, and the change to northern European conditions was a marked one. We wished we had waited and come a month or so later.

It would have been nice to have better weather, but the cruise was not ruined. Canal cruising in Holland, and throughout all of Europe, is far from dull ditch-crawling between restricting banks, like some sections of our East Coast Intracoastal Waterway. There is great variety in sights and scenes, with close-up glimpses of neat, tightly settled, and orderly towns. There are no barren stretches; every inch of the country seems to have been put to some purpose, and gliding out of a town will bring a view, often looking down from the raised canal, across well-tended farm fields. There are frequent drawbridges, where a small toll is collected by hanging a wooden shoe on a fish pole and extending it to the passing boat. There were a few locks, but not as many as in the hillier country of France.

The barge had a van as its shoreside complement so that we could take off around the countryside on occasion, and before we left the Weistender Plassen we took a drive to a tulip nursery, one of Holland's major "industries." It was just past the peak of the spring tulip season, and the vast fields, stretching for acres along the road, had been pretty well stripped of their brilliant blooms. There were enough left to give an idea of what the full display must have been like, and we could imagine the colorful spectacle they had been. We ordered some bulbs to be sent home (that added a nice touch there the next spring), and the greenhouses of the nursery were a riot of blooms in themselves. Although tulip season had passed its peak, there were colorful gardens in a parklike atmosphere along much of the waterways, and May was the month for everything to be in its most lush green glory. And, as I have said, every inch of ground seemed to have been given some purpose. In addition to flowers, many of the waterways had rows of neatly spaced trees of equal height as sentinels along the way.

In Holland, windmills are also an expected part of the scenery, but we learned that almost all of them have been preserved simply for atmosphere; very few are actually working anymore. We did stop at one that is still kept in operation grinding grain as a demonstration, rather than for any serious business reason. It was surprisingly big, with a large central tower, and an enormous grindstone circling around driven by the sails. The sails themselves were very long; we got some perspective on their size when a man climbing up one was only about a sixth of the length of it. This mill was one in a group lined along the canal, and the symmetry of their march into the distance made a memorable picture. If they were only preserved for atmosphere, they were doing their job well.

The canal travel was in a constant stream of small craft of all kinds, and life aboard *Juliana* was very pleasant and easy, with a sun deck for lounging. The captain had his wife and small son aboard, and we were continually entertained watching his "canalmanship," to coin a term for the type of seamanship he displayed; he was a master at maneuvering her ungainly bulk through the tightest squeezes: locks, turns, low bridges, and sharp bends. The barge had a heavy-duty diesel and a bow thruster propeller; and the pilothouse was collapsible, allowing it to go through the lower fixed bridges. The captain's wife and son helped with the deck work, while a cruise director, two chefs, and two stewardesses acted as a very attentive "hotel staff." We were lucky that there were only twelve passengers aboard rather than her full load of twenty-four, as she would have been rather crowded with that number.

As we wended our way toward Rotterdam, we went by a yard where great 150-foot luxury yachts were being readied for delivery to Arab oil sheiks. Our evening stop was at a yachting center called Kaag; we tied up at a marina

Our barge amid decorative windmills

bulkhead and watched the activity of classic-looking gaff-rigged sloops flitting gracefully through the narrow waters. They were rental boats from the marina, and they were obviously very popular and very well handled. After sailing, everyone gathered at the marina's open-air café for schnapps and socializing.

On the way to Rotterdam the next day we stopped at the Delft pottery works, a well-organized canalside tourist attraction with pottery-making demonstrations by master craftsmen and a shop full of the end product right there. The factory was in a town of tightly packed buildings and narrow cobbled streets, a typical example of Dutch urban living.

Moving on, Rotterdam, the world's busiest seaport, was a fascinating study in commercial activity. There is a constant and thick flow of barges, freighters, scows, tankers, yard oilers, fishing boats, and, looking slightly overwhelmed, pleasure craft, on the broad main river, the Lek, which is an extension of the Lower Rhine. Passage from it into canals, tributaries, and docking areas is governed by a large, airport-type control tower, which also has a restaurant on top. Several pairs of eyes are needed to take in all the activity. It was midday when we passed through, so we kept going upriver for a while and then back into the canal system again and the much more peaceful life of the countryside.

While the weather remained cloudy and blowy, with a nip in the breeze reminding us of the nearby North Sea, we were not hampered from sightseeing. This included stops at a cathedral, a moated castle with crenellated walls and darkly paneled interior, and visits to craftsmen in pewter, silver, and pipe making, and the Gouda "cheese factory." Our original itinerary was to come out of the canal northward into the Isselmeer, formerly the Zuider Zee, for an open-water passage across to Volendam, but the northeaster was up to 40 knots and kicking up a good chop on the *zee,* so we stayed in the canals along its perimeter, skirting Amsterdam and continuing on to Volendam. Here there was a big marina, with the Isselmeer stretching off into the distance, and by now the breeze had moderated

Paying a bridge toll into a wooden shoe

and we finally had another glimpse of sun. Cabin cruisers and auxiliaries and fishing boats drying their nets in the marina provided a salty contrast to the canal travel. Much of the Isselmeer has been and continues to be reclaimed as land by pumping, fill, and diking. In a country that is largely reclaimed from the sea, this is not a surprise or a problem for the inhabitants.

Volendam is a resort, and it was crowded with tourists promenading along a shop-lined walkway at the waterfront, reveling in the return of the sun after a windy, dark week. Nearby, Edam, famous for its cheese, was a typical Dutch town of tightly packed stone houses, some leaning a bit as though weary from standing for centuries. It is a new perspective to see such civilization while gliding by at 3 to 4 knots, and, after our week, when we returned to Amsterdam and its highly civilized bustle, again seen differently when viewed from a tree-lined canal, we were convinced that canal barging is a great way to see the countryside, especially a nautically oriented one, and a very pleasant way to relax for a week. And we never had to reef.

Additional Information

British Isles and the Continent

A few years ago, Jane and I were driving around the south of England visiting yachting harbors on a familiarization tour, and we came to Burnham-on-Crouch, one of the major east coast centers, bordering on the North Sea. Over the years, I had read so much in manuscripts submitted to *Yachting* and in British magazines about the famous British centers, and this was supposed to be one of the most prominent ones. It happened to be a dank, drizzly day in September, standard conditions for much of that visit, and we parked the car at a marina and got out to look around.

The tide was out, and the Crouch was a dingy rivulet, bordered by vast mudbanks between it and the shore. It was jammed with boats on moorings, and many of them were aground, crazily careened or standing upright on twin keels, a popular feature in British harbors notorious for extreme range of tide. There was one person in sight. A man in foul-weather gear and rubber boots was plodding up the mud bank toward shore with a dinghy painter over his shoulder, tugging the boat behind him through the mud.

After watching his laborious progress for a while, I turned to Jane and said, "If I lived here, I think I would be a golfer."

Yachtsmen in the British Isles put up routinely with conditions that most Americans would not tolerate. The weather, often damp and penetratingly cold, the tidal conditions, and the lack of attractive cruising areas would be a strong deterrent to anyone used to conditions in more salubrious climes, but the limeys keep at it with fervor and élan, and more power to them. It is not, however, a place for visitors to come cruising unless they have a very special personal reason. Most of the harbors are crowded and busy with commerce and fishing, but there is some attractive cruising to be had on the southern and western coasts of Ireland, and among the islands on the west coast of Scotland.

The same sailing conditions generally apply for the Continent north of the Mediterranean. The coasts of the Bay of Biscay, the English Channel, and the North Sea have extreme tidal ranges and the weather is very often a problem. As noted in the discussion of Scandinavian cruising, many sailors head to those waters for their vacation cruising. The French and British do make the best of the Channel for local cruising, timing their sailing to the tides and the closing of tidal gates that keep the water in many harbors that would otherwise be drained at low tide.

Again, northern latitudes mean long hours for summer sailing, but a short season, and all the waters surrounding the Continent are notorious as storm breeders, with conditions changing rapidly and with little warning. Fog is often a factor, along with strong winds and rain.

My cruising in this area has been confined to barging in Holland, France, and England and day sailing on the Solent, and, after our tour of the south of England and experiences on the Continent's canals, I have to admire the natives for the dedication they do possess to getting afloat. (And I really don't like golf!)

Yachting centers In England, the Solent around the Isle of Wight is the major center, and the birthplace of organized yachting in the English-speaking world. Cowes, Southampton, Lymington, and the Hamble are the chief spots, but every small town has facilities. The Thames out of London supports yachting activity and Burnham is an active center. Channel ports out toward Land's End all have a concentration of yachts, with Poole, Plymouth, and Falmouth among the leaders. Scottish centers are in the Edinburgh area on the east and the Clyde on the west coast. Irish yachting centers on the south coast, and the Royal Cork Yacht Club traces its history back to the Water Club of Cork in the mid-seventeenth century as the original yacht club in the world.

On the south coast of the North Sea in Belgium, Holland, and Germany (whose Kiel is a major base), yachting activity is mostly inland on rivers, canals, and *zees* because of the tidal range and weather patterns of the North Sea. The French, as mentioned, do use their Channel and Bay of Biscay coasts in summer in such ports as Cherbourg, St.-Malo, the Mourbihan, La Rochelle, St.-Nazaire, and the Gironde, and Belle-Île-en-Mer is a favorite offshore target for summer cruising, but they also have the Med to turn to.

Major Spanish activity, except for La Coruña and Santander on the Atlantic side, is in the Med, but the Portuguese do have a lot of local action on the Tagus out of Lisbon, at Cascais, and on the Algarve on the south coast.

Chartering Europeans are avid charterers. In the British Isles, it is mostly of private boats through brokers, who have worldwide connections. A favorite practice in France is flotilla cruising, in which a group of boats cruises in company with a lead boat under supervision, a good way for relative novices to get started. Individual boats and crewed charters are handled through brokers, and the major activity is in the Med.

Weather With its northern and oceanic influences, European weather is not ideal for cruising, as there is a good amount of rain and high winds generated in the Atlantic and moving west to east. The season is early June to early September, again with the advantage of long daylight hours in midsummer. In the fall, some Atlantic hurricanes can make their way as far as the Continent, but an even more dangerous threat is the type of quick-forming storm that was only predicted for a very short time and raised havoc with the 1979 Fastnet Race in the Irish Sea.

Cruising grounds The best of these are in the islands off the west coast of Scotland; the south and west coasts of Ireland; the Channel ports of England and France; the coast and islands of the Bay of Biscay; canal barging and river and lake activity in the interior.

Special attractions Cruising in Europe is cruising with history. Landmarks, historic sites, battlegrounds, castles, châteaux, forts, cathedrals, museums, art galleries, and many more such attractions abound, and a cruising sailor can take in as much or as little as personal choice demands. Barge cruises provide a close relationship with the countryside and the people, and a trip on the Thames brings a new historic site with every mile, from the church of the Vicar of Bray, Windsor Castle, and the Henley Regatta course to the Profumo scandal cottage. Eating ashore with all the varying national cuisines can be an exciting addition to European cruising.

References Robinson, *Where to Cruise*, pp. 89–99, and *Whiskey Run;* Coote, *North Sea Harbors and Pilotage;* Edwards-May, *Inland Waterways of France.*

PART II

SPRING AND FALL header decoration

SPRING AND FALL

In the areas described, summer is too hot, too crowded, or too windless, and out-of-season visits are more rewarding. Most of the areas remain popular and busy in summer despite drawbacks, and it is still possible to cruise in them, but they are at their best during the in-between times.

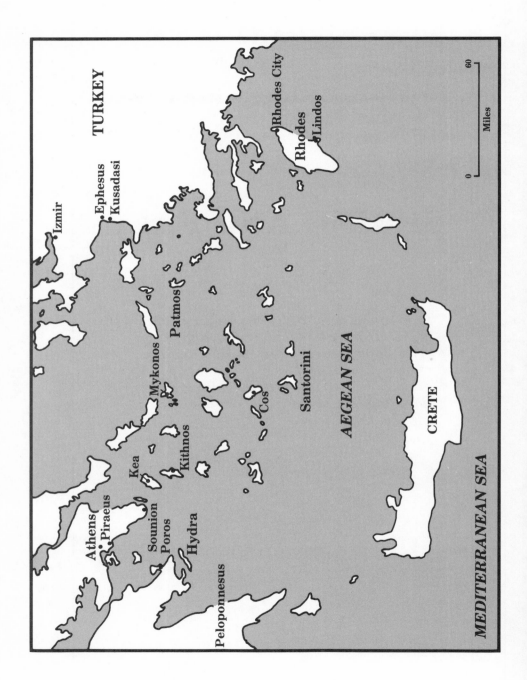

7

▶▶▶▶▶▶▶▶▶▶▶▶▶▶

NOT REALLY WINE DARK
The Aegean of Many Legends

Before starting out on a Greek island cruise, we took a rental car out of Athens beyond the teeming marinas and glitzy hotels of Vougliameni along the shores of the Bay of Faleron to Cape Sounion at the southeast tip of the Greek mainland. The Attic sky was a soft, cloudless blue, and the road was lined with May wildflowers. At Sounion, on the heights above the sea, the ruins of the temple of Poseidon, god of the sea, presided in grandeur, with one row of columns still standing as testament to the original majesty.

Off to the east, the islands of Kea and Kithnos were in hazy outline, and across the bay to the west the mountains of the Peloponnesus bulked mistily. The Aegean, spread below us, was a bright, light blue (I've never seen it as Homer's "wine dark") shining in the sun. A sail or two dotted it, and a cruise ship, gleaming white, looked like a toy below us rounding the cape as she headed for the Dodecanese. Here, in panorama, was one of the most storied, legend-laden maritime areas, rich in history and a beautiful sight on a warm spring morning. The season was too new for the fabled *meltemi,* the wild, monster thermal from the north that sweeps by here in midsummer with frightening authority, and the breeze was a gentle breath from the south. I was reminded of racing past here years before in the Aegean Rally, when our skipper noticed a cloud of butterflies that had blown over the water off Sounion, heralding the first whispers of a mild meltemi. We headed for them and picked up a wind shift that sent us on to victory.

Standing here now, we remembered how, as myth has it, the Aegean got its name. King Aegeus waited on the promontory anxiously watching for his son, Theseus, to return from battling the Minotaur in Crete. Theseus had promised to change his normal black sails to white ones if he was returning in victory. He forgot the vow and sailed home with black sails. Seeing them, Aegeus thought Theseus had been defeated and was dead and threw himself in despair into the sea that thereafter has carried his name.

Every island, bay, and promontory in the Aegean is rich with such myths and legends, adding a fascination to the sailing. Forgetting history, the waters are a prime cruising area in themselves. The sea has a feast of islands spread between the mainlands of Europe and Asia, with hundreds of anchorages and harbors ranging from high-pressure tourist spots like Mykonos and Hydra, to lonely coves hidden away on some of the smaller islands. Standing at Sounion amid the reminders of the god whose realm spreads out below, one cannot help but feel the impact of this world and be taken with an urge to be out there afloat.

That we were soon to be, and in May, one of the better months for Aegean cruising. Although summer months are the busiest, I think of spring and fall as the best times to enjoy the Aegean. We have been there in March, April, May, July, September, and October, and, while we enjoyed the July cruise, the meltemi governed it, the weather was extremely hot, and the towns, harbors and waters were overcrowded. The other months were better. It was in July that I sailed in the Aegean Rally from Piraeus to Rhodes, the top Greek ocean racing event, and we cruised back afterward. We have had shorter cruises and day sails in other visits; twice we have been on cruise ships. Our two most recent visits have been an interesting contrast. After our May visit to Sounion, we sailed down to Hydra and Poros in a 47-foot ketch on a long weekend, and, in a September cruise, we did the eastern Aegean in the four-masted barque *Sea Cloud*. The latter is a cruise ship, but still a fascinating way to experience these waters. She was built in 1931 at Kiel, Germany, for the heiress Marjorie Post, and, at 316 feet, is the largest sailing yacht ever built.

For Jane it is always a special treat to come back to the Aegean, as she majored in Greek at Smith and has had a lifelong interest in its mythology, history, and archaeology. To combine these interests with the wonderful cruising experience is doubly rewarding. I don't have her background in Greek, but it is still a thrill to come in from a stimulating sail to visit something like the ruins of the Aesculapion at Cos, the world's first hospital, set up by Hippocrates, or the eleventh-century monastery of St. Christodoulos at Patmos. Fortunately, we have sailed with Greeks who knew their culture and made sure that we saw the right things ashore, and, one advantage of seeing the islands by cruise ship is that very knowledgeable guides are along to fill in background. When we first sailed to Rhodes, some locals told us that the two stone pillars at the entrance to Mandraki Harbor mark the site of the ancient Colossus of Rhodes, but the professional guide on the *Sea Cloud* pooh-poohed the claim and told us where the statue probably did stand, quite a distance away.

The *Sea Cloud* cruise was a rare experience. We had been transatlantic in her, and later sailed from Easter Island to the Galapagos and Panama (see Chapter 17), so we were completely at home in her special atmosphere. She has powerful auxiliary engines that help her to keep schedule, but when the wind is right, every effort is made to sail. Her captain, Cas Cassidy, a former Coast Guard officer who had been skipper of their full-rigged training ship *Eagle,* loves to sail whenever possible. The breeze must be aft of abeam, as she cannot go to windward because of her rig. Fortunately, we had some good breezes in our September cruise, the last remnants of that year's meltemi sweeping down from the north, and we had fine sailing. A crew of young international adventurers from many countries, who sign on for the fun and experience, works the sails, and it is great sport to see them climb the rigging and man the

Fishermen tending nets, Patmos

yards. When she is under full sail in a good breeze off the quarter, it is an experience unmatched in any other sailing.

Before boarding her, we revisited Ephesus, that impressive ruin of an ancient city on the Aegean coast of Turkey. It was amazing to see how much more had been uncovered in the fifteen years since our first visit in the continuing archaeological program. We had to board in Turkey, as Greece has a law, similar to the one in the United States, that foreign flag vessels cannot carry passengers between domestic ports. Kusadasi, a sleepy fishing village when we first saw it in the 1960s, had become a busy cruise port and yachting center, with a major marina. The ports we visited on the rest of the cruise—Santorini, Patmos, Lindos, Rhodes, and ending with Piraeus—were also not new to us, but it was interesting to see how much they had changed. We had been one of two yachts at Patmos's well-protected Scala Harbor in 1966, and now the entire waterfront was lined with yachts stern-to in Mediterranean-moor fashion. The monastery of St. Christodoulos was much more crowded, but the view from its ramparts across the hills of

Patmos and the spread of the Dodecanese was as breath-taking as ever.

We had the same impression at Lindos, the ancient cap-ital of Rhodes on the south shore, facing the open Mediter-ranean, but again the development couldn't spoil its impressive layer-cake of Greek, Roman, and Byzantine ruins on the Acropolis, with the white cubes of modern buildings a frieze on the lower slopes and along the lovely curve of beach on its little bay. At Santorini, the southernmost is-land of the Cyclades, it was a relief to have a bus tour instead of the torture of a donkey ride up the steep incline from the volcanic crater that forms its harbor; and the ar-chaeological dig at Akrotiri, where a Minoan city has come to light, showed interesting progress.

The city of Rhodes, at the island's northeast tip, has de-veloped into a major charter center, with Mandraki, its yacht harbor jammed with yachts of many nations, as for-

The acropolis at Lindos, Rhodes

eign vessels are allowed to base here by special ruling. Great modern resort hotels line the beach west of the city, a special favorite of sun-loving Scandinavians. They are quite a contrast to ancient buildings and Byzantine fortresses from the Crusades that dominate the old part of town.

We had quite different conditions for our May cruise in the western Aegean. We departed from Piraeus in an Olympic 47, a modern fiberglass ketch beautifully laid out for cruising. The trip was a reunion with Greek friends from previous cruises, George Legakis, a top racing and cruising sailor, and the skipper, George Zaimis, operator of the yacht in charter service. Zaimis had been crew for the then Prince Constantine when he won the 1960 Olympic Gold Medal in the Dragons Class, and I had sailed with him before he was deposed as king when we won the Aegean Rally in 1966. Now we were in a more relaxed mood as we headed out in company with two other yachts for a weekend cruise to Hydra, thirty-six miles south.

Zea Marina, where we boarded, is the major yacht basin in the port of Athens, gunwale-to-gunwale with every form of pleasure boat from sturdy little conversions of caiques, the commercial workhorse of the Aegean, to mammoth luxury power yachts. There were many modern cruising auxiliaries, a few stately schooners from another era, and even two 12-Meter veterans of the America's Cup wars, *Nefertiti* and *American Eagle* side by side. *Nefertiti* had been bought by John Theodoracopoulos, a prominent Athenian yachtsman, and *Eagle,* renamed *War Baby* by her Bermudian owner Warren Brown, was "resting" between long-range cruises.

A pleasant north wind was blowing out of a sky of powdery blue, and we had an easy run down to Hydra along the hilly shores of the Peloponnesus. There was a great deal of traffic of a great variety of vessels, with excursion ferries and hydrofoils threading their way through the sailboats, and a steady stream of tankers and freighters in and out of the commercial harbors of Piraeus.

Hydra probably represents the epitome of present-day yachting in Greece. It has a modest-sized harbor protected by stone jetties topped by old forts, and the town rises in

Yacht Club of Greece overlooking Faleron Bay, Piraeus

tiers on the steep hills above the water. Above the last line of houses, steep mountains rise several thousand feet, with here and there a monastery or snow-white chapel perched on a peak. The promenade along the seawall of the inner harbor is a colorful jumble of open-air tavernas, shops, and restaurants, and, as so often happens in the Med, more yachts than would ever seem possible manage to jam stern-to the quay. We arrived in midafternoon and I thought we were lucky to be able to squeeze into a berth, but more and more boats kept coming in and somehow were able to tie up. It is obviously the thing to do on a spring weekend in Athens to head for Hydra and join the crowd.

It was a friendly, lively scene, and as the afternoon wore

on there was a jumble of sounds: music, both Greek and American, blaring from the tavernas, the chug-chug of motorbikes, the rumble of hydrofoils as they settled down from their lofty run and nosed into the harbor like clumsy whales, and, increasingly, the clink of ice in glasses and shrill peals of laughter from the cockpits and fantails of the yachts. As twilight eased over the scene, there was a gradual exit ashore to the lamplit tavernas and restaurants, and our group made its way to a relatively quiet restaurant up a side street. Feta cheese, octopus, and black olives were hors d'oeuvres as most of us stayed with the local custom of ouzo (but the Greeks went for Scotch); dinner choices were divided between the minced lamb dish, *moussaka,* and a local favorite fish, *barbounya.* Somehow, when we are guests in a foreign country, we seem to get shanghaied into going to discos, something a firing squad wouldn't get me to at home. The evening ended under the flashing rotation of colored lights and the ear-splitting crash of the music at a disco down a dark lane on a beach west of the harbor. Ah well, an experience.

The morning was much calmer as everyone seemed rather subdued, taking *metrio,* that gooey, sweet Turkish coffee, at taverna tables along the quay. They were scanning newspapers, reading books or chatting idly in a relaxed Sunday morning atmosphere of warm sunshine. Things livened up in the harbor as the first hydrofoil arrived from Piraeus, and boats began to extricate themselves from the sardine pack at the quay and head out between the jetties. For a while, all went smoothly until two large power yachts, both about one hundred feet long, started to leave at the same time. They hadn't gone very far when it became obvious that their anchor cables were tangled. They came to a halt and there was a meeting of minds on the two bows, with a great amount of gesticulating. Greeks are constitutionally unable to discuss anything without appropriate gestures, and plenty were being made here as all eyes along the quay watched the confrontation. Finally, a decision was made, between gestures, for one boat to back out of the harbor, towing the other one, and they disappeared through the jetties in this odd fashion.

We left soon afterward, getting our anchor up, fortunately, without incident, and there, outside the jetties, were the two yachts, still bow to bow, still in conference, with gestures. Finally, someone from one of the boats got in a launch and went under the bows, gradually untangling the mess. They were still at it as we sailed away.

The breeze had come around to the southeast, so it was an easy reach back toward the metropolitan area, allowing time for a stop at Poros, the closest Aegean island to Piraeus. It was not as strikingly mountainous as Hydra, and the town was even more oriented toward tourism. Many yachts were at the quay in Med moors, and a cruise-ship-sized one was at anchor. Ferries and hydrofoils were in and out of here, too, as we found ourselves a stern-to berth and went ashore in search of lunch. George Zaimis, who had been here often with charter parties, recommended a certain taverna for its seafood, and it was *barbounya* time again. It is a small, pinkish fish of delicate taste, but I have never particularly cottoned to the Greek custom of showing you the fish in its from-the-water state before it is cooked. This, I suppose, ensures freshness, but I always feel guilty when confronted with the baleful stare of the fish's eye. No matter: The lunch was good.

While we were drifting back toward Piraeus after lunch, the sky began to cloud up, and it was a quiet, gray twilight as we slid into home berth at Zea with the lights, sounds, and smells of the vast city area closing around us.

Additional Information

The Aegean and Mediterranean

These waters on the south of the Continent offer by far the best cruising conditions and the top area for visiting sailors to "go foreign." First of all, the weather is milder and the season is longer, though it may surprise Americans to realize that Venice is at the latitude of Maine and Rome at New York's. As noted, I have placed the Aegean in the "Spring and Fall" category because those are much the best months to sail there. The Aegean and the Med are both very popular summer sailing areas, which is actually one of the reasons to move them out of it for recommended visits.

The summers are very hot, especially in the Aegean, and the crowding, afloat and ashore, here and in the Mediterranean and Adriatic resorts, is horrendous. Also, spring and fall winds are better. In the Med and Adriatic, summer winds are light and capricious, and the reverse is true in the Aegean. In summer, the famous meltemi adds a very special touch to sailing with its unbelievably strong northern blasts down the center of the Aegean. It can very easily keep boats in port for a week or more at a time, and to sail through it is an experience to remember. Generated on the steppes of Russia, it is a giant thermal that sweeps south at up to 50 knots out of a clear blue sky. Its season is July into August, and it blows at its peak during midday hours, slacking off some at evening and in early morning.

I have sailed in the Aegean in July, when it was very hot and the meltemi was very strong, and in May and October, when conditions were ideal. In another July, the Adriatic had very light winds, but a May cruise there saw perfect weather. Early June in the Sardinia-Corsica area was cool and blowy (and ahead of the crowds), and the crowding in Riviera harbors in a July visit had to be seen to be believed.

One drawback to Mediterranean cruising is that Europeans seem to be far behind in awareness of ecology and conservation; they have a very cavalier attitude about throwing garbage overboard. Efforts are under way to improve this, but the waters are unbelievably cluttered with trash. Aside from this, another deterrent to swimming is that the water temperature is also quite cool, even in summer. And, when the spray from meltemi seas hits the skin on a hot summer day, the sting of cold is especially surprising.

The Med and Aegean have very little tidal range, but there are some narrow passages between islands where a current can build up. Fog is very seldom a factor in the summer. There is an impression, because of the hot summers and the idea fostered by British travelers over the years that they were going south to a mild climate on a Med visit, that winters should be warm, but they are not mild enough for sailing, and the effective season is April through October.

Yachting centers Gibraltar, Marbella, Málaga, Barcelona, in Spain; Sete, the Marseilles area, and the Riviera, in France; the Italian Riviera, Sardinia's Costa Smeralda, the Bay of Naples, in Italy; Malta, the Dalmatian Coast, Zadar, Split, Dubrovnik, Kotor, in Yugoslavia; Corfu and Corinth, in the Ionian Sea; Patras, Piraeus, Vougliameni, Hydra, Spetsai, Poros, in western Greece; all Aegean islands, with Rhodes as a major base for yachts; Bodrum, Izmir, and Kusadasi, in Turkey.

Chartering This is a major industry in the Med, with most activity on the Riviera and in the Aegean. There are commercially operated bareboat fleets, flotilla cruises, and crewed yachts, with everything from modest auxiliaries to the largest luxury yachts. Most brokers in the United States, England, and the Continent who advertise in boating magazines have contacts and information on all this chartering.

Weather It is very hot in summer, with light winds in most of the Med and Adriatic and very strong meltemi in the Aegean. The mistral, an Alpine thermal, must be guarded against on the south coast of France; the bora is a strong north wind in the Adriatic; and the sirocco is a southern wind out of Africa. These should be watched for mostly at times of seasonal change.

Cruising grounds The best of these are the Spanish islands in the western Med; the Riviera coast of France and Italy; Corsica and Sardinia; Sicily and Malta; the Dalmatian Coast of the Adriatic; the Ionian Sea and Gulf of Corinth; and the entire Aegean including the Turkish coast.

Special attractions For those with an interest in antiquities and archaeology, the possibilities are endless in all parts of this world. It is a special thrill to sail past the temple of Poseidon at Sounion or to go ashore to visit the dig at Akrotiri; and the cultures of Greece and Rome, of the Venetians, the Moors, and the Turks have left landmarks and reminders in every area. Modern civilization has its attractions in the luxury spots of the Riviera; the scenery is often impressive, especially on the Dalmatian Coast, in the Ionian Sea, and on the Turkish coast, and, again, sampling local cuisines can be fascinating (but avoid an ouzo hangover).

References Robinson, *Where to Cruise,* pp. 90–130; Heikell, *Mediterranean Cruising Handbook;* Denham, *The Aegean: A Sea Guide to Its Coasts and Islands;* Davock and Wilensky, *Cruising Guide to the Turquoise Coast of Turkey.*

8

▶ ▶ ▶ ▶ ▶ ▶ ▶ ▶ ▶ ▶ ▶ ▶ ▶

NEVER IN SUMMER,

*But Otherwise "Yes" for
the Chesapeake*

In the chapter on southern New England, I mentioned that that area might be said to have been invented for cruising. The Chesapeake Bay goes it one better in that one might say it was designed for cruising. This distinctive body of water, stretching almost two hundred miles from the ocean to its headwaters, with a centipedelike profile, *is* an ideal cruising area; there are only a couple of small caveats having to do with the seasons.

The physical conformation is excellent, but it is much better as a cruising ground in spring and fall than in summer, and it is too far north at latitude 37–40° north to offer winter sailing. While loyal locals continue to use it in summer, the characteristic heat, lack of wind, thunderstorms, and, some years, jellyfish, do not make it a strong lure for visitors. My own experience with the Chesapeake extends over many years on many different visits, most of them delightful, and, instead of having one specific cruise stand out as an example, my memories are a kaleidoscope of vignettes and isolated incidents. That is the way I would like to describe its attractions. It is a varied seascape with many different aspects and someone could spend a cruising lifetime on the Chesapeake without taking in all that it has to offer.

Susquehanna River

MARYLAND

Old Canal

Havre de Grace

Baltimore

Sassafrass River

Annapolis

Galesville

St. Michaels

Oxford

Potomac

Chesapeake Bay

VIRGINIA

Back Bay

SMITH ISLAND

Hampton Roads

0   30
Miles

•Norfolk

Except for overnight trips on Bay Line steamers as a youngster, my initial encounter with the Chesapeake was a ticklish one at the end of my first passage as skipper of my new Navy command, SC 743, in March 1943. At the end of a run from New York, we arrived at the entrance to the swept channel, a narrow path through extensive minefields across the bay's entrance, just as zero-visibility fog moved in. We did not yet have radar, and so our advance called for the most careful dead reckoning, feeling our way cautiously from buoy to buoy and hoping fervently that our compass had been correctly compensated (it had). As we cleared the last buoy and were free of the minefield, we could hear the fog bells of many ships at anchor and we gratefully dropped the hook. When the fog lifted after an hour, we found ourselves in a large fleet of merchant and Navy ships, with the low, sandy shoreline of Lynnhaven Roads to the south. Proceeding into Hampton Roads, the 110 feet of my proud command seemed terribly insignificant among the battleships, carriers, cruisers, and even destroyers, and I have had the same feeling every time I move through there in a cruising boat.

In addition to being a major naval and commercial port, Hampton Roads is an important yachting area. I had some pleasant day sails there in prewar Navy days before everything turned grim and serious. It offers good sailing conditions, with sea breezes more prevalent than farther inland up the bay, and its shores are lined with marinas and yacht clubs. It is also the start of the Intracoastal Waterway (ICW) run to Florida. Mile zero of the waterway's 1,090 statute miles, including canals, rivers, bays, inlets, and sounds, is located in Norfolk Harbor off the big Portsmouth Naval Hospital. Marinas in this area cater to the heavy transient traffic of the ICW, especially in spring and fall. Hampton Roads, however, is a world in itself and not really what one thinks of in connection with Chesapeake cruising.

In contrast, one of my most recent Chesapeake visits was to Havre de Grace, Maryland, at the very head of the bay. Here the broad Susquehanna River feeds into it across the Spesutie Flats, a famous duck hunting area, where market gunners used to kill birds by the dozen with one blast of a

great blunderbuss (many years ago). In its contrast to the
salty, deep-sea-port atmosphere of Hampton Roads, this area
typifies the scope and variety of the Chesapeake world.
Havre de Grace is an old town, once an important port for
barge traffic to and from the Susquehanna, backed by
wooded hills. The bay is narrow here, a mere continuation
of the river. Graceful old houses line the grassy shorefront,
and there is now a large, modern marina near the old barge
terminal. I came here to do a "test" sail on a new Hunter
42 cruising sloop. It turned out not to be much of a test, as
the breeze was very light and the water flat on a late May
afternoon. We drifted over the glassy surface in the laziest
kind of way, and it was more a reminder of the Chesapeake's varied charms than an evaluation of the boat.

And varied they are, as these two locations showed, and
as we have experienced time and again in the area in between. Our first cruise was in 1947 when we chartered a
twenty-six-foot sloop out of Galesville, an extremely active
yachting harbor south of Annapolis on the western shore.
It was October, which, all in all, is the best month for
Chesapeake cruising. The thunderstorms have departed,
the breezes have more authority, and the shorelines are at
their loveliest in early fall foliage. For most of the week,
the weather was idyllically summerlike, but we did experience one whooping cold front that kept us in port for a
day and brought out sweaters and windbreakers. Annapolis with its sights was a good port to be stuck in. We also
saw the hustle and bustle of Annapolis at the peak of its
Fall Series activity, and when the weather improved poked
into creeks and byways of the Eastern Shore in the humming peace of summerlike warmth. One memorable day,
the breeze followed us in a near 360-degree circumnavigation from Oxford around Tilghman Island to St. Michaels. It started in the south and gradually shifted
westward so that we were on a reach the whole time.

Two subsequent cruises in late June in the husky, borrowed thirty-six-foot gaff ketch *Horizons,* underrigged for
the Chesapeake but very comfortable, started in Georgetown on the wooded Sassafrass River at the northeast corner of the bay, a popular base for Philadelphia and

Wilmington owners. One cruise was with adult friends and one with our children when they were subteens, and these introduced us to the summer drawbacks of the bay, as well as some interesting explorations of new waters. Both times the cruise started in pleasant weather and good breezes and ended in the deadening calm of a 100-degree heat wave, complete with thunderstorms, and, particularly galling to the kids, too many jellyfish to enjoy cooling swims.

There were enough rewards to make us want to come back, though. A particularly interesting stop was Smith Island. Smith and its neighbor, Tangier, off the Eastern Shore halfway down the bay, are unique communities. When we were there in the early 1950s they survived solely on crabbing, oystering, and fishing. Since then, there has been more tourism, but they are still very much communities that live by and from the water, with their own special life and traditions.

Feeling our way in to Smith Island's harbor through a narrow but well-marked channel, we found a spot to tie up among the work boats. The settlement's houses seemed to be afloat while we approached from a distance, so low is the island. The town is a network of lanes and creeks through marshy land. As soon as we tied up, we were the center of attention, as the only visiting yacht, and we spent an interesting evening with the townspeople and watermen comparing notes and listening to yarns in their soft waterman's twang. When they heard we came from New Jersey, they immediately wanted to know why on earth we called rock fish—a staple there—striped bass; it turned out there were quite a few more regional differences in familiar marine names. The whole place seemed to personify the essence of the Chesapeake to us.

We were at Gibson Island when a heat wave hit. This island is a posh suburb of Baltimore at the entrance to the Magothy River. We figured out one way to beat the heat: At the bay end, a narrow sandspit stretches out across the mouth of the river, and, by anchoring just inside the sand, with an awning rigged over the cockpit, we were slightly cooled by a movement of air caused by the difference of temperature between the bay and the river. It was not much, but it did help in the otherwise stagnant atmosphere.

In yet another spring trip ferrying a Columbia 50 up the bay from Norfolk to Chesapeake City on the Chesapeake and Delaware Canal, which links the two bays from the Chesapeake's headwaters, we had another example of the bay's moods. We left Hampton Roads with a forecast of moderate easterlies on a cloudy, cool day, but as soon as we rounded Old Point Comfort into the open bay, the moderate easterly became a strong northeaster, blowing down the full stretch of the center of the bay, bringing rain with it. A short, steep sea with very determined whitecaps built up in no time, and we decided that continuing was not only folly, but also unproductive. We did not want to turn tail back to Norfolk, and a solution presented itself just to port in a place called Back Bay. We had no chart for it, but it was well described in the *Inland Waterway Guide*, an absolutely imperative publication for operating in the waters it covers. The buoys were easy to pick out, and we found our way into a small marina as the wind piped up to over 50 knots. We were very happy to be there, and were helped into a berth by what seemed like the whole population of the village. With the wind on the beam of a high-sided vessel, this took some doing, and it was a great relief to be snug and safe while the wind howled.

The rest of the passage was in mostly foggy and calm conditions and we learned another fact of life about the Chesapeake, namely that even the annually published *Waterway Guide* cannot always be up to date in every way. In following a "six-foot" channel with our five-foot draft into a marina at the Little Wicomico River, we ran aground smack in the middle of the channel. But grounding in the Chesapeake is always in sand or soft mud, and we plowed our way through. This was not pilot error (which I have been known to commit now and then); the correct markers were right beside us, port and starboard. It was just routine shoaling each season.

During the 1970s, we based our Out Island 36, *Tanagra*, in the Chesapeake for several Octobers before taking her farther south via the ICW, and it was always a pleasant

A well-protected cove on Crab Creek near Annapolis

interlude. That is, except for October 1976, which defied tradition and the law of averages by being almost continually cold and blowy. As any experienced cruising hand knows, there are times while visiting a highly touted area in the perfect season when the locals say, "It never happens like this," and "You should have been here last week."

Through the courtesy of Bill Stone, son of *Yachting*'s longtime editor and publisher, Herb Stone, and himself the magazine's Washington correspondent, we based at his home pier on Crab Creek, a tributary of the South River. It borders the south side of the peninsula that Annapolis sits on. Surrounded by moderately high bluffs and hills, Crab Creek has absolutely perfect protection, and during that nasty October in 1976 it was a great feeling to lie quietly at the pier and listen to the wind moan through the trees high above us on the banks of the creek. This was an ideal base in good conditions for weekending to some of the Chesapeake's top attractions. Near at hand, the South River leads to the West and Rhode rivers, both busy home ports for a great many boats, as well as targets for weekending from other areas. In the fall the foliage above the Rhode River's high bluffs is particularly colorful, and there is a popular anchorage between High Island and the south shore, which we visited several times. Galesville had grown tremendously since our 1947 visit, with major marina installations, as it is the closest bay port to Washington; we would head for it if we wanted to eat ashore at night, almost invariably ordering crab cakes.

The fabled Eastern Shore is near enough for weekending and this we did quite often, usually after a good sail across the center of the bay. On October weekends, with the Annapolis Fall Series in progress and the cruising season at its height, the bay provides an impressive panorama of sail, a floating boat show. The Eastern Shore has a wide choice of anchorages, from the "civilization" of St. Michaels or Oxford and their old houses, to the quiet isolation in some backwater of the lovely Choptank River. Dun Cove, for example, on Harris Creek has bucolic surroundings of browsing cattle, farm fields, and groves of trees. The Choptank, which seems to have its own serene atmosphere, is a cruising world in itself, and Eastern Bay and the Miles River make up another complex with a wide choice of anchorages.

There have been other contrasts, too, to the balmy Indian summer days. Taking part in the Fall Cruise of the Cruising Club of America in a Dickerson 37 one year, we ran into another one of those cold northeasters as we were bringing her up the Choptank to her home base at Trappe. She was a very comfortable "two-person" boat. There could be bunks for four, but she was set up with one stateroom and a main cabin that was like a living room with comfortable armchairs. Jane was happy down there with a book, and I took advantage of another feature of the boat to hide from the elements as well. She had an autopilot with a remote control, and I sat under the protection of the dodger, where I could still keep a lookout, watching the sails while relatively warm and dry and making any course adjustments needed with a twitch of the dial. The creek at Trappe, when we gained its quiet security, was aswarm with geese, a regular feature of fall in the Chesapeake, and a lovely sight when they take off in their great Vs.

Now in the grandparent era, we were reminded of our *Horizons* cruise of over thirty years before when we chartered a Bristol 41 out of Annapolis for a weekend. Annapolis was at its busiest with the fall boat show in progress, a football game at the Naval Academy, and the usual quota of boats on their seasonal way southward via the ICW. Our party of nine managed to squeeze into forty-one feet by means of cozy doubling up of the younger kids, and we took off from Back Creek south of town across the Spa Creek bridge. This Back Creek is not to be confused with the one that was our port in a storm near Hampton Roads. In fact, there are several other Back Creeks in other Chesapeake tributaries, Mill Creeks galore, several rivers with Wicomico in their name, and any number of other duplications, and it pays to be specific in identifying these places.

The Annapolis-area Back Creek is one vast marina on every inch of its squarish outer section, a forest of masts, with sailboats predominating by a big percentage; it makes one wonder what it would be like if the law of averages broke down and they all decided to head for the narrow entrance at the same time. It had been very warm, even for early October on the Chesapeake, ashore in Annapolis, but there was a pleasant breeze as we made our way out through the parade of boats in and out of the Severn and had a good reach across to Eastern Bay in a southerly riffling small whitecaps up the open bay. Tilghman Creek, which cuts into Rich Neck, the sandy point that forms the northwest side of the entrance to the Miles River, was a new experience to me after all our Chesapeake adventures, and it, in its rural setting, was a perfect spot for a quiet evening. A few other boats were at anchor but there was no crowding, and to me, it was a demonstration of how often one can cruise the Chesapeake without running out of new places to explore. The area does, in truth, offer an endless variety.

9

▶ ▶ ▶ ▶ ▶ ▶ ▶ ▶ ▶ ▶ ▶ ▶ ▶ ▶ ▶

A CIVILIZED CRUISE
Florida's West Coast

The Florida west coast is a much better cruising ground than a first glance at the map might suggest. From Anclote Keys on the north, just above Tampa Bay, to Florida Bay in the south, there is a succession of bays and sounds, mostly connected by the man-made Intracoastal Waterway (the remainder by natural waterways) that offers all sorts of opportunities. The Gulf of Mexico itself can provide fine sailing when its mood is right.

Once again, though, the seasons are a key. While a great many people think of semitropical Florida as an escape in winter, I have seen snow in the air in the Tampa Bay area (admittedly a very rare thing), and we have been held up in winter cruising by temperatures in the 30s and winds in the 40s. In contrast, there have been summer days of 98-degree airless heat and thumping thunderstorms every afternoon. I have been afloat here in every month but August, and the best conditions have been in the spring. Fall can also be fine once the hurricane threat is over. Florida can be and is used all year for cruising, but the best times are late fall and March to June.

Two of the cruising boats we have owned, *Tanagra,* a Morgan Out Island 36, and *Brunelle,* a CSY 37, were both

Clearwater

Tampa

Tampa
Bay

St. Petersburg
Bel Air

Tierra Verde

Manatee River

DeSoto Point

Longboat Cay

Sarasota

GULF OF MEXICO

| 0 | 5 | 10 Miles |
| 0 | 5 | 10 Km. |

built in Tampa, and much of our cruising experience here was in shakedown cruises in them, five years apart. *Tanagra*'s maiden cruise was in ideal weather in December (with one morning of fog, not unusual in winter). *Brunelle*'s January shakedown was beset by a series of cold fronts, including the near-freezing, gale-blown day of her commissioning, when the temperature and the wind were both 35.

On another occasion (March 1977), we were loaned CSY 44 Number One for article writing purposes, and the early spring weather was generally good, with two mild fronts coming through in a week.

A Florida west coast cold front is at the bottom end of the strong weather fronts that sweep across North America from west to east in all seasons, but with the severest effects in winter. They come out of the Rocky Mountains with arctic air behind them and gather strength sweeping across the Great Plains. Depending on their path, they can give Florida a good bashing but most of them lose strength and their cold temperatures when they reach the Gulf Stream, though they can still blow with authority in the Bahamas, and one or two a season carry all the way down to the Antilles. In January 1979 we experienced eight cold fronts in bringing *Brunelle* from Tampa Bay around the southern tip of Florida and into the Bahamas, but there are winters when weeks go by without even one.

Our Florida West Coast cruising ended when we took *Brunelle* away from there, as we concentrated on using her in the Caribbean after that, but our last cruise in another boat before *Brunelle* commandeered all our time was in an unusual and interesting vessel, and one especially suited to the area, a Sandpiper 32. Named *Sandpiper* she was the prototype of a model that was in production for a while, a type that has fanatic devotees but that doesn't have wide acceptance, a cat-ketch sharpie. She was designed by Walter Scott, an old friend from the days when we both owned Mount Desert Controversies, who had retired from aeronautical engineering to pursue his real love, boat designing, at Indian Rocks Beach near Clearwater, off Tampa Bay on the ICW.

His idea in designing *Sandpiper* was to create a boat that would be comfortable for cruising, easy to handle, and of shallow enough draft to poke into areas where normal cruising auxiliaries could not go. In increasingly crowded conditions in most cruising areas, this is a real plus, and the Florida west coast's many shallow areas make it a good feature to have. Her dimensions are $32' \times 28'4'' \times 8' \times 1'7''$ (board up). Instead of a centerboard, she has twin bilge-boards housed in the inboard frames of the bunks so that they do not intrude in the sitting-headroom cabin. The four full-sized bunks do have sitting headroom, but 6 feet of standup is achieved at the galley area aft in the cabin by means of a pop-top hatch, a trick Scott learned from his Controversy days in an Amphibi-Con. A 12-horsepower Yanmar diesel tucks neatly away under a bridge deck aft of the cabin. The cat-ketch rig is roller furling on rotating masts and is controlled by wishbone booms. And, as a bit of nostalgia in these inflationary times, in 1978, the Sand-piper marketed for under $20,000.

Aside from her adaptability to shallow water, opening up new cruising prospects, the eight-foot beam is designed so that she can be trailed and, if desired, stored at home on a trailer. Jane and I had been shipmates with a cat-ketch wishbone rig the year before in sailing the prototype Freedom 40, but the 40 could not be reefed. If it blew too hard for full rig in her, you just dropped one of the sails, but *Sandpiper*'s sails, sleeved over the rotating masts, allow partial furling as a reef, or total furling when in port. The masts are worked by a drum at their base, with the control lines, as well as the controls for the bilgeboards and both sheets, all leading to the cockpit on the cabin top.

It was with a feeling of adventure that we went to Scott's waterfront apartment on a shallow lagoon off the water-way, and took off on what proved to be a really new cruis-ing experience for us. There had been a strong cold front the day before; we had walked along the Gulf beach and watched the short, steep waves the Gulf is noted for, pale green under a gray sky. Now it was a brilliantly clear day with a moderate norther blowing, just right for taking Sandpiper down the waterway to Tampa Bay and its mul-

The Sandpiper *in civilized surroundings on the ICW*

tiple choice of harbors. Tampa Bay is actually extensive
enough, with numerous coves and tributaries, to rank as a
cruising area just by itself, and we had spent many days
in the past enjoying it. Walt came with us for a couple of
hours to make sure we understood the intricacies of the
rig, bilgeboards, and so on, and we had a pleasant slide
down the waterway with the sails wing-and-wing most of
the time. With the boards up, we cut corners where the
channel weaved through flats, instead of having to jibe
around sharper turns.

There is civilization all along the ICW here, with a
succession of condos, houses with boats tied up at a bulkhead in front, an occasional marina, and no empty stretches
of woods or fields. We dropped Walt at a prearranged marina stop where his wife was to pick him up and continued
on our way south toward St. Petersburg Beach. There was
moderately heavy powerboat traffic, all at controlled speeds
(I understand it is not that way anymore); and another
form of traffic that is normal here. It is always surprising
in these civilized surroundings to have dolphins (porpoises) as a convoy, breaking surface under the bow and
sliding along beside us as though they wanted to be friends.
The whole Tampa Bay area abounds with them and they
are a common sight. Another natural trademark of the area
is the continual presence of pelicans. They are all over the
place, flying along in formation and diving on targets in
the water. It is great fun to watch them fly along in single-
file formation a few feet off the water, beating their wings
in unison for a while, and then gliding before taking up
the beat again. Their long beaks dowse down toward the
water as they fly, and I always wonder how they coordi-
nate their wingbeats and glides. It must be the same sort
of communication that makes schools of fish swing together in turns and dives, always great to watch.

A rarer sight here, but also a special Tampa Bay feature, is the white pelican. We have only seen them a few
times, and I didn't really believe my eyes the first time I
saw one. They often fly higher than their normal brown
brothers and sisters, and it is an unusual spectacle to see
the sun on their wings as they soar high above in formation.

By late afternoon we had arrived in the St. Pete area, and we rolled the sails up, headed east through a drawbridge, and tied up at a marina we had used quite often, the Sheraton Bel Air, hard by the causeway that is the approach to the Sunshine Skyway. Here we were in a boat in which we were supposed to gunkhole off the beaten path in isolated little coves, and we had picked instead a fully equipped marina in very civilized surroundings. Actually, on our first night aboard, we wanted to settle in at leisure, and we also wanted to eat ashore, which is one of the pleasures of cruising, especially for Jane. It was also fun that the St. Louis Cardinals were based here during their spring training, and the informal bar at the marina was their favorite after-hours hangout. The most interesting game was the young lady "groupies" and the ballplayers interacting at the bar. Oh to be young again!

As is the wont of cold fronts, ours had moved on east by the next morning, and we had a delightfully warm, sunny day, with a mild southerly blowing, and we made our way out onto Tampa Bay. This was a good chance to get familiar with our very special rig, which I was really curious about. First, we figured out the bilgeboards. The best idea was to use only one, the leeward one, in going to windward. They were canted at a 20-degree angle so that they were more or less vertical at a normal angle of heel. Then we had to figure out the balance of the sails. At first, in light air, she moved along very nicely on a close reach.

The shallow, narrow hull slipped through the water so easily that we made almost no wake, both under sail and power. As the day wore on, and we sailed under the Sunshine Skyway, recently reduced to one span by an encounter with a ship, the breeze freshened and we found that balance was critically affected by the trim of the sails. At first we had the main too tight and the foresail a bit slack, and she would round right up and stall out. Once we figured out the right balance by slacking the main and trimming the foresail, she behaved nicely, but it was interesting to see how delicate the balance was, varying rather noticeably in minor changes of wind strength. We played around with partial furling as a means of reefing and found that there was considerable tension on the drum that turned

the mast. In later models, this was corrected by having
two drums, one for furling and one for breaking out.

The ice chest had double access, from below and from
the cockpit, which made it easy to relax over a cold beer
when we figured out the sail combinations, and it was a
fine day of sailing in smooth water, with a good breeze, as
the heavy commercial and pleasure traffic of Tampa Bay
weaved around us.

As the afternoon wore on, we eased back westward to
spend the night at Port of Call Marina at Tierra Verde.
This is a very pleasant marina and resort tucked away at
the inner end of a long lagoon on an island south of St.
Petersburg Beach, connected by a bridge. We have been
there fairly often; it seems almost like a hideaway to us
because of its isolation from busier waterways, and, again,
there is a fine place to have dinner ashore.

The weather held as we made a leisurely start at sailing
the next morning. Now that we knew the sail combinations, we had a good close reach out across Tampa Bay,
past the busy commercial traffic of Egmont Channel, ending up in another favorite Tampa Bay anchorage, DeSoto
Point at the mouth of the Manatee River. This is an excellent anchorage in a horseshoe cove just inside the point
that forms the western side of the mouth of the Manatee.
Legend has it that DeSoto made his first Florida landing
here, though it would not have been a good choice without
the Sunshine Skyway to get him to the other side of the
bay, as it is a long way around by land to the rest of Florida. Anyway, they have named a park on the point in his
honor, which makes a pleasant, unpopulated, natural setting on that side of the anchorage. The other side is a
shoreline of attractive homes and well-tended lawns. The
cove is well protected, and the setting is peaceful.

It is also a fine place to enjoy one of the special features
of Gulf Coast cruising, the sunsets. There is something unusual in the way colors combine over the Gulf in a display
that changes minute by minute, with bright, primary colors in the clouds set against a pale higher background of
apple green sky. We could not see the sun itself but above
DeSoto Point, that evening's spectacle was spread out across

the sky. Despite the civilization all around Tampa Bay and along the shores of the Gulf, there was a pleasant sense of isolation here that was a nice contrast to our two previous marina evenings. One or two boats shared the anchorage but were not close, and the lights of the houses on the southern side of the cove were softly subdued. Jane cooked a simple supper on the propane camping stove, and nightcaps made a relaxing coda to a day of the best the Gulf Coast has to offer.

We had made arrangements to turn *Sandpiper* in at the Buccaneer Marina down the waterway on Longboat Key, and, with the weather holding nicely, our last day was spent in a sightseeing sail up the Manatee to the bridge at Bradenton, with an escort of pelicans and busy schools of fish breaking the surface of the river all around us. Turning at the head of navigation, we reached back out and, since the breeze was in the east, it allowed us to reach south behind Anna Marie and Longboat keys. Because of our shoal draft, we never worried about depth of water as we cut corners in the channel, and we nosed into Buccaneer in late afternoon. It is one of the most attractive and best-run marinas we have seen, a good ad for the type of cruising the Florida west coast offers best. It had been a short cruise but one that introduced us to an interesting boat, a boat that put new dimensions on cruising possibilities, in an area that we have always enjoyed when the temperature was somewhere above 35 and below 98 degrees.

Additional Information

The Intracoastal Waterway and Florida

Chesapeake Bay is part of the Intracoastal Waterway, but the image that comes to most sailors' minds when the ICW is mentioned is that measured stretch of 1,090 statute miles from the Portsmouth Naval Hospital to Key West, Florida. Boats heading south via the ICW in the fall and back north in the spring do traverse the Chesapeake, and wise skippers allow time in the process to stop off, poke around, and enjoy the Chesapeake.

The smart skipper will also allow time to enjoy the rather subtle charms of the ICW south of there, rather than treating it as an interstate highway. While it is that for delivery crews taking powerboats to Florida and back, and for tug and barge crews and other small commercial vessels, the cruising yachtsman will find good reason to make a cruise out of it.

True, there are sections that are strictly utilitarian ditches to be gotten through at best cruising speed, but there are many more regions that call for relaxed exploration. I have never done the whole Norfolk–Florida ICW in one cruise. I break it up by leaving the boat for periods of time or having friends take her over for part of the way, but I have seen most of it at one time or another. Our daughter and her husband brought her through from West Palm Beach to New Jersey in two weeks once, pushing through rather steadily, and a determined delivery crew can take a powerboat through in a week of hard pushing, sometimes ducking outside between inlets for a faster passage offshore, when the weather allows. In spring and fall, Florida traffic is at its peak, and the weather is at its best. Summer can be hot, with thunderstorms, and winter cold waves can reach down the whole length of the ICW on occasion. Ice can be a problem from South Carolina north in midwinter, and can sometimes close it, though commercial traffic usually pushes through and keeps it open. We left *Tanagra* in winter wet storage in Oriental, North Carolina, on the Neuse River. An exceptionally cold spell in January 1977 had her frozen in solid for three weeks, which the marina operators claimed was very unusual.

One factor to consider about spring and fall is the difference in daylight hours, which is important for pleasure boat operation. Commercial vessels push through at night with great searchlight beams stabbing the darkness to pick up markers and landmarks, but I don't recommend it for the cruising yacht. In May, at the height of the northward migration, up to fifteen hours of daylight can be used, while October only provides ten or a little more for the southbound fleet.

In sailboats, there is a great amount of powering, but there are quite a few chances to hoist the sails in some sections. The Chesapeake, of course, provides good sailing, as do the North Carolina sounds. We have had some interesting side cruises there out to Cape Lookout and other Hatteras areas, well worth the time taken, and it is possible to jump the season by a couple of months over New England cruising.

There are marinas for overnighting after almost every day's run, with the Alligator River in North Carolina one of the few areas where auxiliaries cannot make a marina-to-marina run in one day, especially in the fall. But those who prefer to anchor out for peace and quiet (and cost saving) have endless opportunities. Some of the longer canals with unbroken banks are about the only places where this is impossible.

Once in Florida, the ICW down the east coast gives little opportunity for conventional cruising, except on the St. Johns River inland from Jacksonville. South of Miami, the Keys offer some good cruising, although this is limited for sailboats by shallow water.

Yachting centers Among the Chesapeake's many harbors, the major centers are Georgetown, Annapolis, Oxford, Galesville, Solomons, and Hampton Roads, Virginia; with a wide choice of other ports as well. On the ICW, Great Bridge, Belhaven, Oriental, Morehead City, Beaufort, Wrightsville Beach, North Carolina; Georgetown, Charleston, Beaufort, Hilton Head, South Carolina; Savannah, Brunswick, Georgia; Fernandina Beach, Jacksonville, St. Augustine, Daytona Beach, Melbourne, Vero Beach, Stuart, West Palm Beach, Fort Lauderdale, and Miami, Florida, are major stops, again with many more choices. On the west coast of Florida, Marco Island, Naples, Fort Myers, Venice, Sarasota, Tampa Bay, Clearwater, and Tarpon Springs are the top ones.

Chartering There is considerable chartering of individual boats, both bareboat and crewed luxury yachts, out of Fort Lauderdale and some from Miami, with the Bahamas as the intended cruising grounds. There are several fleet operations for bareboats, as well as individual charters through brokers, on the west coast. Many fleet operators and individual boats are in Chesapeake centers.

Weather Summer is hot, relatively windless, and there are frequent thunderstorms in the Chesapeake and south. Winters are cold as far south as the Carolinas, with occasional cold fronts reaching Florida. Spring and fall are the best seasons, though hurricanes are a threat into late October.

Cruising grounds These include the entire Chesapeake; Albemarle and Pamlico sounds; the Neuse River and the Cape Hatteras-Cape Lookout area; the St. Johns River; Biscayne Bay and the Florida Keys; Florida Bay and the west coast from Naples north to Clearwater.

Special attractions There are quiet creeks and byways on the Chesapeake; quaint towns like Annapolis, Oxford, and St. Michaels; local seafood (crab cakes); interesting towns and historic cities like Charleston on the ICW; fishing and gunkholing in the Florida Keys and parts of the west coast.

References Robinson, *Over the Horizon*, Chapter VI; *Where to Cruise*, pp. 181–207, and *South to the Caribbean*, Chapters 1–7; Mid-Atlantic and Southern Editions, *Inland Waterway Guide;* Stone, Blanchard, and Hays, *Cruising Guide to the Chesapeake;* Young, *Cruising Guide to Coastal North Carolina* and *Cruising Guide to Coastal South Carolina;* Papys, *Cruising Guide to the Florida Keys;* Moeller, *The Intracoastal Waterway.*

10

▶ ▶ ▶ ▶ ▶ ▶ ▶ ▶ ▶ ▶ ▶ ▶ ▶ ▶

MAKING THE MOST OF THE COAST
Northern and Southern California

Cruising in California is a very different kettle of *mahi-mahis* from eastern and southern cruising grounds and the Pacific Northwest. The few islands offshore from southern California are largely restricted, and the rest of the coast is long and straight, with no real bays until San Francisco, and no other islands. There are no areas for relaxed, easy cruising in short hops. The use of cruising boats is largely confined to weekending, or time-consuming jaunts to Mexico. In San Francisco there is river cruising in the Delta area inland from the San Francisco Bay. The latter is best suited to powerboating, although auxiliaries can find some cruising waters when the wind is right.

I have had no extensive California cruises, but what I have done there could, I guess, be considered rather typical. After an Ensenada Race a few years ago, we did get a chance for an overnight cruise in one of the 563 participating boats. I have been to Catalina; and I have cruised the Delta region out of San Francisco, but a lot more California experiences have simply been in day sails off San Diego and Newport Harbor or on San Francisco Bay. I'm not sure what kind of boat I would want to own or where I would keep it if I lived in California. Because of limited

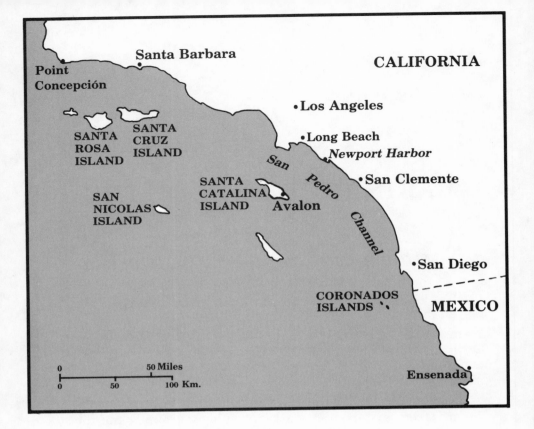

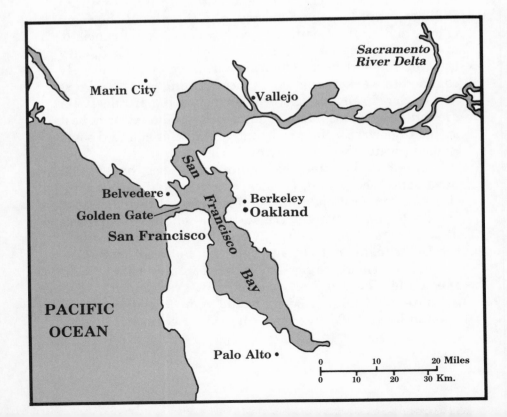

harbor shoreline, marinas have traditionally had waiting lists for slips, and transients also have to make specific plans for coming into a harbor as a guest. There is no such thing as casually moving around from harbor to harbor.

Day sailing in San Francisco Bay is an unusual experience, and provides a graphic demonstration of the contrasts of conditions there. Its avenue to the open sea, the Golden Gate, is prey to wild extremes in weather within a few miles because of the special conformation of the land. The ocean outside the gate is cold all through the year, and the onshore winds from it are cold and damp a good part of the time. When they are funneled through the narrow gate by the high land on both sides of it, they suddenly clash with the much warmer conditions inside, especially in the summer when the country on the inland side of the bay heats up in desertlike fashion. The result is the familiar fog. In winter, the differences are less dramatic, and there can be pleasant sailing days in any month.

I have boarded the sixty-foot ocean racer *Orient* for a day's sail at the St. Francis Yacht Club, right on the gate. With a raw wind of over 20 knots freighted with fog and 50-degree temperatures, we needed windbreakers and foul-

A small part of the mammoth Ensenada Race fleet

weather gear. Within a couple of miles, however, in a short passage through Raccoon Strait between Marin County and Angel Island, with the grim facade of Alcatraz just off to starboard, there was a remarkable change. The northern half of the bay lay placidly under the sun in a soft northwest wind, the temperature shot up into the 70s, and we stripped out of our heavy gear right down to T-shirts.

The Delta cruise was in a large motorsailer as a means of taking part in the SFYC's unique Stag Cruise, an annual September event, to the club's upriver station at Tinsley Island. The phrase "Stag Cruise" might conjure up images of nude *Playboy* bunnies and riotous orgies, but it is far from that. There is plenty of social drinking, but excess is frowned on and likely to bring a polite but firm request to leave. The food situation is elaborate over the four-day event, but the emphasis is on special sailing symposiums conducted by famous designers, sail makers, and racing skippers, with dinghy racing, singalongs, and amateur theatricals of a broadly comic music-hall nature. A hardworking Dixieland band plays continually, starting at sunrise with a wake-up launch cruise through the large fleet of club boats moored and anchored in the area.

The half-day cruise there and back is an interesting part of the affair. Although we had a good sailing rig, and we saw some smaller boats under sail, we powered the whole way. From the bay, the route goes up the Sacramento River and then through a network of sloughs, canals, and creeks to Tinsley, where the main feature is an old lighthouse. Most of the year, the area is used for weekend cruises, junior sailing camp, and other family activities, until the Stag Cruise has its day.

This is strange "countryside" cruising, at times reminiscent of barging in Holland, as the waterways are often higher than the surrounding fields, held on course by dikes and levees, and the view is downward across the land. When at a distance from the main course of the river, it is an odd sight to look across farm fields and see the superstructure of an oceangoing freighter seemingly moving across the land. The dominant feature of the landscape is an endless array of tules, the tall cattaillike reeds that are a trade-

The Golden Gate from Belvedere

mark of the area. Bay boat owners come up here for a week
or more of vacation cruising, taking life very easy and tying
up to a bank whenever the spirit moves them. There are
small settlements along the banks, and a wide choice of
routes through the network of waterways. This kind of
cruising is best in spring and fall, as the summers can become unbearably hot, and winter weather is often chilly
and damp.

In the other direction, going south to Mexico, summer is
to be avoided because of heat and the threat of hurricanes.
Winter is best, and spring and fall are all right. The Ensenada Race, from Newport Harbor, is an enormous catch-
all for every kind of boat that could be considered an ocean
racer, and some that never should be. Ensenada is the
northernmost port on the west coast of Mexico, and Mexican it (barely) is, but it is much more southern Californian
than truly Mexican.

The race I sailed in was a typical example of California
sailing, as we had a mild southwester at the start, a rous-
ing westerly sea breeze in the afternoon, and a night of
absolute calm, in which the dew was so heavy that it
streamed off our foul-weather jackets. We sat motionless
on the oily surface gazing sleepily at the amazing array of
lights along the shore during our unproductive watches.
Then a whooping northwester gave us a surfing spinnaker

run the next day—and a laugh at the boat's spinnaker. Our boat was a Cal-40 named *Whisper,* and her owner had just bought a brand-new spinnaker. To advertise the boat's name, the letters "SH-H-H-H" were strung across the sail, but when it was broken out for its maiden appearance, there, at the end of the sewn letters, a couple of pixies in the crew had secretly added the taped letters "I" and "T," much to the owner's horror.

Under it, we had a hull-speed-plus screamer of a run, anticipating a quick slide to the finish six miles inside the bay of Ensenada. As we jibed and rounded the point, heading in, we were caught so swiftly by a land breeze blowing out of the bay that the spinnaker was knocked aback and we shuddered to a halt. From there it was a long slow beat against the fitful easterly into the line.

After a night and day of Latin-tinged festivities, Jane, who had come down by car with other wives, and I were invited to cruise back to San Diego in a Columbia 50, which gave us a quick taste of what the area offers. There are two island groups on the way that have anchorages of a sort. The Coronados, standing boldly a few miles off the international boundary, have a couple of coves of questionable protection, suitable only in settled weather. Closer to Ensenada, just outside the bay, is Todos Los Santos, a striking collection of rocky pinnacles and cliffs. It was an easy jaunt out to them after a late-afternoon departure, and the long May twilight led to a typical Pacific sunset of quickly changing colors flashing across the western sky. Our cove there was a quiet hideaway after the fun and games at the end of the race, and the sheer pillars of rocks that formed our protection were a dramatic backdrop, quite different from any other anchorage I have been in.

It was a quiet reach back toward San Diego in a light westerly that gradually faded; we ended up powering into port over long Pacific swells that are so far apart as to be almost imperceptible. San Diego is typical of California harbors in that every inch of water surface is designated for a specific purpose. In Mission Bay there are areas for sailing, water-skiing, and fishing—but no place to anchor overnight. Mission Bay and the main San Diego Harbor are lined with marinas and yacht clubs in the designated pleasure boat areas, and San Diego also has major commercial and naval port areas. The prime attraction here is the equable climate, and San Diego yacht clubs boast that they conduct sailing races fifty-two weekends a year unless Christmas falls on a weekend.

The cruising, though, is limited to the Coronados and Ensenada for weekending, or marina hopping northward up the coast, unless time can be taken for a cruise down to the Gulf of California.

But you haven't seen California cruising at its most typical without experiencing Catalina. This island, twenty-two miles long on a roughly northwest-southeast axis, from eight miles to a few hundred yards wide, twenty-six miles off the teeming Los Angeles metropolitan area, is the be-all and end-all of cruising opportunities in the area. It is one of a string of offshore islands, the Santa Barbaras, that look inviting on the chart but are mostly off limits for military or private ownership reasons, and have very few usable harbors anyway.

Catalina is actually Santa Catalina, discovered in 1524 by Juan Cabrillo, the Portuguese explorer, but named in 1602 by the Spanish Sebastian Vizcaino, who sighted it on the eve of the Feast of Saint Catherine and named it for her. It is privately owned and controlled by a corporation, but open to the public with certain restrictions. Avalon, at its southeastern end, is a major tourist attraction, visited by thousands by ferry and small plane, but the rest of the island is largely uninhabited. It has one all-weather harbor at The Isthmus, on the south side, but its cruising harbors include nine coves strung along the north side. Each is filled with mooring buoys and access is controlled by various mainland clubs and the corporation. Rights to a Catalina mooring are as coveted as a lifetime ownership of a special box in a sports stadium.

At just above 33° north, its weather is as reliable as that of the rest of southern California, with a few special features. Although it is most popular on summer weekends, there can be severe heat then, and the threat of the Santana. This is a virulent desert wind, whose name is a cor-

ruption of Santa Ana which sweeps out across the coast
from inland with temperatures in the 90s and velocities
up to 50 knots and more. It can also strike with amazing
suddenness. When this happens during the night on a
summer weekend, the resultant chaos in the jam-packed
northside coves is something special. In the twenty-six mile
stretch from the mainland, a short, steep, vicious sea builds
up, making the anchorages untenable, and there is a panic-
stricken exodus followed by a tough slug to windward to
get back to the mainland.

Fortunately, my visit was under much pleasanter conditions. For years, the smog in the area, along with regular sea fogs in winter, kept me from seeing Catalina even
once during several visits to Newport Beach. Then one April
I was invited to sail out to Catalina by Bill Lapworth, the
naval architect who made such a fine reputation with
his various Cal-boat models and custom yachts. He and his
wife Peg wanted me to see the Cal 2-46, a cruising motorsailer of Lapworth design, and the day I arrived was so
smog-free that the Los Angeles newspapers had front-page
pictures of the city's skyline in celebration. Catalina's purple bulk loomed large on the horizon across a sparkling
sea, and a fresh northwester was blowing in from offshore.

When we poked our bow out between the breakwaters of
Newport Harbor into the open Pacific, we were greeted by
steep, whitecapped seas. The boat took them well, and we
made sail and headed off close-hauled on the port tack.
But we soon realized that the twenty-six-mile slug to the
island would be a tough one. After determining that, despite being a motorsailer, the Cal 2-46 could make good
progress to windward in a lump of sea, we turned back
through the inlet, mast swinging wildly as the seas built
against the ebb tide, to the smooth water of Newport Harbor. I decided that full-cruising auxiliary was an apter description than motorsailer after this little test.

We went back to the Lapworths' waterfront house and
moored at their pier for a pleasant evening of visiting and
yarn spinning, and by morning the bluster had gone out
of the wind. The wallop had also gone out of the seas when
we poked out the inlet again, and we had a pleasant sail,

still to windward, across to the ever-increasing bulk of the island, which gradually changed from purple to green as we neared it. It had been a wet winter, and Peg and Bill said they had never seen Catalina so green. Also, on this midweek day in spring, we ranged along the shore looking at the coves we passed, and saw only one or two boats in the whole area. The multiple buoys that would all be taken by their lawful tenants on busy weekends, bobbed in neat rows, and we had a wide choice. Howland's Cove was it, one whose buoys are controlled by a mainland yacht club, but open for the taking on a day like this, and we had the spacious cove all to ourselves. Ashore, the grass was green and dotted with wildflowers, and great blobs of rubbery brown kelp could be seen between us and the shore.

Poking the dinghy through the kelp, we landed at the cove-head beach and hiked inland up a dry riverbed. The higher we got, the more trees there were. While the lower slopes had been dotted with flowers and clumps of cactus (and buffalo dung, though we did not see any buffaloes, which roam wild over the hills). On the upper heights, great stands of Australian pine and eucalyptus gradually cut off the view of the water completely. It was cool and quiet amid the trees, with the soft soughing so special to Australian pines blending with the hum of insects. It was hard to imagine that more than ten million people lived just across the way on the mainland. On our way down, back in the open, we stopped on a promontory and had a rare panoramic view from Santa Barbara off to the north, to Oceanside, a spread of almost one hundred miles. Above the deep blue of Catalina Channel, the skyscrapers of downtown Los Angeles reflected the late sun, and everyone agreed that it was rare to be able to see this sight in southern California. Back on the boat for a relaxed supper, as darkness settled over our lonely cove, the vast spread of lights to the east seemed a million miles away.

There was no breeze for a while in the morning, and we powered over a gently heaving surface until the expected westerly came in and we had a pleasant run back to the inlet. The passage between the Newport Harbor breakwaters must be one of the busiest waterways anywhere, and even on a weekday there was a constant stream of boats in and out as we made our way through the heavy flow of traffic inside to the Lapworths' pier.

I was glad I had not only seen Catalina at last, but had the chance to visit it in such unusual conditions. I doubted that southern California could do any better for me.

Additional Information

California and Mexico

As I have already pointed out, there is very little opportunity for conventional cruising on the Pacific Coast between Puget Sound and Baja California. Inland from San Francisco Bay and island-hopping off southern California are the only possibilities along California's long, relatively unbroken coastline. Because of these limited opportunities, many California sailors become long-voyagers to Hawaii, the South Pacific, and down the coast of Central America to the Panama Canal and the Caribbean. Long-distance cruising along the West Coast is a relatively rugged operation, with very few good harbors to put in to. It is simply a means of getting somewhere, not the pleasant relaxation that cruising is supposed to be.

The major cruising activity is to head down the coast to the Gulf of California behind Mexico's Baja California peninsula. This is a winter venture, as summers are too hot and hurricane-prone. Getting there is a relatively easy slide in prevailing winds. It is the long voyage home against the prevailing northwesters along Baja that makes the adventure a major project.

Once there, Baja offers unlimited anchorages in spectacular scenery, with the diving and fishing to go along with the climate, and the atmosphere is truly "going foreign." Recently, The Moorings has been able to open a charter operation in the northern part of the gulf, a real breakthrough, as the Mexican government has not allowed such operations before; it is now much easier for visitors to enjoy this unique area.

Yachting centers There are centers, in California, in all of San Francisco Bay, Monterey, Santa Barbara, Marina del Rey, Long Beach, Newport Harbor, Mission Bay, and San Diego; and, in Mexico, in Ensenada, Cabo San Lucas, Guaymas, Mazatlán, Puerto Escondido, and Acapulco.

Chartering Many agencies charter in San Francisco, the Los Angeles area, and San Diego; and in Puerto Escondido. Individual boats are available through brokers.

Weather California weather is less changeable than on the Atlantic coast. San Francisco, with fog a famous factor sweeping in from the cold offshore waters through the Golden Gate, has a mild climate year-round. Southern California also has a mild climate year-round with some heat waves in summer and fog in winter, but boating is possible all year. That hot land wind, the Santana, is a disruptive factor in the Los Angeles area and can hit without warning. Baja's climate is tropical, with high summer heat and thunderstorms and the threat of hurricanes; it is mild and pleasant in winter.

Cruising grounds The best of these are the Sacramento Delta, Catalina and the other offshore islands, the Ensenada area, and the Gulf of California.

Special attractions The main one is the opportunity to visit another culture in Mexico.

References Pacific Boating Almanac 1989: Northern California and Nevada; *Pacific Boating Almanac 1989:* Pacific Northwest and Alaska; West, *Cruising the Pacific Coast;* Fagan, *Cruising Guide to California's Channel Islands;* Scott, *Cruising Guide to the Sea of Cortez.*

11

▶ ▶ ▶ ▶ ▶ ▶ ▶ ▶ ▶ ▶ ▶ ▶ ▶ ▶

ONE-CITY CRUISE
Sydney, Australia, Has the Makings

It is a seldom-noted fact that all the major cities of the world are located on the water (except Teheran). A few are on just a river or a lake, but many are important ports. I don't know of any city that takes better advantage of its waterfront location, and is more boat-minded, than Sydney, Australia. Its harbor is a marvelous combination of coves, bays, and rivers, and it is entirely possible to spend upward of a week cruising just in the waters inside Sydney Heads, where the harbor meets the Pacific. I don't know of another city that can make this claim.

It is not the kind of cruising that would rate a special trip but it could be a highlight of an extended visit to Australia. I have included it in the "Spring and Fall" section, since those are the best times to enjoy it. A Sydney summer is inclined to be very hot, and its winters are raw and windy, with occasional nice days; but its in-between seasons, which are naturally just the reverse of the North American ones, are especially delightful. Sydney sailors do make full use of their facilities all year round, and it is always strange for a Northern Hemisphere denizen to realize that Christmas is a major summer holiday when everyone goes sailing or to the beach. The latitude of 33°

south, the antipodal reverse of southern California, means
that the overall climate is similar, except having a continent to the west and the sea on the east does make the
extremes hotter and cooler. On several visits, I have been
there in March (late summer) and September (early spring),
and in both months the weather was delightful.

Aside from its unusual opportunities for cruising, Sydney Harbor is a perpetually fantastic nautical spectacle. It
is a busy commercial and naval harbor, and much of the
area's commuter transportation is by high-speed ferries and
hydrofoils. They ply its routes in a constant display of motion, with their wakes arrowing across the surface, and big
white cruise ships make frequent visits, tying up in the
heart of town near the ever-busy ferry terminal.

The harbor is always dotted with pleasure boats, mostly
sail, even on weekdays. It is on weekends, however, that
the yachting scene expands into a multifaceted panorama.
Various races take place in the main body of water and in
many coves, and day sailers and cruising boats are out in
force. I have never seen this sort of display so close to a
big city, and there is always something to watch. There
are major yacht clubs like the Royal Sydney Yacht Squadron and the Cruising Club of Australia, and many local
dinghy-racing ones.

On my first visit to Sydney in 1962 to report on the
preparations for their first-ever America's Cup challenge
with *Gretel,* I was told that *Gretel* and her trial horse, *Vim,*
would just be taking individual practice sails for crew
training and familiarization. Supposedly, *Gretel* was not
yet ready for serious racing trials. I was out on one of the
tenders on a Saturday morning, watching *Gretel* start out
on a training run, when the word was suddenly flashed
that there would be a race, *Gretel*'s debut. Sir Frank Packer,
the publishing tycoon who was head of the Aussie challenge effort, was entertaining guests for lunch at his home
in Vaucluse, a suburb on the southeast arm of the harbor,
and he wanted to give them something to look at as they
gathered on the lawn.

A man of impetuous whims and iron will, he had suddenly decided to race *Gretel* against *Vim,* catching the crews

The Cruising Club marina, Gretel I in foreground

by surprise, but they were soon all eager for action. The idea was to stage a brush in the north-south stretch of the harbor just inside the Heads, starting off Vaucluse, in a fresh easterly that was blowing in from the Tasman Sea. Somehow the word spread around the harbor, and by the time the two 12-Meters were lined up and ready for action there was an amazing flotilla gathered for the spectacle. Packer had chartered *Vim* from her American owners, as she was a proven campaigner and had almost beaten out *Columbia* for the 1958 defender's berth, even though *Columbia* was the brand-new brainchild of Olin Stephens, and *Vim* was a 1939 product of his design board. *Gretel* had to prove herself against her.

There was excitement and tension in the air as the boats squared off for a reach northward between the great rafts of boats that had assembled. Very gradually, *Gretel* began to inch ahead, and she had a lead of a couple of lengths when they arrived at the top end of the harbor off Manly. There was real jubilation in the *Gretel* support group as we all gathered for a raft-up lunch just inside the North Head. "She's fair dinkum," was the word. And time and again someone would say, "At least she's no *Sceptre*," referring to the British challenger that had laid a complete egg in 1958.

It is a memory that has stayed with me of the kind of excitement that is being continually generated on Sydney Harbor's waters; and I had other glimpses of the colorful variety during the visit. One day I had a sail on *Vim,* and it was interesting that I understood less of what the crew was shouting to each other in Strine, the colorful Aussie slang, than I did when sailing with that Greek crew in the Aegean Rally. As the afternoon wore on, the breeze kept increasing until they decided to call off operations, and all hands piled aboard the tenders to watch the 18s racing. These sailing dinghies, commercially sponsored, with advertising logos on their sails, stripped down to the ultimate in planing speed, are a colorful feature of Australian and New Zealand sailing. Called Eye-deans in the Strine lingo, they are professionally sailed, and large ferryboats loaded with bettors follow them around the course, although the betting is technically illegal. With all the passengers lined up on the side of the race, the ferries proceed with an alarming list. On a day of strong breeze, the races are fast and furious. The boats plane at amazing speeds and the action around marks is particularly hectic, with last-minute jibing and sail handling, and lots of screaming and yelling.

The 12-Meter sailors were like spectators at a prize fight, howling and cheering and placing bets, and I thought that the stakes must be high in pounds (still the currency then), so fierce was the yelling. It was a laugh to find that the usual bet was a shilling.

Every weekend the 18s are an important part of the harbor spectacle. When we came back years later, we made sure to be in their vicinity while we were using a charter boat loaned to us, a modern twenty-eight-foot, locally built fiberglass auxiliary. The 18s were still at it, and just as colorful, and, if possible, the harbor was even more crowded and active.

On this visit we started with a few days in Sydney before going twelve hundred miles north to Australia's special cruising grounds, the Whitsunday Islands inside the Great Barrier Reef. We were guests of the government tourist agency, which put us up at the elegantly understated Sebel Town House Hotel in the King's Cross section of Sydney.

We had a very nicely appointed suite there, and when we came back from our Barrier Reef junket, the desk greeted us like long-lost friends and said that they had our old room back for us. This was in midafternoon, and the bellboy ushered us up to it with great ceremony, unlocked the door, and bowed for us to precede him into the hall. It was a narrow one about twenty feet long, with a kitchenette and dressing room off to the right, leading to a large bedroom-sitting room. The big double bed was just to the right of the end of the hall, and, as I walked in, I could see two pairs of bare feet at the bottom of the bed.

"Hey, there's somebody in here!" I cried, turning to the bellboy, and a deep masculine voice from the bedroom echoed, "There bloody well is!"

We beat a hasty retreat back to the front desk to learn that we had been one floor off, and the room we had invaded was occupied by a Sir Somebody Robinson: Never got to meet him otherwise.

Our cruising featured quiet explorations of coves in the more remote corners of the harbor, and a one-day junket by taxi up to Pitt Water and the Hawkesbury River about thirty miles north to sail on a day-charter yacht. The taxi driver was a "new Australian," the term for Europeans who have immigrated in considerable numbers since World War II, mostly from central and southern Europe. Our driver was an Italian, and his accent was an incredible mix of Italian and Strine. We asked him how he liked Australia (Aus-tryl-ya to him), and he said he was quite happy except for one thing.

"The only trouble with Aus-tryl-ya is too bloody many Aus-tryl-yans!"

Pitt Water is a resort area that has many boats based there and semiwild hilly shores, covered with eucalyptus and Huon pines. It is a pleasant, get-away-from-it-all type of place, and we had a good day as the charter yacht poked into its many coves. We had a fine lunch of the tender little oysters Australians are so proud of, and lobster, served by a husband-and-wife team of captain and mate dressed in spotless whites. The boat was a classic clipper-bowed ketch reminiscent of the *Tioga-Ticonderoga* breed of Herreshoffs. Sydneyites can take a good week or two vacation cruise up here, but there are no other cruising areas nearer than the Barrier Reef. The Hawkesbury, which runs inland for over twenty navigable miles from Pitt Water, is home to an enormous fleet of powered hire-cruisers, very popular with vacationing Australians.

Back on our charter boat in Sydney, we would have good sails every day in the open water of the harbor and then tuck into a different cove each night. The 22 square miles of the harbor make 190 miles of shoreline, so it would take more time than we had to explore all corners. The Parramatta River inland from the main harbor, which is known as Port Jackson, is mostly industrial, but the other tributaries, like Middle Harbor, have handsome private houses along the wooded bluffs, with boats at private moorings in every corner. Most of the houses have a pen in front for swimming, enclosed by mesh as protection from sharks. These are evidently an ever-present threat, but we never saw one. No one seems to swim from boats, but when the 18s capsize, the crew is usually in the water for a while. Perhaps the mess of sails and rigging in the water is protection enough.

At Middle Harbor, we tied up at a seafood restaurant to try the local favorites, ordering John Dory and barramundi and sharing each other's dishes. Oysters are another specialty, and everywhere you go people run down all the ways they can be served. They can be treated with sauces like Mornay, fried, or breaded, but I think they are best "natural."

There are good, deserted luncheon coves on the undeveloped shore inside the North Head, and Manly, just north of it, is a busy beach resort with ferries constantly in and out, and active dinghy racing. On one day of mild breeze, we poked the bow out between the heads just to get a feel of the open sea. There is no in-between here, you are either in the harbor or out in the Tasman Sea, noted for its boisterous conditions. Local sailors tell convincing stories of the kind of seas that their winter storms, called southerly busters, can kick up here.

It was gentle and pleasant, though, for our couple of miles out and back, and then, by way of playing up the contrast that cruising here provides, we went to the Sydney Opera House that night. This is a unique building on the shore that, along with the great arched Harbor Bridge rising just west of it, is the hallmark of Sydney. Sections of the opera house, curved and pointed, represent drawing sails, and it was interesting to see a sail-training schooner go by it and have the curve of her sails match beautifully with the lines of the building. The harborfront terrace outside the opera house, with a garden and an open-air cafeteria, is a delightful place to spend a few hours watching the constant flow of harbor traffic. For our evening visit, we were taken to dinner at an indoor terrace restaurant with a panoramic view of the harbor (and the best lamb chops I have

Sydney Harbor symbols: the bridge and the Opera House

ever tasted) and then to a performance of *Simon Bocanegra.* The auditorium and the staging were marvelous, but, as an operatic ignoramus, I would have been happier to be back on the boat. In another visit, we saw a beautifully staged and costumed performance of *The Mikado,* which was great fun.

The next day, our last, was a Sunday. It was a wonderful way to top off our visit to be a part of the great armada of sail, with every shape and size of boat, and the Eyedeans at it in their best planing, swooping show of speed. We still like get-away-from-it-all cruising when we can find secluded harbors to enjoy in solitude, but this taste of urban cruising had been a very special adventure.*

---

*For added information on Australia, see Chapter 19.

PART III

///

WINTER

The places described in this section offer an escape from the rigors of northern winters. Those in the Southern Hemisphere are sometimes better during their winter, but Northerners don't feel the urge to change climates then. All of the following could be classed as year-round areas, with an understanding that their conditions vary.

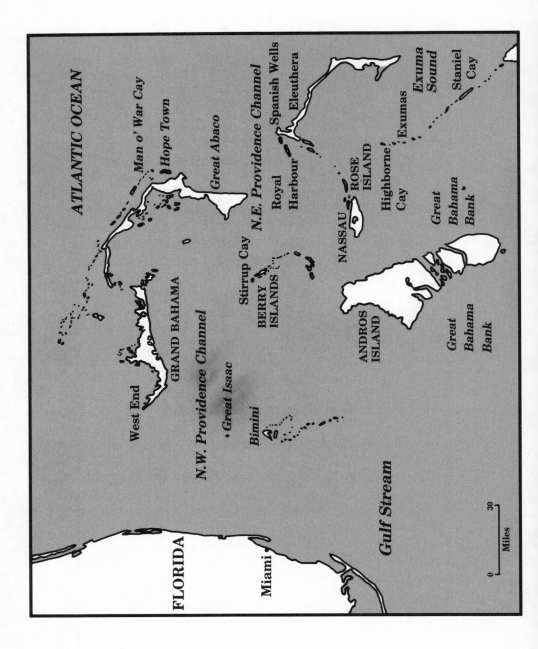

12

▶ ▶ ▶ ▶ ▶ ▶ ▶ ▶ ▶ ▶ ▶ ▶ ▶

HUB OF THE BAHAMAS
Fanning Out from Nassau's Central Location

In airline operations, certain airports are "hubs," and travel through them radiates out to all points of the compass. In the world of cruising, Nassau is a hub for all Bahamian operations; it is situated at the strategic center of this vast archipelago, which covers almost fifty-four hundred square miles of the Atlantic (note, not the Caribbean) between 21° and 27° 30′ north in a seven-hundred-mile arc. From it, good cruising grounds in all directions can be reached in a one-day sail. It has great opportunities for short excursions as well and it is the center for supplies, services and transportation, restaurants, night life, and shopping.

From 1957 to 1979, I managed to get to the Bahamas at least once a year, sometimes for the Southern Ocean Racing Circuit and, more often, for cruising. In three of our boats, *Mar Claro, Tanagra* and *Brunelle,* we followed the practice of basing at Nassau and fanning out, cruise by cruise, to the outlying areas. These used to be known as the Out Islands, a geographic description, but have, for political reasons, been given the wishy-washy title of Family Islands. To me, they remain the Out Islands (*Tanagra* was an Out Island 36), and following the hub theory, we have had some great cruising to them in all these boats. After operating *Brunelle* there for the better part of the winter of 1979, we shifted our base of operations to the Virgin Islands and I have since missed the charm of the Bahamas.

The islands suffered briefly in the 1980s from a combination of drug traffic, political problems, and local crime, but I understand that things have settled down considerably, and the very real attractions of cruising there are as strong as ever. Because of government policy, there is no crewed chartering and very little bareboat chartering, but the Bahamas still rate as the most accessible waters for southern cruising for private boats. They can remain, without having to pay duty, for up to six months.

For years, I used to answer the oft-posed question as to my favorite cruising grounds by saying it was a toss-up between the Exumas and the Grenadines. Both still rate among the top areas in the world, but other Bahamian areas can be placed right up there with them, and this is one of the main advantages of "hubbing" out of Nassau.

We spent the most time in the Bahamas in *Tanagra* over two separate winters. She had gotten there on her own bottom, after north-south ICW trips, and she was a fine boat for the area, well-named as an OI36 by Morgan. She was a centerboarder with a three-foot-nine-inch draft, which allowed her into many areas that are especially appealing. A draft of six feet is considered the maximum for Bahamian cruising, but anything less opens up a lot more possibilities. We used both Yacht Haven and East Bay Marina in Nassau as bases. Yacht Haven is a major facility and very popular, but we ended up spending more time at East Bay because of finances (translation: it was cheaper) and because of its location, right opposite a shopping center with supermarket, chandleries, and all conveniences. It is also right next to the native landing of Potler's Cay, which always had interesting goings-on.

Nassau Harbor is a constantly vibrant slice of marine life, with boat traffic of all descriptions, including native work boats in every state of repair, commercial traffic, and large white cruise liners. Despite the crowded conditions, it can be used very well as a base for one-day excursions

Busy marinas in Nassau Harbor

in a variety of directions. Just outside the harbor, the seaward side of Paradise Island (which used to be Hog Island
until tourism gentrified it) offers fair-weather coves for
beaching, and there are some diving spots along Athol Island, just to the east. Lyford Cay, an enclave of wealth and
privilege, is an easy sail to the west at the tip of New
Providence, with a well-protected marina. Salt Cay, just
north of Paradise Island, is private and does not have a
real harbor, and the best day-cruise area is just to the east
of it. Tiny Sandy Cay, frequently photographed as the essence of tropical glamor with its golden sand and small
stand of palms, has a daytime anchorage, but no landing
allowed. The best spot of all is at the western end of Rose
Island, south of Sandy Cay. There is a gorgeous beach here,
backed by a stand of stately casuarinas. While there are
numerous coral heads off the beach, it is easy to spot them,
eyeballing in sunny weather. The water is so clear that
the anchor and its rode can be clearly seen against the
white sand of the bottom in about fifteen feet, close enough
to shore to swim to the beach. Only about four miles from
Nassau's marinas, it is a marvelous escape, and we went

there many times. It also became our standard foolproof way to impress guests right off the plane with the charms of the Bahamas. There are also some pleasant anchorages on the south side of Rose Island at East and West Bottom harbors. A week or more can be easily spent just daysailing or overnighting out of Nassau to these nearby anchorages.

For longer cruises, there is a wide choice, wide as the compass card. To the west lies Andros, largest landmass of the Bahamas, and relatively undeveloped. We happen never to have gone to Andros, as locals warned us off it in easterly weather which was the predominant condition while we were there. The Berry Islands and the Abacos are to the north, Eleuthera is to the east, and the Exumas and the Family Islands, farther on, are to the southeast. The Abacos are better approached from Florida, as it is a long pull across Northeast Providence Channel to open-sea cuts into calm water, and timing is an issue. We have enjoyed them in a separate cruise, but in our Nassau operations, we concentrated on the Berry Islands, Eleuthera, and the Exumas.

The Berrys and Exumas are made up of small cays in a closely knit pattern. Eleuthera is one big, rather hilly island, with a few small off-lying ones, and quite different in atmosphere and feeling. It is a perfect day's sail from Nassau of about thirty miles, depending on the chosen landfall, and Eleuthera is long enough north-south so that the approach to one end of it or the other can avoid windward work. With the prevailing winds in the southeast, the trip is usually a delightful reach in the lee of a string of cays all the way from Rose Island to Royal Island at the northwest tip of Eleuthera. Northeast Providence Channel has the royal blue hue of deep water, and it is especially pleasant sailing to be surging along on an easy reach with the feeling of the open sea, but in calm water, making good knots as the hard-to-identify little cays, just above awash, slide by to starboard. The nice part about this route is that, should the wind be in the north, calm water can be found for the same course on the Bank side of the cays, where the water is a pale, translucent green.

A wrecked freighter on the reef off Egg Island, gleaming in the slanting afternoon sun, loomed up as we swept northeast, and soon Egg Island's lighthouse and the hills of Royal Island appeared. Royal Harbour at the center of the south side of this private island, is an ideal landlocked anchorage, hemmed in by hills and completely peaceful. The next day we threaded our way across the Bank, careful to follow the directions in the *Yachtsman's Guide* with the bottom always in full view through the pale waters, into the narrow entrance to Spanish Wells. This island, barely separated from Eleuthera, is unique. Its name comes from the days when Spanish galleons on their way back to Europe stopped off to take water from wells that have long since disappeared. Eleuthera (from the Greek word for freedom) was named by Tory loyalists who fled the American Colonies during the Revolution and sought asylum there. Their descendants make up most of the population of Spanish Wells, a completely white community of distinctive character. There is a characteristic Spanish Wells look of sandy hair, many freckles, and gaunt features with prominent nose and chin and rather sunken mouths. The men look so much alike that you feel you are talking to the same person no matter how many different ones you deal with.

It is a very prosperous community, based on fishing, lobstering and seafaring, and the houses are brightly colored, modern, and well tended with TV antennas on tall masts and new cars in every driveway, though the island is only two miles long. The people are very religious. Sunday is a day of complete quiet, and hymn singing can be heard drifting across the harbor waters from the churches on many week-nights.

Once through the tricky approaches, the long, narrow harbor is completely protected, and Sawyer's Marina, now called Spanish Wells Yacht Haven, well up the winding channel, is well tended. In one of those typical midwinter weather patterns that sweep through the Bahamas, the southeaster that had given us such a good sail on the way up had swung into the south and then southwest, heralding the approach of a front, and we were in the perfect spot when blasts of northwest air, carrying a few dashes of rain, hummed harmlessly through the rigging that night. Spanish Wells is an interesting place to spend a day in port, as we wandered around on a casual sightseeing walk, intrigued by the neatness of the houses and the general air of purposeful activity on the fishing boats along the town seawall.

The front behaved properly and brought a clear northeaster the next day, ideal for a run down to Eleuthera's Hatchet Bay. A cut from the open Bank waters into an inland pond has made a fine harbor here, a popular stop, and the little yacht club served up a good supper of cracked conch and crawfish.

The wind, now in the east in its normal clockwise moves after the passage of a front, gave us an easy run back to Nassau. We had a shortened spinnaker pole on *Tanagra,* making runs more fun with a wung-out jib.

It is unthinkable to operate out of Nassau without going to the Exumas, and that was our next move after a crew change (one of the obvious advantages of a Nassau base is the direct air connections with New York and Miami). Sailing over the Yellow Bank on the direct course of 133°M to Allan's Cay is said to be dangerous, as there are reportedly coral heads with as little as three feet over them, but I have crossed more than a dozen times and never saw anything that shallow. The recommended procedure is to be out on the Yellow Bank no earlier than 1100 so the sun is high enough for good visibility on the heads, and a draft of six feet can be carried. In deeper boats, or in times of poor visibility, the safe route is to go south for eleven miles from a point two miles south-southeast of Porgee Rocks outside Nassau and then head over to Allan's on 113°, which avoids all heads.

The day we wanted to start for the Exumas, the wind was fresh on the nose from the southeast, and we had to power there, as a beat under sail could not be accomplished in good light. As usual, we did not see a head to frighten us, and Highborne Cay's three hills soon appeared on the horizon. When we first came to the Exumas in the 1950s, there were no facilities in any of the harbors.

Everything was completely natural and primitive, but by the late 1970s Highborne had a small marina installed, and we headed to a good berth there in late afternoon, a bit spray-blown but happy to be in the Exumas.

The weather remained stable, giving us a chance to range down the chain as far as Staniel Cay, which had also grown into quite a cruising center in the years since we first saw it. We had a night in the lee of a favorite spot, Shroud Cay, where the snorkeling is good along the shore (as in most Exuma harbors).

Of all the places I have been in the world, there is nowhere that can quite match the Exumas for the clarity of the water and the shades of delicate color. The shimmering water of the clear pale shallows is like sailing through air. Slightly deeper water is a delicate green, which darkens with depth. The tongues of water come through between the cays from Exuma Sound, are a brilliant blue of startling contrast. We sailed through these shadings the next morning, and headed into Sampson Cay for a lunch stop in the tight little harbor. This is on a remarkable stretch of cruising water called Pipe Creek, which is really just a narrow channel between a double row of cays. Glimpsed through the breaks between them, Exuma Sound is a rich, deep blue to the east, and the Great Bahama Bank's pale, endless expanse, spreads off to the westward. We threaded our way southward, ooh-ing and aah-ing in a continual chorus, finally ending at Staniel Cay Yacht Club's pier, where a number of boats had gathered. In contrast to the previous night's isolation, this was an evening of eating ashore and calypso-style merrymaking with crews from other yachts.

The return route took us up to Allan's for our last Exuman night. Strangely, the next day there was a flat calm and we were again powering across the Yellow Bank, this time without spray. In calm water, there is a strange illusion that the bottom is tending uphill, and that shallow water lies just ahead. Conditions were perfect for head-watching, and despite our worries we did not see any that looked dangerous.

By early May, it was time to think of heading north, and

we decided to make a leisurely cruise across to Florida and the ICW. At first we contemplated the Abacos, but, with family aboard including four-month-old granddaughter Julia on her first cruise, the deep-sea beat of almost sixty miles to an open-sea entrance to the Abacos' eastern side did not seem advisable. We chose the Berry Island route instead, and it worked out well. We had been to the Berrys earlier in the year on one of our short excursions out of Nassau, taking in the pretty but surge-plagued anchorage off Little Whale Cay and then the totally protected and very civilized marina at Chub Cay, where dinner ashore was especially good. On this visit, we had planned to head north to Little Harbour Cay the next day, but it was blowing fresh from the east, with prospects for an even stronger breeze more in the southeast the following day, which would have meant a real slug of over thirty miles back to Nassau. We took the easy way, and had a brisk sail on port tack over whitecaps to Lyford Cay.

Lyford's luxurious ambience was impressive after the smash and bounce of open waters, and, again, we enjoyed eating ashore. When we have guests aboard, one night ashore is the "Captain's Dinner" and another one the "Crew's Dinner," easing the financial impact and making a pleasant ceremony. When the next day brought the expected strong southeaster, even stronger than predicted and close to 30 knots, there was smug satisfaction in being on New Providence. We had a ten-mile starboard tack thrash to Nassau Harbour, with one-cloud rain squalls adding stinging sheets of rain. *Tanagra* was a stiff and able sailer and took it well.

Now we were ready to head to the Berrys again, and the breezes of May were milder than the winter ones. In calm seas and a gentle easterly, we slid easily along, heading into Little Whale on the last zephyrs of the day for a solo night in the anchorage that was minus surge this time. It was a lovely evening with a newly waxing moon which was perfect lighting for steak cooking on the hibachi. The easterly was back in the morning for a leisurely start and a reach northward along the islands.

Because they are relatively limited in scope and somewhat off the main cruising routes, the Berrys are not as popular a cruising area as the Abacos and Exumas, but they contain, on a reduced scale, all the same charms. The water may not be quite as dazzlingly clear as in the Exumas, but the colors are still very impressive indeed. The cays are typically featureless, and they have to be carefully ticked off to keep a navigational track. Occasional strands of pure white sand vary with low, rocky cliffs, and the vegetation is minimal except where encouraged by human effort in places like Chub and Little Whale cays.

A late start, no pressing schedule, and the urge to explore cut the day's run to about six miles as we chose Frozen and Alder cays as a likely spot, and eyeballed our way in through the entrance and a turn to port into a picturesque oval of an anchorage. Frozen Cay evidently is named for the white rocks that line its shore, evocative, perhaps, of ice. Both were uninhabited and Alder is a bird sanctuary, with lots of activity to watch and hear. The crew's plans for snorkeling had a sudden shift, when, just as they were ready to enter the water, the long silver menace of a barracuda slid out from under the keel. Operations were shifted by dinghy to inshore waters along the beach. Again we had the place to ourselves, and the only slight glitch was a gentle surge coming over the cut between the cays at high tide.

Our weather held for another easy reach north to the top of the Berrys where Stirrup Cay and its tall lighthouse and radio tower marks the turn at the elbow of Northwest Providence Channel. From the Gulf Stream to Stirrup, it runs almost east and west, and then bends southeastward toward Nassau. The light is an important landmark in the Miami–Nassau Race, and, as we glided toward it over the gentlest of seas, drifting easily in balmy sunshine, I couldn't help but think back to some of the more rugged SORC races. Then the channel had been a welter of whitecaps, and driving through them in racing trim was a wet, bouncy test of boat and crew. I liked our present relaxation better.

There are several anchorages inside Stirrup; we chose the closest one, a short run in to the westward at Goat Cay, a small island with high bluffs just south of Stirrup.

Tanagra at Frozen-Alder Cays, Berry Islands

We dropped the hook off the southwest corner, with a view down the back side of Lignum Vitae and Great Harbour cays. Off to the west under the lowering sun was the vast, empty expanse of the Great Bahama Bank. I still have a basic sense of unease when anchored in such an exposed bearing, wondering about cold fronts and northwesters. The Bank is fine protection, however, in anything but a really heavy front, and none were in the vicinity on this mild May day.

In the years since we were there, Great Stirrup has become a picnic stop for cruise ships, and I imagine the atmosphere must be a bit different. But on this calm evening, we watched the sun dip down to the Bank, alone and very glad that we had chosen the Berry Islands to savor before leaving the Bahamas.

Additional Information

The Bahamas and Caicos

The Bahamas have a special attraction for Atlantic coast sailors in that they are the easiest way to go foreign south of Canada, and the closest tropical location. Stretching as they do over so many miles of the Atlantic, they extend down below the Tropic of Cancer at about 23°30' north into the true tropics. Their scope is surprising and they span an area comparable to that between New York and Atlanta and from Cape Hatteras across into the Appalachians. Adding the Caicos would stretch the area down to Louisiana.

In this vast region, there is a profusion of good cruising waters, although, as I have pointed out, most of the activity centers on Nassau. It is relatively rare for visitors to go beyond the popular grounds in the Abacos, Berrys, Eleuthera, and the Exumas down to Crooked, Acklins, Mayaguana, Inagua, and the Turks and Caicos. Facilities are more primitive, and supplies and repairs are harder to come by, but for those who have the time, these far-out reaches of the Family Islands retain the atmosphere of days gone by, a world still relatively untouched by the modern influences evident in Nassau.

There is a price to pay in cruising the Bahamas, and that is the Gulf Stream crossing from Florida. It is only fifty miles across this turbulent ocean river from Florida ports to Bimini or West End, but it is one of the most challenging stretches of water anywhere, never to be taken lightly. Sea conditions are rough as a rule, and the weather can change rapidly. Gauging the speed of the Stream is difficult, especially in a slow-moving auxiliary, and entrance into ports on the Bahamian side can be tricky, especially in onshore winds. The best advice is to play weather forecasts very carefully and then get across as quickly as possible. If a norther is blowing or forecast, the Stream is no place to be in a cruising boat, as the wind against the 2–3 knots of current shouldering northward can raise a nasty, short, steep sea. In two years of subchaser duty in the Navy between New York and New Guinea, the roughest, nastiest sea I experienced was in sight of Fowey Rocks Light just outside Miami. In twenty crossings by sail and dozens more in the Navy, only twice were conditions pleasant.

The Gulf Stream rim of the Bahamas, from Cat Cay and Bimini on up to West End and Walker's Cay is sportfishing country, famous worldwide as such, but not good cruising. It takes another long plug via the Northwest Providence Channel or across the Great Bahama Bank, to get to the heart of cruising country in the central Bahamas.

I have listed the Bahamas in the "Winter" section, as this is the time when most visitors like to go there, but they are actually one of the best year-round areas anywhere. The drawbacks are continental northers in midwinter and the threat of hurricanes from late summer into autumn. But the good days win out by a large margin, and there is not a violent change in climate between seasons. There was one crazy day in January 1977 when snow actually fell on Grand Bahama, the only time in recorded history, but most northers are not that extreme. The wind cycle when one is approaching makes for fairly easy predicting, as the wind clocks down from its usual easterly quadrant into the south and southwest, often increasing in strength, and it is a sure thing that a front is on the way. The onslaught of a front and its first day are usually good times to be in port, and then the wind settles down and goes into its clockwise action again, moving to northeast and east. Sometimes it will hold in the east for days on end, but the cycles are prone to be quicker in January and February. In January 1979, we had eight cold fronts, with the complete cycle each time, while we were moving from Florida across the Gulf Stream and on to Nassau.

The other three seasons see weather that is much more stable as a rule, and cruising conditions average out as delightful unless a hurricane is brewing. These are well tracked and reported, and forecasts are usually continual, so there is no excuse to be caught unawares by a hurricane.

There has been publicity about "piracy" in the Bahamas, which is just a glamorous term for robbery, and there have been unpleasant incidents over the years, but these should be put in the perspective that no area in the world is guaranteed crime-free, and someone's chances of being robbed or assaulted while afloat in the Bahamas are about the same as having an intruder in the house at home. It is unpleasant to think of crime in such delightful surroundings, and the sensible thing is to take all precautions possible and to be security-conscious. This brings up the question of firearms on board, and I feel that that should be handled according to one's own philosophy. I personally have never had a firearm on board my boats (or at home), as I think their presence is more likely to lead to trouble than to avert it, but there are many people who think differently, and that is their own concern. The only time I questioned my decision on guns was in a curious episode leaving Antigua (see Chapter 15), but otherwise we (knock wood) have not been bothered by anything worse than the "rowboat Mafia" of young kids in the harbors of the lower Caribbean.

Some of the best cruising we have ever done has been in the Bahamas, and their scope is so large that it would be almost impossible to run out of new places to explore. Although the Caicos are not politically in the Bahamas, they fall into the same geographic area.

Yachting centers Nassau, Bimini, West End, Marsh Harbour, Hatchet Bay, Staniel Cay, George Town, Clarence Town, Providenciales, and many more excellent harbors have some facilities for home-based boats and transients.

Chartering There are bareboat fleets in the Abacos and Hatchet Bay, Eleuthera, but crewed yachts usually operate out of Florida for Bahamas cruising. Some Florida charterers permit bareboats to go to the Bahamas.

Weather Climatic conditions are tropical and semitropical, mostly controlled by easterly and southeasterly trade winds that prevail year round, but are interrupted by cold-front northers in midwinter and the threat of hurricanes in late summer into autumn.

Cruising grounds The best of these are the east coast of Abaco, the Berry Islands, the east coast of Andros, the cays to Eleuthera and Eleuthera, the Nassau area by the day, the Exumas, with longer cruises to Long Island, Acklins, Crooked Island, San Salvador and Mayaguana, the Turks, and Caicos.

Special attractions The brilliant colors of the waters, as well as the beaches, snorkeling, scuba diving, local seafood, and native culture, all make the Bahamas worth cruising.

References Robinson, *Over the Horizon,* Chapters XIII, XIV, XV; *Where to Cruise,* pp. 208–226; and *South to the Caribbean,* Chapters 7–11; Fields, *Yachtman's Guide to the Bahamas;* Dodge, *The Compleat Guide to Nassau.*

13

▶▶▶▶▶▶▶▶▶▶▶▶▶▶

LEARNING FROM CHILDREN
A New Look at the British Virgins

In all the years we have cruised in the British Virgin Islands, starting with charter cruises in the 1960s and 1970s and continuing in our own boats since 1979, it would seem that there could be no new discoveries or surprises. We have been to every harbor many times, experienced every type of weather, and done all the things there are to do (except scuba diving). What new experience could there possibly be?

Ours came from seeing the same places through new eyes. Our most recent BVI action involved a cruise-in-company in two boats with five grandchildren in the crews, and it was wonderfully refreshing to see the area from their perspective. The familiar ports and routines took on whole new aspects, and it was, in a way, as though we were first-timers ourselves instead of having an aggregate of well over two years of BVI cruising. It also added a whole new catalog of cruising activities to our rather settled ways.

The children were at an age to mix well with both juvenile and adult doings. Kate, Sam, and Danny were twelve, and Julie and John fifteen (almost sixteen). Their parents are our daughter Martha and husband Dan Bliss. Danny and John are his by a previous marriage as Martha's three

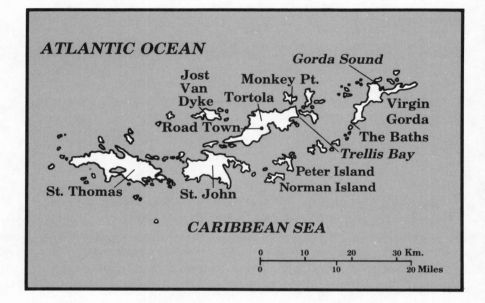

ATLANTIC OCEAN

Gorda Sound

Jost
Van
Dyke

Monkey Pt.

Tortola

Virgin
Gorda

Road Town

The Baths

Trellis Bay

St. Thomas

St. John

Peter Island
Norman Island

CARIBBEAN SEA

| 0 | 10 | 20 | 30 Km. |

| 0 | 10 | 20 Miles |

are for her (Sam and Kate are twins). Completing the party was Uncle Bill Doniger, everyone's favorite uncle and an interested observer of the activities of nieces and nephews.

The boats were *Helios,* our CSY 42 from CSY's charter fleet, and a sister ship, *Sapphire Star.* We took the cruise on a school break in January, and the weather cooperated with an idyllic week between two weeks of those legendary Christmas winds. The group was split with Bill D., Jane, the two girls and I sleeping on *Helios,* and Martha, Dan, and the boys on *Sapphire Star.* During the day, at meals, while under way or in port, the groups formed and re-formed in all sorts of combinations. We rafted at anchor in most places, at least during the day, splitting at night if there was a surge, and we managed adjacent berths in marinas.

The traffic between the boats was a constant Katzenjammer comedy, as the cold soda, snorkeling gear, books, video camera, CB walkie-talkies, items of clothing, snacks, suntan lotion, and dark glasses, to name just a few items, always seemed to be on the "other boat." Each boat felt as busy as a subway station at rush hour, with a steady up and down the hatches. This contrasted with the typical adult activity of relaxing over a book or a drink in the sedentary cockpit "potato" mode.

The CSY 42s also have special equipment that adds a whole new dimension to cruising life and was enjoyed to the full by the children, such as a cassette player, TV with VCR, microwave oven, and a hard-top Bimini. The latter has subjected us to some ribbing from traditionalist friends, who ask us what we are doing in a "roll-top" boat, but we never imagined what a hit it would be with the younger generation and how it would work. To us it is a welcome shade from the tropical sun, but to them it became sort of a tree house clubroom. While in port they repaired to it for reading, playing games, telling stories, and just relaxing. It also served as a diving platform, which made a special romp out of swimming interludes. The squealing and splashing were continual. Of course the hard-top was off limits while we were under way, but it was still a totally unexpected addition to juvenile cruising fun.

Some "toys" that the kids brought along also provided added action. Each one had personal snorkeling gear, but they also got great mileage out of the walkie-talkies and the video camera. The radios were an early hit, and there were almost continuous conversations between boats, with special coded "handles" for each kid, for the first few days, but the novelty wore off before the week ended. We let them use the regular VHF, with proper procedure (most of the time), when we wanted to communicate formally.

The video camera saw continual action, and many evening hours were spent in giggly appreciation of a recap of the day's events. How much was preserved for posterity, I'm not sure, but there was one special production of Uncle Bill's birthday party at the Last Resort restaurant, where Tony Snell, the inimitable proprietor and post dinner entertainer, made special note of the occasion. There was the obligatory "Happy Birthday to You" and some other special song favorites and allusions. The Last Resort, by itself on a tiny island, is the perfect eating-ashore place for a multi-generational crew, as the buffet is easy and good, the show is broadly entertaining for any generation, but above and beyond that, there is "Chocolate" the donkey! She has a special window giving onto the restaurant, with a handsome frame drawn around it, through which she visits with the customers, braying on occasion and eating and drinking whatever is offered her. Going to a "night club" is exciting enough, but how many are there with a donkey?

All these special features contributed greatly to the success of the cruise, but the basic factor in the success was the type of cruising the BVI offer. Nowhere else boasts such a complete round of activities in such a compact area, and this applies no matter what the generational makeup. Although there can be exceptions, the weather is, on average, most likely to make operations easy. One of the few "downers" we found during the cruise was in sailing for more than a few hours, and that is seldom necessary in the BVI. At the start of a sailing passage, there was competition for the helm, a lively interest in the course and scenery, time spent riding the bow pulpit, roller coasting

over the bow wave, and activity with the radios; but the
enthusiasm would gradually slack off, and there would be
a retreat to a book or a bunk and the usual when-are-we-
getting-there? questions. Fortunately, we only had one sail
longer than three hours, and it was only four, and excitement would mount again at the prospects of a new harbor.
It isn't only the younger set that reacts this way. I have
noted the same general psychology with adult guests, which
makes short passages a plus. On many days, we break the
day with a stop for a swim and lunch. This is a distinct
contrast to the interisland sailing in the eastern Caribbean, where daily passages of forty and fifty miles are
sometimes necessary in getting on to the next port.

The specifics of our cruise reveal even more about the
attractions of the area. Our group tumbled in on a Saturday evening, with everyone keyed up at the weather change
from Pennsylvania and the spectacular up-and-down-hill
taxi ride from the airport to the CSY base in Road Town,
and there was a great bustle of settling in on the boats
and straightening out what went where. Rather than de-
lay for shopping on Sunday morning, which would involve
taxi rides and be time-consuming, we put enough supplies
from *Helios* on *Sapphire Star* for lunch and took off for
Virgin Gorda Yacht Harbour, where we could do all the
marketing needed right at the marina. It was a brisk thrash
to windward in the usual 18–20-knot easterly trade, punctuated by a good lashing from a one-cloud rain squall just
before we got in, and everyone knew they had been sailing. Although we had taken a long starboard tack and
Sapphire Star had gone off to port, we arrived within a few
minutes of each other and took adjoining berths in the marina, assigned by Denise, whose friendly radio voice from
the marina office has been a VGYH hallmark for years.

The interboat traffic began immediately, amid individual exploratory forays around the marina by foot and by
dinghy, and dinner was a two-boat operation, with the
younger generation eating on the *Star* and adults on *Helios*. All five children had saved Christmas money and al-
lowances for the trip, and the morning saw them take off
to case the various shops, while the adults did food shop-

ping in a three-store combination. Road Town would have had ampler selections at lower prices (not counting taxi ride), but this was much more convenient under the circumstances, and quicker.

By midmorning we were supplied and organized, and Martha and Dan took the whole tribe on the *Star* to The Baths, Virgin Gorda's virtually obligatory lunch stop at the southwest tip of the island, while Jane and I dallied over lunch at the marina and then sailed straight to Trellis Bay to meet Bill Doniger's plane. The Baths were a great hit, with excellent snorkeling and lots of exploring caves and climbing around the fantastic boulders that tumble along the beach like a carelessly strewn Stonehenge. The boys were brave enough to do some high diving from the rocks, and they were full of their adventures when we reunited at Trellis.

Trellis, an excellent anchorage at Beef Island, hard by the airport, is dead to leeward of VGYH, and we had a lazy man's sail by just unrolling the jib. It is handy and fun to meet guests arriving by plane, as it is only a couple of hundred yards from the town dock to the terminal. Knowing the percentage of on-time arrivals here, I always take some crossword puzzles with me to kill waiting time, and this was a two-puzzler. Bill was settled aboard when the *Star* wafted in from the Baths adventures, and she anchored parallel to us, close aboard. We then pulled the boats together into a raft that lasted until we went ashore to the Last Resort for the birthday festivities. It was in Trellis that the kids first discovered the extra dividend of diving off the hard-tops, though they had already used them as clubrooms at VGYH.

It was just as well that we split the raft for the night, as there was a slight surge in the anchorage, a rather rare occurrence. The morning was beautiful, and we headed in company to a favorite stop for snorkeling and lunch, Monkey Point on Guana Island. It is only about an hour's run from Trellis, threading our way between Great and Little Camanoe, and, exercising one of the prerogatives of grandparenthood, I let Dan go ahead and anchor, and then we rafted up. Nice to have strong-backed younger people do the work.

Monkey Point, a little neck of land at the south end of hilly, isolated Guana, has a small beach, a protected anchorage if there is no northerly swell, and is ringed with great snorkeling reefs. It has not been too well known, although we do see more boats there than we used to. This day two other boats were there, one a dive boat giving instructions to beginning snorkelers. The woman conducting the exercise called out to her half-dozen pupils, assembled off the stern of the boat, "Now put your faces in the water," and Martha and I had a laugh. When she was taking her first swimming lessons at the age of three, her teacher used to say, "Now put that facey in the water; stretch those hannies out," and it has been a family joke ever since.

The second and third generations all snorkeled around the cove, ranging along the shore in "buddy" pairs or groups, and they came back after a good half-hour session full of enthusiasm, describing the varieties of fish and coral they had seen. Pelicans had flown patrol over them, occasionally making their own dive-bomb attacks. After a leisurely lunch from the larders of both boats, we powered back through the Caminoes to Marina Cay, a mile to the north of Trellis Bay.

Marina Cay has a colorful background, as it was the subject of Robb White's book, *Our Virgin Island,* about the adventures in the 1930s of a young couple building a honeymoon cottage. The book was later made into a movie that marked Sidney Poitier's debut in the role of a helpful local, and was followed up in the 1980s with White's retrospective book called *Two on an Isle.* When we first cruised the Virgins in 1964, Marina Cay was the only place where cruising sailors could eat ashore, and it still has a restaurant, and a small resort built around the original honeymoon cottage. The anchorage in the lee of the little cay is protected by a fringing reef on the southeast, and rather iffy anchoring conditions have been helped by the placement of a few ten-dollar-a-night rental moorings. Close to shore, in shallow water, soft sand is not very good holding ground, and farther out, in deeper water, there is a cross tidal current and a surge. Even in the inner section, there is quite often a surge at time of high tide. The range is only a little over a foot, but this is enough to cover the reef and take away its protection. Years ago on earlier cruises, this was an excellent snorkeling reef, with live coral, but Hurricane David in 1980 broke up the coral and killed it.

All the rental moorings were occupied by the time we got in, but we hailed Fritz Seyfarth, who lives on his classic ketch *Tumbleweed* on a mooring just inside the reef, to invite him over for dinner, and he pointed out two private moorings that were not going to be used that night, so we didn't have to anchor. Because of the possibility of surge, we didn't raft, and it turned out to be a wise idea, as the surge developed with some authority before dawn.

Fritz is a boating writer (*Tales of the Caribbean,* among other books) and a colorful character full of local lore. The twins had a treasure map that he had sent them from a previous cruise of ours, and all five kids dinghied over to *Tumbleweed* for a visit and ended up in a good sea-story session. Fritz had been aboard her during Hurricane Hugo's onslaught, riding to seven anchors. Six of them pulled out, one by one, but the seventh held and she rode the storm out safely, one of the many wild tales that local sailors were full of in the post-Hugo season. The sea-story session continued when Fritz came over for dinner, a tradition we always enjoy at Marina Cay.

There was a good fresh trade wind for the beat to Gorda Sound the next day. We had the three 12-year-olds on *Helios,* and they spent a good part of the passage riding the bow pulpit out through the rocky islets called the Dogs, and around the northwest tip of Virgin Gorda. As we cleared the lee of Virgin Gorda, the waves became steeper, with authoritative whitecaps, and they cheered and laughed as the bow did its elevator action. This was obviously more fun than steering, though they did take their turns. We had real open-water sailing, and a good thrash that ended with the boats rafted for a late lunch on one of the rental moorings off the southwest point of Prickly Pear Island. Prickly Pear forms the northeast side of Gorda Sound, also called North Sound, which is the real cruising mecca of the Virgins, a two- by three-mile landlocked body with Mosquito Island on the northwest and the towering hills of Virgin Gorda on the south and east.

The entrance from the north is between two impressive reefs. The eastern one, off Prickly Pear, breaks and boils in any kind of surge, and the one on the other side is a long, wicked-looking stretch of brown. The water pales from the deep blue of the open sea to a translucent green where two buoys mark the narrowest part of the entrance, then darkens again on the inside, as Gorda Sound is rather deep. It has several anchorages around its perimeter.

Drake's Anchorage off Mosquito Island is reached by doubling back to starboard around the western reef and two smaller reefs that lurk between the big reef and the island. It takes its name from Sir Francis Drake having used it as a rendezvous point for a fleet he was gathering for an attack on the Spanish settlement at San Juan, Puerto Rico. When the fleet had assembled, it set sail down what is now Sir Francis Drake Channel on its way to San Juan, but Indians friendly to the Spanish sent a warning on ahead, and the attack was repulsed. Had it succeeded, the history of Puerto Rico would certainly have been different.

Across from the entrance, Leverick Bay has a resort settlement and a marina, and Gun Creek, the native settlement, is on a cove just to the east. The Biras Creek resort is on a cove at the far eastern end of the sound, and the rest of the eastern shore is taken up by the Bitter End Yacht Club complex. This is where most of the visiting yachts gather, at anchor, on rental moorings, or at a small marina called the Quarterdeck Club, and the entire stretch of shoreline is taken up with BEYC installations, topped by the hillside bedroom units.

On our 1964 cruise, we were the only boat in Gorda Sound, and the Gun Creek settlement had the only buildings. In 1973, the BEYC was in its first years and had a small restaurant and a few bedroom units along the beach. We were one of four tables at dinner in the restaurant when we came ashore from our charter, and it has been fascinating over the years to watch the complex grow.

The BEYC is very boating-oriented, as the guests can use Windsurfers, Lasers, Sunfish, Rhodes 19s, and Freedom 30s, and its two restaurants are heavily supported by visiting yachtsmen.

Lively sailing on Gorda Sound in a Bitter End Freedom 30

After lunch on our arrival, a typical one-cloud squall, an expected feature of the Virgins, swept in from Anegada Passage. One minute there is a bright clear sky, and the next, a cloud will scud over the eastern hilltops, lash the area with a brief but hard avalanche of rain, and then speed off to leeward, leaving clear skies again. We had a couple on our way in to the Quarterdeck, but they cleared up by late afternoon.

The Quarterdeck is a bit of an extravagance, but it has always seemed worth it to us for the convenience of showers and bathrooms in the clubhouse and the easy access it provides to all the things there are to do on shore, especially so for the younger generation. They were immediately off on explorations of the beaches, the gift shops, and the "aquarium," a netted enclosure in front of the main clubhouse that contains some sharks, tarpon, turtles, groupers, parrot fish, and schools of bait fish. When they found that there was a good movie (free) at the Sand Palace Theater, they opted for a quick pizza supper and then the show, instead of joining the adults for Uncle Bill's dinner treat, and all generations had a good time.

The next day had been designated for in-port activities. We had a morning snorkeling expedition in both dinghies to the reefs out in Statia Sound. That was a moderate success, hampered a bit by rough water, but in the afternoon the children spent their savings renting their choice of small sailboat, and conditions were ideal.

Again, the evening option was for an early supper aboard and another movie for the kids, while the adults, who had gone to the Carvery the night before, ate at the clubhouse in a table right by the water. Julie had a social triumph in being invited to a party by a young man from one of the charter boats, but she wouldn't go without John, and John preferred the movie.

All in all, the BEYC was the perfect spot for a break in the cruise and a typical example of the BVI's ease of cruising options. About all it lacked was a donkey. After a success like this, the rest of the cruise might have been an anticlimax, but that was not the case. Once the BEYC has been achieved, it is all downhill to anywhere else, so there

Late afternoon on Gorda Sound; cruise ship Wind Star, *sister ship of* Wind Song *(Chapter 18) in the distance*

is no more slugging it out to windward. We took off downwind the next morning, regretting that we could not negotiate the "back door" out of Gorda Sound through the little cut between Mosquito Island and Virgin Gorda at the western end of the sound. In *Brunelle,* with a four-foot-nine draft, we could handle it easily, but the CSY 42s are too deep, at six feet, to make it safely. We took the northern route out and had an easy run down Drake Channel to Road Town. Despite all the attractions they had taken in, the kids had not been to the "metropolis" of the BVI, and some of them still had some mad-money funds available. Village Cay Marina was target of that day's run. Having been based there for nine seasons, we look on it as home-away-from-home, even though it has been gentrified since our first days there. The minute we tied up in adjacent slips, the younger generation was off exploring the shops and other attractions. The sleepy little village on first acquaintance has added more and more shops, restaurants, and marine facilities, and the masts of several hundred yachts dominate the area known as Wickham's Cay, which was a mangrove swamp when we were here in the 1960s.

Village Cay Marina has added a pool, and that became an attraction after the shopping forays ended. For the evening, we signed up for another must-do of a BVI cruise, dinner at the Cloud Room. This is a restaurant one thousand feet up on a hill on the east side of Road Town. It is so high up that the only way to get there is by a van driven by the Tortolan proprietor, Paul Whatley, as no taxi will brave the climb. The ascent is exciting, and the view of the spread of Road Town harbor, ringed with lights, is increasingly spectacular. Once there, the Cloud Room's balcony seems to hang out in space over a fantastic panorama that extends all the way to St. Croix, thirty-five miles away to the south.

Dinner, all managed by Paul's family, measures up to the surroundings, and the grand climax comes halfway through the main course, when the roof is silently rolled back to expose the stars. Hard as it was to outshine Chocolate, and free movies at Bitter End, this was another highlight that could not be forgotten; the ride back, of course, even though it is downhill, is a suitable coda.

We had hit most of the highlights, but we were not through. There was one more day for adventures, and the next morning the two younger generations took off for the caves of Norman Island. Typical of the easy accessibility of all the BVI, this is a reach of six miles from Road Town. The caves, supposedly the inspiration for Robert Louis Ste-

venson's *Treasure Island,* are great fun to explore, both by
snorkeling on the reefs around them, and by poking inside
by dinghy.

We followed later and met at Little Harbour on Peter
Island for a final rendezvous. This has been one of our favorite anchorages in the BVI over the years, partly because there was a private mooring there, set out by the
late Percy Chubb of the insurance family, whose winter
home was on the point above the harbor for fellow Cruising Club of America members. Unfortunately, it is no longer
there, and we had to cope with the special problems of anchoring like everyone else. The difficulty is that the harbor is rather deep and ringed with steep hills. The trade
wind does not blow evenly across it, but swoops down from
the hills at unpredictable angles and, often, backdrafts, so
it is a challenge to set an anchor properly, with enough
swinging room to avoid neighbor boats. We chose a spot
close under the south shore, in fairly shallow water, and
when *Star* came in, she rafted with us and ran her anchor
off her stern to the shallows along the shore. We were far
enough away from the swinging circle of any other boats,
and we rode securely in one spot through the night.

This was a final extravaganza of rooftop diving for the
kids, and the two younger generations also had a final session of snorkeling on the rewarding reefs that ring the shore
of Little Harbour.

As a gag during cocktail hour and preparations for dinner, I started keeping count of the number of times each
kid went up and down the hatch on *Helios.* "You're the
champ," I told Danny. "You've been through nine times."
I thought this might slow things down a bit, but instead,
a frenetic contest developed to see who could negotiate the
hatch the most. Ah well, it was all in fun.

And fun it was, for the whole week for all of us, and a
marvelous example of how the BVI lends itself to almost
any type of cruising except long open-sea passages.

14

▶ ▶ ▶ ▶ ▶ ▶ ▶ ▶ ▶ ▶ ▶ ▶ ▶ ▶ ▶

THREE-NATION CRUISE
In the St. Martin Area

As a change from her normal routine of summer layup at Road Town, Tortola, one year we arranged for *Brunelle* to stay in St. Martin (or actually Sint Maarten, since this was the Dutch side of this two-nation island), and it worked out very well. She was in the care of Robbie Ferron, an experienced boatkeeper who had worked on her in years past, and who has a service out of Bobby's Marina at the head of Philipsburg Harbor. We stripped her of all valuables and removables, and gave them to Robbie for storage at his office, and she spent the summer at anchor in Oyster Pond. This is a landlocked harbor on the east side of St. Martin that is completely secure in a weather sense, and it meant that she had no dockage fees.

When we came back in December, she was sparkling clean and in perfect running order. We had a day or two to get her back together and supplied with food before Phil and Dolly Minis joined us. We had promised Dolly that we would find her some good birding. She is expert enough to have a working arrangement with the Cornell Ornithological Laboratory, and she came equipped with tape recorder and boomed mike to pick up "cries and whispers."

It is always an adventure to explore food markets in a

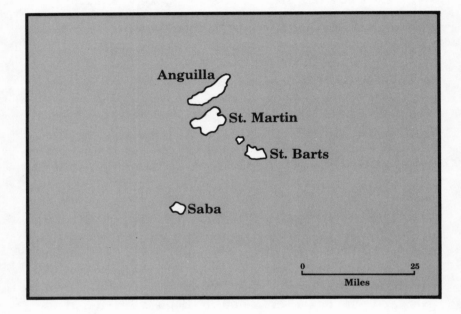

new place, and it took a day or two to get what we wanted together. The price tags were in Dutch guilders even though dollars were welcome, and liquor prices were pleasantly low. Food prices were not, but supplies were plentiful and mostly familiar. Refrigeration problems on board that had plagued us the previous spring had been solved.

It was too blustery to take off for one day, and we relaxed aboard and explored in town. When we first came to Bobby's Marina in 1980, it was wide open to the constant surge in the bay of Philipsburg, which is not a good natural harbor. It is only in recent years that it has been used as an anchorage. When I first saw it on a 1958 visit, there was not so much as a rowboat in it, and a modest surf was piling onto the long curve of beach. Yachting started to develop in the 1970s, but we took an unpleasant smashing around at Bobby's pier in *Brunelle* in 1980. Since then, jetties have been built at Bobby's and nearby Great Bay Marina, and the protection is much better. Boats in the marinas managed to ride out Hurricane Klaus when it made its freak rampage through here in November 1984, and we were comfortable on this latest visit. I still remember, though, a day a few years before the jetties were built when six-foot rollers sweeping in from the south provided surfing for kids on the breakers on the bar in the middle of the bay, while boat masts were swinging like crazy pendulums.

Aside from food markets, Philipsburg is a good duty-free shopping spot for such items as optical gear, cameras, electronics, and perfume. The main street, a narrow alley that was just a dusty path in 1958, is lined with shops displaying credit card decals and is a madhouse scene on cruise ship days. I'm not much of a shopper, but I did find a good pair of 7×50 binoculars for twenty-eight dollars.

After our day's wait of shopping and browsing, the next morning was clear and not so windy, and we took off on the standard cruising start from Philipsburg, a direct run westward along the south shore past the big hotels that have built the island into a major tourist mecca. They make quite a contrast to the two small hotels that were all there were in 1958. The airport there is a busy jet field with

direct service to the States and Europe, making this a good
port for crew changes.

The fanciest hotel, La Sammana, is on French land near
the western tip, overlooking a lovely stretch of beach. At
the point, Basse Terre, we jibed, set the jib, and rounded
up to beat along the north shore toward Marigot, the main
port on the French side.

This is a lovely wide bay that has perfect protection in
trade wind weather but is completely exposed to a northerly surge, which we have only experienced once there. To
starboard on the way in, standing in lonely splendor, are
the abandoned buildings of La Belle Créole, a large resort
development, which failed. They looked like a picturesque
Mediterranean village until a closer view through binoculars showed that they were starkly empty. More recently
they have been restored and the place is in business.

Year by year, I have watched Marigot grow from a completely native fishing village in 1958, when there was not
a single inn or restaurant along its ramshackle waterfront, into a sophisticated and very French resort. It now
has smart boutiques, classy French restaurants block by
block, and a marina in the lagoon, reached by a drawbridge that opens twice a day. While the Dutch side is almost completely Americanized, Marigot retains its Gallic
aura despite the developments, and there is something of
the feeling of being on the Riviera.

The bay gets gently shallower approaching the shore,
and we like to anchor close in off a small break in the reef
that fringes the beach. The dinghy can be landed here near
the *pâtisserie*. I make a ritual of going ashore every morning, on awakening, for fresh croissants, and the native
market strings along the beach a few feet away. Jane and
Dolly had a fine time here loading up with cristofine, okra,
eggplant, tomatoes, bananas, limes, and lettuce, waited on
at each booth by native women with small children peer-
ing shyly around their legs.

We explored the town for a while and were back on the
boat and ready to leave when a rain squall swept in over
Marigot's hills, and we waited it out over lunch. By 1345
it was clear again, with a pleasant southeaster, and we

had an easy reach the six miles across to Anguillita, the little cay off the western tip of Anguilla. From there, as the wind freshened, we had a beat along the yellow bluffs of Anguilla's north shore into the main harbor, Road Bay. Anguilla is the most northerly of the north-south Antilles string and seventeen miles long. It was named by Columbus as he sailed by on his second voyage in 1493 and means eel in Spanish, fitting its long, slender shape. Relatively low compared to its mountainous neighbors in the Antilles, it is only three hundred feet at the highest point. It made news and history in the late 1960s when it reverse-revolted out of the St. Kitts-Nevis-Anguilla associated state back into the arms of Mother England as a colony. The dictatorial government in St. Kitts was giving Anguilla, sixty miles away on the far side of St. Martin, the wrong end of the stick on many deals, and the Anguillans, normally peaceful and tractable farmers, fishermen and seamen, got fed up. After a series of events that sounded like comic opera to the outside world but were very serious locally, their revolt was successful, and Anguilla, Montserrat, and the British Virgins remain the last colonies of Britain's once-vast empire in the Caribbean.

It was also our third country in about twenty miles of sailing, and formal entry into Anguilla had become something of a game for us. A capricious, to say the least, customs man named Ambrose had been very difficult to deal with on our previous visits. His decisions seemed to depend on the number of empty beer or rum bottles on the top of his desk, and he could be anything from downright nasty to archly playful. Sometimes he would tell us that we could only stay in Road Bay, and then, on another visit, he would let us visit other harbors at will. The drill at Road Bay is to check in first at the Police Office, which acts as Immigration, right at the town dock, and then walk half a mile along the beach to Ambrose's domain. The police officer, always friendly and helpful, knew of my run-ins with Ambrose, and sometimes, when I checked with him, he would wink and say, "Better go to customs quick. Ambrose out to lunch."

This day Ambrose was there in all his cantankerous glory

and particularly unpleasant, and, feeling that something should be done about it, on my way back along the beach, I stopped at a beachfront restaurant called the Barrel Stave and asked if I could use the phone. It was behind the bar, and I got through to the minister of tourism and told him of my reactions to Ambrose in what I hoped was a constructive manner. While I was talking, I noticed that the barmaid slipped away, and I thought nothing of it until my next check-in with Ambrose a week or two later.

He gave me a cold stare and said, "Why for you go talkin' 'bout me to the Minister? You give me bad name. I don't like that." He entered me quickly and in surly silence, and I decided not to say anything. Later on I found out that the Barrel Stave barmaid had had three children by him, though they were not married. Such is life on a small island of seven thousand people.

A pleasanter side of our visits to Anguilla was getting together with the Emile Gumbs family. Emile and his Canadian wife are among the few white residents of Anguilla. Emile was the latest in line of a family that had lived there since the eighteenth century, and, stemming from the time of slavery before it was abolished in 1834, the name is a very common one throughout the population. We had met them on our first visit in 1980, having been told to look him up as a congenial sailor, only to find from an offhand comment that he was the Chief Minister of the Anguillan government. He is a dedicated sailor, very interested in visiting yachts, and for years he was skipper of the grand old schooner *Warspite*. She was a colorful addition to the Road Bay scene; her last duty had been to supply lonely Sombrero Light far out in Anegada Passage, the first sentinel of the approach to the Caribbean from Europe or the north. Now we were sad to learn that she had been a victim of Hurricane Klaus, whose maverick behavior of moving eastward out of the Caribbean had sent it right across Anguilla with hurricane-force winds smashing directly into Road Bay. Not only was she lost by dragging ashore and breaking up, but she also demolished the town pier, a rickety old structure that was a reminder of what the Caribbean looked like fifty years ago, before the great tourist influx began.

We had dinner at the Barrel Stave, with conch as the main course. Ambrose's lady friend was still behind the bar, but we didn't communicate. The Gumbs joined us for a drink, and Emile and I had a little discussion of the Customs problem. He knew of it and said that they had tried Ambrose at every post with pretty much the same results, but, evidently and inexplicably, he had job security.

We had promised Dolly some birding, and so we went in search of the prominent species here, the tropic bird, a graceful, ternlike creature with long forked tail and red beak. In previous visits, we had seen them swooping around the cliffs on the way in from Anguillita and also in great profusion at Crocus Point a couple of miles east of Road Bay. We headed there the next morning, anchored close in off the postage stamp of beach set between craggy cliffs, and Dolly got out her boom mike and tape recorder. In the noonday sun, the place was strangely quiet, and she had a hard time getting recordings from an occasional bird flying by. She stopped while we had lunch and then a nap, with her tape exhausted, and when we woke up at 1500 the sky was aswarm with swooping birds, and their cries filled the air. They were operating on and off rookeries in niches in the cliffs. There were thousands of them, now that Dolly had no more tape. It was an impressive sight nevertheless, and the explanation of their scarcity at noon, according to Emile later on, was that they fish at midday.

It turned out that Emile is also an ardent birder, the only one on Anguilla, and when he heard of Dolly's interest, he took the Minises on a birding-sightseeing trip by auto that afternoon after we got back to Road Bay. They said it was a fascinating excursion not only for the intended purposes, but also to see him stop frequently at a house, or talk to someone walking along the road, asking about a sick child, a farming problem, or some other concern a political leader should have for his constituents. They hit it off so well that they later came back to Anguilla and stayed in an apartment at the Gumbs' house for a concentrated session of birding.

Jane had been bothered by a bad toothache, and Emile again came to the rescue, taking her to the dental clinic, a facility run by the national health service; a very pleasant and caring young dentist, a Welshman, gave her some medication that soon took effect; and the whole thing was covered by the British government. We had found the same kind of caring (and free) service for a medical problem at a little clinic on Virgin Gorda in the BVI.

It was time to move on, and we scooted before a fresh easterly to Anguillita along the cliffs where the tropic birds swooped, and where there were the beginnings of two superluxury resorts that have made Anguilla an "in" place without taking away from its unspoiled charm. Emile had told us that the policy of the government was not to expand beyond resorts and installations that could be handled by local labor, resisting rather strong pressure to put in a jet airport and large hotel-casinos that would have been controlled by (rather unsavory) outside interests. We said amen to that policy.

Hard on the port tack in a whole-sail breeze, we stood across to the bay at Marigot and then short-tacked around the point to the next harbor to the east, Grand Case. This was an interesting place for Dolly and Phil to explore ashore, with the town spread out in a long thin line on the coastal road where some of the best restaurants on the island stand along the beach. It turned into a squally, windy night, with williwaws sweeping out of the gap in the hills behind the beach and a bit of a surge building in the anchorage. It was still that way in the morning as we reefed the main and fought our way past Baie Marcel and around North Point. Marcel at the time was an unspoiled duplicate of a South Seas hideaway but has since been built up with a big hotel and marina. We used to love to duck into its isolation for lunch.

Rounding North Point, there is a sneaky little menace called Spanish Rock about a mile ENE, with only seven feet of water over it. It sometimes breaks in heavy seas, and even with a draft under five feet I am always careful to check its location as we go by. The open-sea sweep is broken here by a low island called Tintamarre that has a rather odd history. It was rumored (unconfirmed) to be a secret fuel base for German U-boats during World War II, and more recently it has been the site of a private airfield, with many derelict planes strewn around. We have never

Ile Pinels anchorage, St. Martin

landed there, but there is a pleasant lunch-stop anchorage, a bit surgy, off a white stretch of beach on its west side. We were headed just down the coast for a favorite spot, Ile Pinels, at the north end of wide open Orient Bay. Sweeping into Orient Bay on the big, deep-sea rollers that suddenly build steeply as they come into shallower water, is always a thrill. The choice is then to swing to starboard to Pinels or to port to a less secure spot behind Green Cay. The major "attraction" at Green Cay is nude windsurfers, who look extremely ridiculous exposed to the breeze.

Pinels is our favorite, and we slammed over in a jibe and eyeballed our way through its reefs into a lovely, calm, round dollar of a harbor, beach-girt with shining sand and stands of palms, to anchor in about eight feet. There is only room for half a dozen boats, so an early arrival is a good idea, and departure before 1100 is recommended, as that is when several day-trip boats from Philipsburg arrive and take over. The only blot here is the piles of garbage left on the island by native picnickers.

The breeze eased off and we had a typically peaceful evening watching the moon rise behind the palms, before beginning the twelve miles to St. Barts the next morning. The breeze came back, and the seas were steep and dark blue out in the open for a good solid sail. As we eased into Gustavia Harbor to tie up stern-to at the commercial cay, there was a clunk in the lower depths of *Brunelle,* and I soon realized that we had no propulsion. Just in time, we were able to toss a line over to the boat alongside, and they ran the line ashore for us so that we could tie up. It turned out that the bolts of the propellor shaft coupling had sheared. At least we were secure for the moment, and could easily sail back to Robbie Ferron's ministrations at Philipsburg on the morrow.

Meanwhile, Dolly and Phil explored the quaint byways of Gustavia, which gets its name from the fact that Sweden owned St. Barts until the late nineteenth century, when it was sold to France. St. Barts's full name is St. Barthelemy or Bartolomeo, named by Columbus for his brother. In the recent past, entry formalities were minimal or nonexistent, but now there was a proper Port Office with an official in white uniform and epaulets manning the desk and collecting the fee of $3.50. He was impersonally businesslike until, in going through the form I had completed, he came to Jane's birthplace of New Haven, Connecticut.

"What is this CT?" he asked. "I am French. How am I supposed to know CT?"

Although there are good French restaurants here, we ate aboard and had an early bedtime after the excitements of the day. It is also smart to go to bed early, as everything gets going in the tight little surroundings at a very early hour, with hymn singing from a nearby church, bells ringing, dogs barking, horns tooting, trucks rumbling past, and local fishermen roaring off to work with their 50-horsepower outboards at full throttle. Aside from its general quaintness, St. Barts is unique in the Caribbean for its population ratio of about 95 percent white to black, the exact reverse of most other islands.

After some quick shopping for local delicacies at the waterfront market, which has more customers arriving in dinghies than in autos, we were ready to leave. Our saviors of the previous afternoon in the next boat, *Mon Ami,* a Beneteau 42 just in from San Diego, were kind enough to tow us out of the traffic jam in the harbor to make sail outside. The wind was enough in the south to give us an easy reach by the series of landmarks such as Barrel of Beef, the Groupers, Ile Fourche and its nice little harbor, and Rocher Table, and on to Philipsburg. VHF brought Robbie out to meet us in his work boat to tow us into Bobby's. It turned out that the problem had been the use of metric bolts in United States-sized holes in the shaft coupling, done by the yard, not Robbie, and the loose fit caused vibration to shear them. Not a very dignified way to end a fine cruise in this compact area of three nations.

15

▶ ▶ ▶ ▶ ▶ ▶ ▶ ▶ ▶ ▶ ▶ ▶ ▶

THE HIGH ISLANDS
The Mountainous Lesser Antilles

The moonless predawn, with clouds scudding before the strong easterly trade and blotting out most of the stars, seemed especially dark. Perhaps it was because we are so seldom under way at 0400, but we had made up our minds to get to St. Barts in a one-day passage, seventy-two miles, and we had eased out of Deep Bay, Antigua, made sail of reefed main and jib just outside, and were leaving a phosphorescent trail of sparks in our wake as we winged off on course 320°. This departure from the norm of casual mid-morning cruising starts lent an extra excitement to the sailing, and *Brunelle* was flying through the darkness.

Jean and Nev Conyers, Bermudian sailing friends of long standing, were along, and all four of us were in the cockpit, silently enjoying this departure from routine. Looking back to check the dimming lights of Antigua, I caught a glimpse of a green running light off our starboard quarter and wondered idly why no red light showed. The glimmer of green dipped out of sight in a moment, and I gave it no more thought for a while. Gradually, though, the low rumble of a motor could be heard, and I started looking back more often. I didn't say anything, nor did Nev, but I noticed that he had become aware of the stranger too. Every

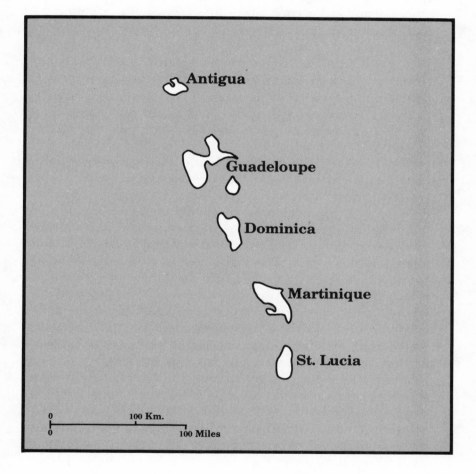

Antigua

Guadeloupe

Dominica

Martinique

St. Lucia

0   100 Km.

0   100 Miles

so often, the green light would wink for a moment as the engine noise gradually increased, and I began to look steadily over my shoulder.

I have never been particularly bothered by security considerations, and we had never had the faintest hint of trouble in all our Caribbean cruising, but there had been rumors, and even corroboration, of incidents of "piracy," and one very disturbing case in Bequia, written up in Betsy Holman's book *Sitting Ducks,* of a boarding and assault. Perhaps it was the night-shrouded start and the unusual sensation of being alone, except for the lurking stranger, that brought an increasing tenseness. None of us said anything for a while, but I finally murmured something like, "I wonder what he's up to," and Nev grunted an acknowledgment.

Now we could see the dark outline of a powerboat, and the green light no longer showed as she came closer. She was traveling at only a fraction of a knot faster than we were, so the approach was very slow, and the increase in motor sound came in spurts with the uneven gusts of the trade wind. I began to have Walter Mitty-like fantasies of what action I would take if the boat came too close, but I didn't want to say anything. The only "arms" I had on board was a flare launcher, not even a pistol, as I have never wanted to have anything to do with firearms at home or on my boat. I had had my fill of them in the subchaser Navy, and I was firmly convinced that the only casualty of my having a firearm would be my own left foot.

While the stranger was creeping up on us, a welcome streak of light began to appear on the eastern horizon. Quite close now, it could be seen that she was a low, native-type powerboat with a small pilothouse and long open cockpit. Several figures were huddled there. I figured that daylight would soon take away the cover of darkness she had been under and lessen the chance of something happening, and we all now watched the boat, and the growing light, with anxious curiosity. The hull was now in our wake, and the boat veered a bit to starboard, away from us, and drew up almost even. A native man was at the wheel in the pilothouse, and the huddled figures in the cockpit were three women and a man. As they crept by and moved slowly on

ahead they all smiled and waved cheerily. We waved back
with great enthusiasm, feeling rather silly, and only then
acknowledged what we had all been thinking. The port
running light was obviously not working, the boat was on
a routine passage to Nevis or St. Kitts, and, as she pulled
ahead, the whole thing seemed a silly anticlimax in the
broad daylight. Darkness and mysterious lights can work
wonders with the imagination, and the routine rumble of
an engine can take on a subtle menace when that imagination is working. We all admitted how silly our fears had
been, but we also admitted that they had been very real
for a while.

And somehow this incident seemed to symbolize the
quality of cruising the "high islands" between St. Martin
and Grenada. Actually they are the Lesser Antilles, and
there is a very different feel to sailing in them than the
more easily managed BVI, Grenadines, or St. Martin area.
The islands are mostly mountainous, as high as five thousand feet, and the passages between them are from thirty
to fifty miles over open ocean. Trade wind seas sweep in
all the way from Africa, making for a lumpy ride, and the
breeze usually has an extra heft to it. There is a day-long
panorama of watching the island astern fade from green
to blue while the one ahead reverses the process, and one-
cloud squalls can bring a sudden dash of cold rain, slashing in quickly to be gone in a few moments. Towers of
cumulus build over the mountain peaks during the day,
and sailing in the lee of the islands is a hit-or-miss business of calms, sudden, brief williwaws, and even a backwind westerly. The civilizations vary radically and colorfully
from island to island depending on their colonial background, and there is a shortage of good cruising anchorages.

Cruising is not the casual business of a short sail to a
luncheon stop for a swim followed by a lazy afternoon sail
to an easy anchorage. The days are long and often rough,
and they should be broken up with lay-days when possible,
but it is a fascinating world, the scenery is gorgeous, and,
for those who like deep-sea sailing, the interisland passages can be exhilarating.

Our brush with the "suspicious" motorboat was near the

Brunelle (right center, bow-to) at Marigot Bay, St. Lucia

end of a winter's round-trip excursion for *Brunelle* down
the chain to Grenada and back. Jane and I had not been
able to do the whole route. Friends took *Brunelle* from the
Virgins to St. Lucia, we went from there to Grenada with
adventures in the Grenadines similar to those described in
Chapter 16, and daughter Martha and her husband Dan
sailed her from Grenada up to St. Lucia. From there, we
took over for the run back to St. Martin. There had been
mechanical problems for Martha and Dan, and we spent a
couple of days at Marigot Bay, St. Lucia, getting them
straightened out, remembering our first visit there in the
charter schooner *Mollihawk* in 1962 when we were the only
boat in the bay. Now it is the base for a Moorings Company charter operation, with two hotels and restaurants
and full marine service, and crowded with boats.

Phil and Dolly Minis, world travelers, experienced sailors and expert bird-watchers, were our crew again for the
passage to Antigua, and, once the stamp-banging of Customs and Immigration clearance was done, we ducked the
few miles into Castries to stock up at a very handy waterfront grocery hard by Vigie Airport, and then took off for
Martinique at 1315. The trade was just right for an easy
sail over the thirty-one miles to Anse d'Arlet on the southwest coast of Martinique. This was April, and the days were
a little longer than in midwinter, and we eased into the
excellent anchorage at 1745 after a delightful passage. We
have had blustery, wet going in the past on this route, but
this was a piece of cake at close to hull speed. The impressive Martinique peaks glowed in the slanting sun, and as
we neared them, the scruffy buttress known as Diamond
Rock began to take shape and definition against the background. This pockmarked, scrub-covered pile of stone, a few
miles offshore and almost six hundred feet high, is famous
for having been a British Royal Navy "ship" for a year and
a half. Starting in 1804, it was manned by a team of British tars, who kept tabs on French fleet movements and
heliographed them back to Admiral Rodney in St. Lucia.
An added attraction for us was the sighting of three whales
fairly close by on this passage. April is a migration month
for whales moving north from the southern Caribbean, and

most of our sightings over the years have been in April. The ubiquitous flying fish seemed larger than most on this run.

Anse d'Arlet, a favorite weekending harbor six miles south of Fort-de-France, had plenty of boats even on a weeknight. The center of the harbor is marked off for fishing activities by rows of yellow buoys, an addition since our last visit, and the anchored boats were strung along the southern shore. To welcome us, there was a green flash on the clear horizon at 1817 sunset, and a full moon soon rose over the hills.

A short power trip to Fort-de-France the next morning gave us almost a full day to explore its civilized delights of sophisticated shops and fine restaurants. It is the most European of Caribbean cities, with beautifully dressed women of every skin tone and lovely carriage, and a tremendous bustle of traffic. Food shopping here can be an adventure, as all brands and labels are French, while most of the non-French islands have familiar American brands on their market shelves. La Grande Voile, an imposing building near the shore, provided a fine dinner (on the gourmet menu, not the standard house one) and sent us early to bed for an 0625 start on the long run to Dominica, sixty-five miles to the only passable harbor at Portsmouth.

It is almost impossible to sail in the lee of Martinique's peaks, and we powered till 1000, passing infamous Mount Pelee. This is the volcano that erupted in 1902 and wiped out the forty thousand inhabitants of nearby St.-Pierre. The only survivor was a criminal in the innermost cell of the jail. There is a great smooth apron of green down the southwest slope of the peak that shows where the lava flowed on its deadly path.

Coming out of its cone of calm, was like entering a wind tunnel, and, with porpoises romping around us, we were suddenly in a 20-plus-knot trade and a confused lump of sea. With reefed main and jib we made a fast passage, occasionally dusted by bursts of spray when a wave thumped us just so. A quick black squall halfway across called for dousing the jib and switching to staysail, but she still tracked along well and we were off Scotts Head at the tip of Dominica by 1330. We managed to carry the trade half-way up the leeward side of Dominica until we got beneath its highest peak, Diablotin, about forty-seven hundred feet high, and were forced to power the last miles into Portsmouth.

Dominica is the least developed and most scenic of the Lesser Antilles, and the story goes that Columbus described it to Queen Isabella by crumpling up a piece of paper and throwing it on the table, as it is a succession of craggy ups and downs. It has had economic difficulties over the years, and hurricanes have damaged it badly. A trip into its interior is an adventure in "jungle" sightseeing, and its peaks are almost perpetually covered in rain clouds. It also has no really good cruising harbor. The capital, Roseau, at the southwest end, has a rolly, open roadstead, but we were able, on a previous cruise, to tie up fore-and-aft to the beach at a hotel called the Anchorage just to the south. Portsmouth is the only place that has something approaching a conventional anchorage, but its bay is wide, with a constant surge, and very windy.

It is also home for some of the most persistent members of the "rowboat Mafia." We found that the poorer the economy of an island, the pushier the rowboat boys are. The first ones met us way off the point, promising ice, so we signed them on as our reps and towed them into the anchorage. This usually serves to deter later approaches, but we were surrounded when we anchored in a chorus of cries of "Hey, Skip! Hey, Skip!" the universal hail. "I get you ice," " I bring you bananas," "I take you on river trip," "I your best boy." They finally settled down, realizing we had picked our crew, after a spell of water fights and gunwale bashing with oars, and I asked whether John and Glenroy were still around. This brought giggles and shouts to other boats, and soon these two were alongside.

Five years previously, on our first down-island *Brunelle* cruise, John had been our "boy" for a day, and Glenroy, then nine years old, had taken our garbage on a tiny homemade raft that was barely afloat. He had promised then that he would be in charge of the anchorage when we came back, and now he was a deep-voiced teenager and

obviously one of the leaders. John had grown into a man
and was about to set sail for Europe as crew on a large
yacht. I had written them both up in my book *South to the
Caribbean*, including a picture of John in his boat. I had a
copy aboard and showed them their "publicity" and they
were astounded, amid a gleeful gale of giggles and whis-
tles from the assembled Mafia fleet.

As so often happens in Portsmouth, it was a restless,
windy night, with heavy, uneven gusts, but mercifully not
as much surge as there can be. The rowboat fleet brought
us ice, bananas, tomatoes, grapefruit, and cabbage in the
morning, and, despite the blustery conditions, we decided
it was time to leave. Under reefed main we tore out of the
harbor to find an incredibly confused bobble of chop, short
and nasty and every which way, off the north point of
Dominica, fought our way through, set the staysail, and
took off on a rough, bouncy but quick reach the twenty
miles to the Iles des Saintes.

We had first seen this little archipelago ten miles off
Guadeloupe in 1960, when it was a colorful transplant of
a Breton fishing village. The islanders were Europeans,
their boats were gracefully sheered canoes, and there was
a marvelous vibrancy to the scene when the fishing boats
came into the beach in late afternoon and the whole town,
including wives and children, came down to meet them.
We had been the only yacht there on our first charter cruise
in the Caribbean.

Now it was a disappointment to see what a quarter century of touristic development had done to this picturesque
enclave; the anchorage, of course, was full of boats. We
picked a spot off Pain de Sucre, a miniature version of Rio's
Sugarloaf, and had just settled in peacefully when a local
boat dropped its hook right across our anchor line. I have
written before about the anchoring habits and harbor
manners of the French, which are terrible, and this was
just another example of it. Guadeloupe and Martinique are
departments of France, not colonies, with large French
populations and, in recent years, a great number of local
yachts. This was a Saturday, and the weekend influx from
Pointe-à-Pitre and other Guadeloupe ports, was on.

We finally untangled, moved to a less crowded spot, and had no more trouble as the weekenders continued to flood in. I had the feeling that this could be Price's Bend, Cuttyhunk, or Catalina. Through the late afternoon, visibility kept decreasing, with a hazy cast to the sky. This turned into one of those earlier times that we experienced the African dust phenomenon we were later to see in the Grenadines (Chapter 16). We had another fast slide across to the lee of Guadeloupe the next morning, and the trip up its back side was a typical example of leeward side sailing. First of all, the waters are pimpled with a profusion of fish pots, and a constant lookout is needed. Because of them, night operation within five miles of the coast would be difficult. For a while we carried the strong trade around the bottom of Guadeloupe and its slim white lighthouse, one of the few in the Antilles. Then the wind quit for a while, followed by a strong westerly backwind for several miles; at last we gave up and powered into the handy harbor of Des Hayes for good protection on another windy night.

By departure time for the forty-mile crossing to Antigua, visibility was down to about three miles in the dust, and the sun was a fuzzy lemon in the haze. This was a strange experience as Antigua usually looms sharply on the horizon all the way from Guadeloupe. Once more a reef was in the main and the waves were big and bouncy. I held a bit high of the course because of reefs to the west of English Harbour, and because of the poor visibility, which took away any visual checks of a possible westerly setting. We sighted Antigua's Shirley Heights in early afternoon a bit off to port. Remembering the busybody hassle of checking through Customs and Immigration at English Harbour, where the head man caused so many complaints from yachtsmen that he was finally removed, I decided to head for the new facility at St. James's Club a few miles to the east. It was advertised as a port of entry (which is now no longer the case), and I thought it might be worth a try. Its buoyed entrance channel starts out in the open sea, exposed to the big rollers charging in from the Atlantic, and it was a bouncy few minutes before we slid into calm waters inside and tied up to the new marina at the club, with a

The Curtain Bluff anchorage, Antigua

great sense of civilization after all the windy nights at anchor since St. Lucia.

This was crew change time, with the Conyers replacing the Minises, and we had a relaxed few days puttering around Antigua's delights, first by rental car, and then with short boat hops to English Harbour, Falmouth Bay, and Deep Bay. Antigua is a yachtsman's haven, and it is fascinating to boat-see around the Dockyard at English Harbour, ogling large, glossy power yachts, ocean racers, character vessels weeping rust, and just about every kind of cruising yacht imaginable, with flags of perhaps two dozen nations in evidence. St. James's was comfortable but expensive, exemplified by a bill of seventy-four dollars for a normal batch of laundry.

Finally it came time for our departure from Deep Bay and the encounter with the temporarily spooky motorboat. After that excitement, the rest of the sail to St. Barts was almost an anticlimax despite a few squalls that caused rather rough, splashy going and called for a reefed main. On arrival at St. Barts, we found that the water pump was not doing its job, calling for a very careful anchoring under sail in the jammed, surgy roadstead of the outer harbor.

There was an interesting interlude in getting the water pump fixed, as the mechanic we located via recommendation from the smartly uniformed harbormaster was really a garage mechanic who started to get seasick in the surge of the roadstead. He quickly took the pump ashore and repaired it in the solid security of his garage.

After a pleasant morning swimming and picnicking at Baie Colombier at the west end of St. Barts, the short run to St. Martin ended *Brunelle*'s round trip down the islands. She had earned a rest after all her travels.

16

▶ ▶ ▶ ▶ ▶ ▶ ▶ ▶ ▶ ▶ ▶ ▶ ▶ ▶

THE LOW ISLANDS
The Well-Situated Grenadines

There was a time, as I have mentioned, when the Exumas and Grenadines were tied in my affections as the best cruising areas. Later experience in the British Virgins has changed that somewhat, but the Grenadines still have to rank at or near the top. With their combination of special anchorages, reliable breeze, colorful waters, and general charm, they have just about everything a cruising sailor could ask for except one ingredient that they have recently lost: isolation.

Our most recent visit in 1987 was our eighth, and all the old charms were still there. But each of our successive visits had found the islands more popular, and crowded. On our first Grenadines cruise in 1962 in the venerable charter schooner *Mollihawk,* we had the Tobago Cays, the major attraction of the Grenadines, all to ourselves. This last time, there were well over fifty boats in the several Tobago Cays anchorages, and two large cruise ships in the bight outside the cays.

Their popularity is deserved. The colors of the water match the Exumas for clarity and delicacy of tone, the snorkeling and diving are the best, the trade wind flowing in from Africa is fresh and authoritative, unblocked by the relatively low hills of the islands. It was in the Tobago Cays on an easily accessible reef off Petit Bateau, one of the cays that encircles the main anchorage, that I first snorkeled and every spot since has been an anticlimax.

That the trade winds here originate in Africa was brought home to us in the Tobago Cays in dramatic fashion on this last cruise. Along with the forty-five other boats in the anchorage, lying in well-protected water but wide open to the trades sweeping in across the complex of reefs to windward, we had a wild and windy night, with the rigging humming tautly and the slap-slap-slap of little wavelets against the hull punctuating our sleep. The breeze was 30 knots or more, and in the morning there was graphic evidence of its transatlantic sweep from Africa. Instead of the clear blue of a Caribbean sky, there was a smoky haze in the atmosphere that was more like a summer afternoon on Buzzards Bay, and visibility was down to about three miles. The phenomenon, mentioned in Chapter 15 was caused by dust from African sandstorms carried all this way on the trade. African weather often spawns the hurricanes that sweep across to the Caribbean, and the hazy atmosphere was another evidence of this relationship.

Our boat on this cruise was a CSY 42 sister ship of *Helios*. As owners we can use CSY boats in either of their charter areas, British Virgins or Grenadines, and this was actually our first experience with a 42, as we had not used *Helios* yet in the BVI. They are cookie-cutter sister ships, so it is a minor difference whether you are using your own boat or another one in the fleet. This one was named *Xanthous Nomad,* and we were rather glad that we never had to use the VHF and get that name across.

We had her for two weeks; it was an interesting example of how, even in an area of the most predictable and consistent weather, there can always be surprises. The first week we had heavy trades, typified by the night in Tobago Cays, but the second week the wind was so light that we had to do quite a bit of powering. Both weeks started at the CSY base in Blue Lagoon at the southern tip of St. Vincent and took us down through most of the sixty-mile chain and back.

For the first week, with Genevieve and Al Gagnebin as guests, we had an extra added attraction to give us more local color. Although I had bareboated through here many times, we were able to get Basil Hazell as a shipmate to provide it. He is a Bequia professional captain with CSY with vast local knowledge and happened to be free that week. It was great to have him aboard for his husky physique, his fund of sea stories, and his many connections throughout the Grenadines. He seemed to have at least one cousin in every port, others as captains of other charter and fishing boats, and more as lobstermen in the Tobago Cays. It is always fun in the islands to compare how the natives talk with visitors and among themselves, and Basil's chatter with his cousins was a prime example.

We picked him up in Bequia (pronounced Beck-wee) after a fast, spray-blown scoot across the seven miles of Bequia Channel from Blue Lagoon to Admiralty Harbour. The harbor is rather deep, about forty feet, with a wind tunnel effect through a gap in the hills at its head, and always crowded, but we managed to squeeze into a spot. The mix of yachts, commercial boats, and cruise ships here is quite a show, and, because there are so many boats, visits from the "rowboat Mafia" are not as much an intrusion as in some islands. These, as I have said, are local lads in beat-up old skiffs who make a business of hassling visiting yachts, selling fruit, fish, services and "protection" with an insistence that can become very annoying, one of the minor drawbacks of cruising the lower Caribbean.

Basil joined us in the morning and immediately guided us out of the harbor via a route I never would have taken. The western tip of Bequia is a long, rocky promontory known as Moonhole. High up on its cliffs there is a natural moonhole, a vertical open circle in the rocks, with a distinctive house centered in it that had to be abandoned when a rock crashed on it from above. Other vacation houses have been built in equally unlikely perches along the cliffs. We went right under them, almost close enough to be served a drink from their patios, and then skinned through a cut, only about one hundred feet wide, between the tip of Moonhole and the first little rocky lump of a string of cays

CSY 42 Xanthous Nomad *in a good Grenadines breeze*

running off from it. I would have gone around all of them before heading south, but Basil steered us through, so close we could practically touch the rocks. There was plenty of water under the keel, but the depth sounder pinged with a quick echo from the rocks on both sides as we rolled our way through.

Out in the open, we made sail and had a fast reach for twenty miles to Mayreau, covering it in less than three hours. Through most of the Grenadines, there are islands or reefs to windward, and the sea is relatively smooth even in a strong breeze, but every once in a while there is a stretch exposed to the open Atlantic and its trade wind seas, and there will suddenly be an exciting part of an hour of deep-sea conditions, with blue, whitecapped rollers looming up to windward and rushing on by for a real roller-coaster effect and great sailing. We had not been to Mayreau before in all our previous cruises, and Salt Whistle Bay at its northwest corner proved an idyllic anchorage with the proper background of an arc of white beach and graceful palms behind it. There is only room for a dozen or so boats, but it was not too crowded on this night. As in most Grenadine harbors, the horizon is open to the west, and our happy hour was made memorable by a perfect green flash as the sun dipped to the cloudless rim of the sea. In fact, in our two weeks, we saw four green flashes, the most I have ever seen in a similar time span. This is a phenomenon seen only in an unclouded sunset in the tropics when the upper limit of the sun turns green as it dips the horizon.

We had a pleasant dinner ashore at a small inn where we were just one of two tables—no overcrowding here— and the night was a quiet one in the lee of the palms. Basil did set a Bahamian moor in case the wind quit and we tended toward the beach, as we were anchored quite close, but the breeze held firmly all night. The swimming and beachcombing here were especially good, making a relaxed morning before we headed the few miles across to the Tobago Cays and our windblown, haze-shrouded stop there. Looking back at Mayreau, we were glad we had been at Salt Whistle, not Saline Bay at the other end, as a large white cruise ship anchored off there had put about three hundred people ashore for a beach barbecue.

Salt Whistle Bay, Mayreau

Basil found a cousin selling lobsters, and another one with a pot big enough to cook them, and we had a fine feast as the wind howled through the rigging. Tobago Cays is the center for Grenadine lobstering, and temporary camps for the fishermen are the only shore installations in what is now a protected national park, but we wondered how long the lobstering would last while supplying fare to three-hundred-person beach barbecues.

By morning the wind had eased down to about 20 and the haze began to dissipate. We had a quick jaunt the few miles down to Petit St. Vincent, ranging along the beach at Palm Island, where many charter boats were anchored on the narrow ledge of sand off the beach and another big cruise ship's white bulk loomed farther out at anchor. Petit St. Vincent, the southern end of St. Vincent's jurisdiction, is completely taken up by one resort, an informal but luxurious haven with widely spaced guest cottages on hilltops fronted by their own little beaches. A mile away across the international boundary is Petit Martinique, a part of Grenada. For years it was an isolated and very independent smugglers' headquarters where visitors were not welcome, but it now provides most of the staff for Petit St. Vincent. Its distinctive cone has a tier of bright lights at night, thanks to a new power station the United States provided after the 1983 Grenada "intervention."

All the islands of the Grenadines are so close together that it is never necessary to make long passages; we could have ducked over the three miles to Union and then a couple of more miles down to Carriacou if we wanted to go through the double fuss of Customs and Immigration. Banging rubber stamps is a major industry in the Caribbean, and we decided to stay in St. Vincent waters rather than go through the red tape.

PSV has a blindingly white beach along its anchorage. There is something of a surge, but it has lovely views off to the south with Petit Martinique in the foreground and Grenada's graceful blue bulk in the distance beyond Carriacou. It was our turnaround point for heading back to Blue Lagoon, and we made another passage under Basil's guidance that I probably would not have taken on my own.

We wanted to go to Mustique, another of the Grenadines we had missed before, and the most direct route to it from PSV is on the windward side of the reefs protecting the Tobago Cays: Horseshoe Reef and the appropriately named World's End. We headed out there hard on the starboard tack in a still-fresh easterly trade, perhaps 20 knots, and *Nomad* was soon plunging across deep-sea rollers in a good test of her sailing qualities. She took it well with an easy motion and only an occasional dash of spray into the cockpit from a maverick wave.

In the open, the waves were spaced well, but as we neared World's End they became shorter and steeper as they hit shallower water. We couldn't quite make the windward tip of the reef, but a short hitch on port tack took us clear. We watched with awe as the great white horses reared up and self-destructed, baring the pale menace of the coral as they surged on and off in a welter of foam and spray. Whoever named the reef had a fine poetic sense, and it was a striking contrast to the limpid waters in among the cays just a few miles to leeward.

Once clear of the reef's influence in deeper water, the wave patterns evened out, and we were able to ease off to a close reach toward Mustique, a blue shape up ahead with the white mansions of the rich and famous on its hilltops looming like fortresses or Greek monasteries. Mustique is famous for jet-setters from Princess Margaret on down, and it is somewhat isolated off to the east of the rest of the Grenadines. The anchorage, which is just an open roadstead in the lee of its hills, can be surge-prone, but Basil knew a mooring we could use, well under the hills, and by anchoring fore-and-aft from it we were end-on to what surge there was and hardly felt it. Shore birds came out to greet us, hopping along the lifelines, but we saw no evidence of jet-setters in the anchorage or at dinner ashore that night at a raffish restaurant on a pier. They did show up the next morning to board a large yacht nearby with everyone, male and female, decked out in matching white caps, jackets, and slacks or skirts.

Just off Mustique on the north side is the wreck of the French cruise ship *Antilles,* which inexplicably ventured into reef-strewn waters far off a normal course for large ships, ran aground in broad daylight and calm seas, and eventually caught fire from ruptured fuel tanks. That was in the 1960s, and the hulk is now a rusty, misshapen skeleton. We ranged right alongside, and it was an awesomely sad sight as the waves sloshed into the gaps in her plates and gulls strutted along the top of the hull.

The trade had come back to its most boisterous, and we had a wet, splashy sail to windward of Bequia on our way back to Blue Lagoon. On the seaward side of the island, two little Bequia sloops with their low aspect, long-boomed rigs, were moving along in company, and Basil said that they had probably had a whale sighting reported. There is a small whaling operation out of Bequia and it is considered a good year if one is caught. I suggested getting closer to have a look, and Basil quickly demurred.

"If they knew I was aboard and we happened to spook a whale while they were chasing it, I couldn't go back to the island. I would be a dead man, mon."

I saw his point.

Our hard thrash across notorious Bequia Channel to finish up the week also finished up the heavy trades. Neil and Connie Lindeman joined us for the next week and a near reprise of the same itinerary, without Basil this time, and conditions were radically different. It was so calm that we had to power most of the way to Mayreau, and the African dust had given way to crystal-clear visibility in which both St. Vincent and Grenada stood out boldly from the central Grenadines. It was on this week, with its clear horizons, that we saw the three added green flashes, and, unruffled by the blustery trades, the waters of the Tobago Cays showed their most beautiful pastels when we revisited them.

We joined the winter cruise of the Cruising Club of America for part of its itinerary, and met up for a beach picnic in a grove of palms on Petit St. Vincent. The fifteen boats of the CCA fleet were a colorful addition to the anchorage. The next organized event was a dinner ashore at Bequia, and the harbor, so blustery on our previous stop, was mirror calm, the only time I have seen it that way.

Bequia, long the scene of local boatbuilding and a base for interisland freight boats, is now oriented primarily toward tourism without becoming garish like some of the other once-picturesque Caribbean hideaways.

It was time to wind up our session with *Xanthous Nomad* and we made a leisurely start the next morning on the seven miles back to Blue Lagoon across what had always been the roiled and bouncy waters of Bequia Channel. This is one passage to get over as fast as possible, but this day was different. A moderate easterly had filled in after the overnight calm, and the usual eccentric chop had given way to the gentlest of little waves. I couldn't help but remember the previous week with the Gagnebins, when we had spent much of our time ducking the bursts of spray sweeping across the center cockpit and were delighted to reach the shelter of Blue Lagoon.

Now we set out in the most idyllic conditions, expecting to make Blue Lagoon for lunch, but three quarters of the way across, I suggested that it was silly to come in early on such a beautiful day, so why didn't we keep sailing? As the reefs around Blue Lagoon became clearly defined, we came about and headed back toward Bequia's uneven profile. Conditions remained ideal as we swept easily across the gentle little chop, and we had lunch under sail instead of in port. Back at the northeast tip of Bequia, it was finally time to make the last tack back and head for port. We had seen the Grenadines in a remarkable variety of moods for a two-week cruise, and all of them had added up to an experience that kept the Grenadines right up near the top of the list.

Additional Information

The Caribbean

The Caribbean is nirvana, the dream area of dream areas, for a large percentage of cruising addicts, and very few of these sailors feel that their experience is complete unless they have sailed its waters. It deserves the praise, as its multitude of fine cruising grounds can match almost any others, worldwide, and it seldom fails to live up to these expectations. It has the trade winds, the climate, the scenery, the variety of cultures, the sense of history, that combine to make a rare and rewarding experience. For centuries it was a faraway land of exotic promise, but only the truly adventurous, and those with the time and means to break away from routines, were able to know it. Now, with jet planes and fiberglass charter fleets, a cruise is easily possible in the average vacation time.

This, of course, has lessened the sense of the exotic, as once-empty anchorages of legendary charm fill with boats each afternoon, but the basics are still there, and the Caribbean's scope is such that there is still room for everybody (well, most of the time).

I first experienced the Caribbean in the subchaser Navy early in World War II, and on those wet and uncomfortable vessels the first thing that impressed me was the strength of the trade winds and the size of the seas. This, of course, was in the open sea on passages along the coasts of Cuba and Hispaniola, or from Guantanamo Bay to Panama, and we did not tarry in such great cruising areas as the Virgins or the Grenadines.

My first yachting visit was in 1960 on a crewed charter out of Antigua, and we have been returning almost steadily since then, basing *Brunelle* there as a winter live-aboard for nine seasons, and still going back every chance we get to use *Helios,* our CSY 42. We have seen great changes in those times, starting from a fleet of a dozen crewed yachts at Antigua in 1960, and eleven bareboats out of St. Thomas in 1966. In Chapter 22, I discuss some of these chartering developments and how they have changed life for the visiting sailor.

Given its great spread, Caribbean cruising has many variations and choices, and the real heart of its sailing, both in charter yachts and private boats, is in the Virgin Islands, both American and British. As reported in Chapter 13, this is a compact area with a minimum of problems and an unbelievable choice of anchorages so close to each other that no long, hard runs are needed. Admittedly, from

the Christmas holidays through Easter the popular harbors are crowded, but the sailing is still great, with the
full range of activities.

Someday, the Greater Antilles may develop as a cruising area, as Cuba has some fine cruising waters, but Hispaniola has rugged coastlines, and most of Puerto Rico is
too developed to provide pleasant cruising. Its satellite islands of Culebra and Vieques provide a few limited but
nice little enclaves on the way to the Virgins.

Beyond the Virgins, there is the only passage between
islands all the way from Cuba to Grenada that is long
enough to lose sight of land, Anegada Passage. It is eighty
miles from Virgin Gorda to St. Martin of rough, unpredictable waters that rank with the Gulf Stream as a challenge. The currents and weather systems of the Caribbean
and Atlantic meet here, and conditions can change mo-
mentarily. Almost every one of our dozen or so crossings
has been an ordeal, and, again, the idea is to get there as
quickly as possible.

From here on down to the Grenadines, cruising is very
different from the close-in operations of the Virgins and
Grenadines, where there is always an island nearby to pop
in to. From St. Martin to St. Vincent, a stretch of about
four hundred miles, the distances between islands are from
thirty to fifty miles. It is almost always a reach across the
trade wind in seas that have had a chance to gain authority all the way from Africa, deep-sea sailing at its most
exhilarating, but a far cry from close-in gunkholing of more
protected areas. Each island has a distinctive culture based
on its colonial history, and the towering, cumulus-crowded
peaks, are always impressive. A not so rewarding alternative to the open-sea passages between the islands is the
challenge of getting through the unpredictable areas of
calm, sudden williwaws, and backwinds in the lee of the
big islands.

While the eastern Caribbean sees the bulk of cruising,
there are many more wonderful areas in this great, island-
girded sea. The Venezuelan coast has attracted more and
more visitors recently, and knowledgeable charter skippers in the eastern Caribbean head there during hurricane

season, as this area on the historic "Spanish Main" is typically hurricane-free. Isla Margarita, a resort center, is also a yachting center for locals and visitors, and it has a bevy of satellite islands. Los Testigos, between Grenada and Margarita, are a haven for passage-makers, and Los Roques, eighty miles out in the Caribbean off La Guaira, are genuine South Sea atolls and a favorite escape for yachtsmen from the mainland.

The truly adventurous can explore the San Blas Islands off Panama. There you can have a fascinating glimpse of the pre-Columbian civilization of the Cuna Indians, but conditions are extremely primitive, and facilities are virtually nonexistent. Between Venezuela and the San Blas there is a stretch of about six hundred miles, after leaving Curaçao and Aruba, Dutch islands off Venezuela, that is a sailing no-man's-land. Colombia is off limits because of the drug activity, and boats cannot get insurance for operating within its territorial waters.

In the western Caribbean, there are two prime cruising areas, the Bay Islands of Honduras and the reef off Belize. Above that, the Mexican resorts on the Yucatan Peninsula are mainly for fishing. For a while, Belize and the Bay Islands were the coming place in the cruising world, but the political troubles of Central America dissuaded many people from sailing there. They remain attractive and interesting, awaiting a more peaceful time. I have had very pleasant and interesting cruises in both places in years past.

Yachting centers The major bases include Fajardo, Charlotte Amalie and environs, Road Town, Virgin Gorda Yacht Harbour, Philipsburg, English Harbour, the Pointe-à-Pitre area, Fort-de-France, Rodney Bay, Marigot Bay, Blue Lagoon, Bequia, St. George's, La Guaira, Colon, Roatan, and Cozumel.

Chartering This is big business in the Caribbean, with St. Thomas and Road Town as major Virgin centers and Philipsburg, English Harbour, Fort-de-France, and Blue Lagoon also figuring. There is a wide choice of bareboats and crewed yachts in the major centers.

Weather Pleasantly warm, trade wind tropical weather prevails for a major percentage of the time. Easterly waves can cause rainy periods in the winter, the autumn is relatively unsettled and inclined to be rainy, and hurricanes must be carefully monitored in season. It is really an all-year area except for hurricanes.

Cruising grounds The whole Caribbean is one great big cruising area. The major subdivisions are the Virgin Islands; the St. Martin area; the Antigua area; south from Antigua to St. Vincent; the Grenadines; the Venezuela coast; the San Blas Islands; the Bay Islands of Honduras; and the Belize Reef.

Special attractions The sailing is it, just pure, good sailing. Other attractions include beaches; diving, both snorkeling and scuba; sightseeing; scenery; native cuisines; and native cultures.

References Robinson, *Caribbean Cruising Handbook, Over the Horizon,* Chapter XII; *Where to Cruise,* Part V; and *South to the Caribbean,* pp. 123–323; Fields, *Yachtsman's Guide to the Virgin Islands;* Scott, *Cruising Guide to the Virgin Islands;* Street's, *Cruising Guide to the Eastern Caribbean;* Wilensky, *Cruising Guide to the Bay Islands of Honduras;* Eiman, *St. Maarten/St. Martin Area & St. Kitts and Nevis;* Scott, *Virgin Anchorages;* Bobrow and Jinkins, *St. Vincent and the Grenadines.*

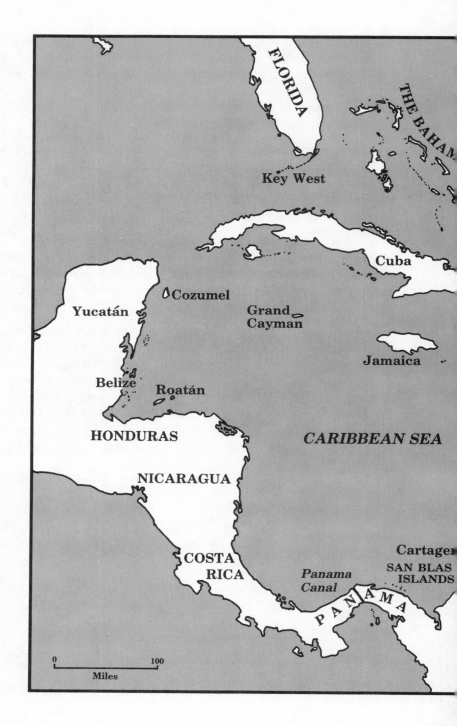

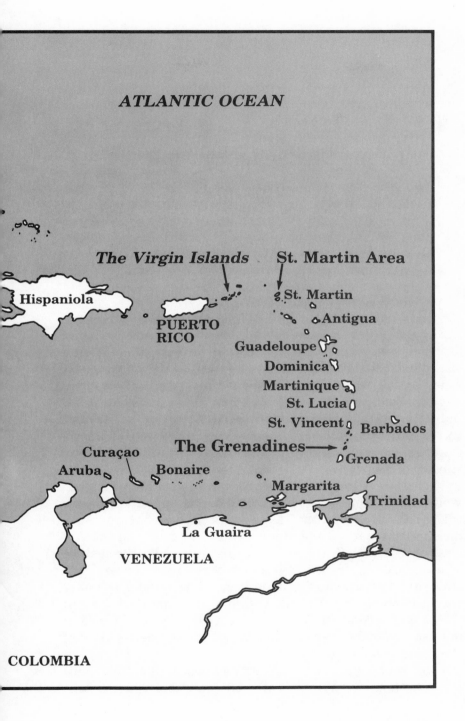

ATLANTIC OCEAN

The Virgin Islands   St. Martin Area

Hispaniola   St. Martin

                          PUERTO   Antigua
                          RICO
                                        Guadeloupe

                                        Dominica

                                        Martinique

                                        St. Lucia

                                        St. Vincent   Barbados

                          The Grenadines   Grenada

            Curaçao
Aruba   Bonaire   Margarita
                                                          Trinidad

                          La Guaira

            VENEZUELA

COLOMBIA

17

▶ ▶ ▶ ▶ ▶ ▶ ▶ ▶ ▶ ▶ ▶ ▶ ▶ ▶ ▶

TALL SHIP IN THE TRADES
From Easter Island to the
Galapagos

Rapa Nui, or Easter Island to non-Polynesians, had dropped over the horizon astern, and we were alone on one of the most deserted stretches of ocean in all the wide sea lanes of the world. The Galapagos lay some 1,900 miles ahead, South America was 2,300 miles to starboard, and Tahiti another 2,500 miles to port. The four masts and thirty-four thousand feet of *Sea Cloud*'s twenty-nine sails towered above us, and a fresh southeast trade was on our starboard quarter.

This, like canal barging in Holland, was not your conventional cruising experience, but it was one of the nautical thrills of a lifetime, a very special adventure. As I mentioned when telling of our *Sea Cloud* cruise in the Aegean in Chapter 7, there is nothing quite like the feeling of a square-rigger surging before a favorable breeze, her sails taut and drawing, a bone in her teeth under the long thrust of the bowsprit, and a slight tilt to her decks. Even if this was a commercial cruise, it was a rare and exciting moment, and the good sailing lasted for the better part of the ten-day passage.

There were thirty-six passengers aboard, just about half her complement, and most of them were experienced sail-

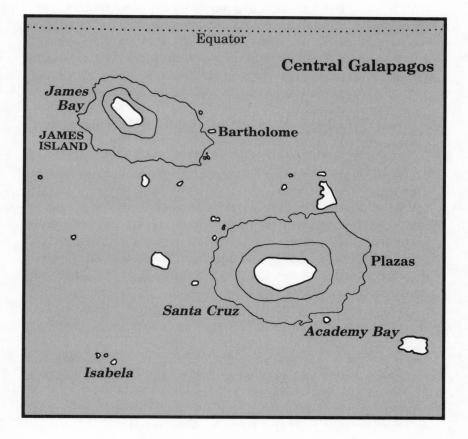

Equator

Central Galapagos

James Bay

JAMES
ISLAND

Bartholome

Plazas

Santa Cruz

Academy Bay

Isabela

ors, since Mystic Seaport Museum was one of the sponsors of the trip. As a shared experience with congenial seafarers, this cruise had a special aura to it, and the ports—Easter Island and the Galapagos were among the most out-of-the-way and exotic anywhere on the seven seas. For us it was also especially pleasant that the whole trip was "on the house," as I was earning my way as lecturer. It had been arranged in a rather unusual manner the previous spring (this was November). I was in the BVI setting up the sale of *Brunelle* when I got a message to call Vasos Papagapitos at Travel Dynamics in New York, the company that had *Sea Cloud* under charter for sponsored cruises by special groups.

When I got hold of Vasos, he explained that he was in something of a bind getting a lecturer for the *Sea Cloud* cruise the following autumn. I had had frequent dealings with him while running the travel program at the Princeton Club of New York.

"We thought we had Walter Cronkite lined up," Vasos said, "but we haven't been able to get a definite commitment from him, and we have to send our brochure to the printer on Friday." It was Tuesday. "We would be pleased if you could take over. Could you think it over and let us know as soon as possible?" he asked.

After a slight pause, maybe eight seconds, I answered, "I've thought it over, and the answer is yes."

The trip started with a flight to Santiago, Chile, a handsome city in the shadow of the Andes, where we had an interesting day of sightseeing before we took a five-hour flight via 707 jet to Easter Island. The United States had built a jet strip there as part of the space shuttle program, so this isolated dot, the most remote inhabited island in the world, has good air connections with Chile.

The single runway goes almost all the way across a narrow part of the island near its western end. The rest of the island is hilly, with several cones and craters of small, extinct volcanos. It is about sixteen by three miles, located at latitude 27°09′ and longitude 109°26′ southwest. The population of a little over two thousand people is two thirds of Maori descent, though the island belongs to Chile. After centuries of isolation, with only an occasional passing ship, the air service has brought a small flow of carefully administered tourism, which is taken care of in guesthouses and one hotel, the Hanga Roa in the settlement of that name, the only real town on the island.

Easter Island is best known for the huge stone statues called *moais,* whose origin and purpose were a mystery for many years until Thor Heyerdahl of *Kon-Tiki* fame brought an expedition to Easter in the 1950s, written up in *Aku Aku,* followed by archaeologists and anthropologists who applied a scientific approach to the Easter Island legends. In the process they restored many *moais* to their original locations.

Easter Island's moais

It has been established that the island was settled in
about the fourth century A.D. by Maoris who were evidently fleeing from conflicts in islands to the west, and for
about twelve centuries they lived in complete isolation under the impression that they were the only people in existence in the whole universe. At times the population was
as high as 15,000 or 16,000 people, and they lived out a
microcosm of human history, divided into factions of "long
ears" and "short ears" and other family clans who had their
own territories, and who occasionally carried on civil wars.
The *moais* were a form of ancestor worship, carved out of
stone from a quarry on the flank of the highest mountain
and dragged by massive manpower to their special locations, where they were placed in exact relation to the sun
at the seasonal solstices. They were painstakingly ele-
vated from a reclining position by the insertion of stones,
first no more than pebbles, then larger and larger, underneath them to lever them up, again with massive manpower as the final force.

It was not until 1722, when a Dutch ship came upon the
island on Easter Sunday and gave it its European name,
that life here was touched by foreign influences. Over the
years more explorers came by, including Captain Cook in
1746, and the culture, isolated for centuries, was gradually undermined. The islanders contributed to their own
problems by deforesting the land almost completely, and,
after South Americans came in 1770, the population was
decimated by foreign diseases and by slave raids. More recently, a benevolent government has introduced some
modern solutions while at the same time preserving the
traditional culture, and Easter is one of the most unusual
places to visit anywhere in the world.

It is not a good stopover for vessels, as there is no harbor. One small, shallow cove, surrounded by beaches, on
the north coast, supposedly where the first Maori canoes
landed, is the only break in the shoreline. At Hanga Roa,
there is a tiny boat-basin behind a concrete mole, but it is
subject to open-sea surf when that happens to be the windward side. Visiting vessels have to seek a lee and anchor
in the open. While we were there, one yacht, *Tangaroa,* a

Swan 65 with a delivery crew aboard, headed for the Caribbean from New Zealand, was anchored off the hotel, and her masts were a steady metronome against the horizon. Easter is on the best wind route for this trip, avoiding the steady easterly trades at a more northerly latitude, but it is not much of a haven for yachts on the long passage.

For Jane and me it was completely different from anywhere we had ever been, and we had three days of highly rewarding sightseeing under the leadership of a knowledgeable guide, a German archaeologist. Some of the roads were paved but many were dirt or just a pair of ruts as we ranged from the *moai* locations and quarry to some of the volcanic craters in pleasantly sunny weather. A BBC TV crew was staging an enactment of the original Maori landing at the beach-girt cove, an interesting stimulus to the imagination.

Easter has the reputation of being an unlucky island for ships, as so many have been lost when the wind shifted, catching them on a lee shore. Bad luck is even supposed to follow a ship after it leaves there, but *Sea Cloud,* undaunted by these legends, arrived on schedule from Tahiti, after stopping at Pitcairn Island. Some of her passengers debarked to fly home, while our group joined those aboard who were remaining for the rest of the cruise to the Galapagos and Panama. I, the poor man's Walter Cronkite, replaced Bill Buckley as on-board lecturer, and after a one-day stopover, the ship was ready to leave.

Boarding was quite a thrill. There was a good run of surf into the entrance of the boat basin, a tricky business for the inflatables that are *Sea Cloud*'s launches. One of them capsized, fortunately with no passengers aboard, and the only damage a very wet coxswain, and it was tactfully suggested that it might be wise for island boatmen to handle the landings. This they did with great skill, and it was a good lesson to watch them gauge the series of breakers and pick a lull to make their approach in and their trip out. Holding on tight, all of us stayed dry.

It became rainy and semifoggy by the time we left, but we were soon out into the trades for ten days of straight sailing. The southeast trades blow almost constantly here, and we had a fine session in them. Cas Cassidy was again *Sea Cloud's* captain, extremely happy with the great conditions, and the days went by in a pleasantly relaxed routine. It was always a show to watch the young crew members, male and female, climbing the rigging to handle the sails (passengers are not allowed aloft), and to chat with them and learn their enthusiasm for their special tasks. They were from many different countries and backgrounds, united by a love of the life afloat.

At happy hour in the main saloon, which still had elements of the glory days when she was Marjorie Post Hutton Davies's yacht, such as stained glass, an elaborate fireplace and mantel, and carved paneling, there was time for swapping sea stories and casual piano sessions with the ship's entertainer. That is also where I gave my lectures, including a couple of slide shows of cruising in various areas, and talks on the history of *Sea Cloud* and other luxury yachts written up in my book *Legendary Yachts*. I also read from excerpts of literature on the area from such a diversity of writers as Melville, Joshua Slocum, Heyerdahl, and Irving and Exy Johnson, and told of my experiences in World War II in my subchaser in the South Pacific, and of my Uncle Sam Robinson's ordeal of getting his command, the ocean liner *Empress of Australia,* out of Yokohama in the 1923 earthquake. With an audience of less than forty, these sessions were very informal, with much give-and-take and questioning, which I enjoyed, and Captain Cassidy also gave a talk on the workings of a squarerigger that was especially interesting.

The rhythm of the ship, accompanied by the diurnal doings of the sun, moon, and stars, made a euphoric blend and time seemed of no importance except for meal hours (the food was good). An upper deck area atop the main cabin was a daytime focus, with a noonday bar and a chance to look up at the sails from relaxed comfort. We watched the crew with interest as they occasionally climbed the ratlines to make some sort of adjustment aloft, and the steady rhythm of the trade-blown seas was a hypnotizing influence off the starboard quarter. It was a wonderful demonstration of the constancy of the trades, and this was

Manning the sails: Sea Cloud *getting under way*

one of the best places in the world to be on a square-rigged barque.

Before we raised the Galapagos, there was an obligatory day of fun and games when a crossing-the-equator ceremony was held, even though we hadn't quite reached it. The rule of the day was that crossing the line by air did not count, and everyone for whom this was a first surface crossing, albeit northbound, had to undergo the Shellback initiation. Since Jane and I had long since become Shellbacks, she was a member of the bucket brigade, dousing initiates as they knelt before King Neptune, and I took pictures. Everyone took it in good spirit, but the ceremony for the passengers was a gentle spray compared with the later ordeal that members of the crew, who had joined south of the equator, were subjected to.

The Galapagos appeared on the horizon as low, purple lumps, not very dramatic from a distance. Close up they are amazingly distinctive with bare, lava-covered hillsides, soaring cliffs, crags and pinnacles of rock, uplands of dusty brown vegetation, and occasional oases of green higher on the hills.

Over the years, I had read many published and unpublished works by earlier voyagers like the Johnsons, Bill Crealock, W. A. Robinson (no relation), and many others, going back to Charles Darwin's chronicle of his historic visit in *Beagle* in 1835. From them I got the impression of a primitive never-never land where strange beasts and birds lived a life without fear, and pioneers carved out a rugged living from the wilderness. There were tales of an Austrian baroness and a murder mystery; of the hardy Angermeyer family; of the dentist, Dr. Wittmer, who replaced his own teeth with steel false ones before coming here; and of the hand-to-mouth existence they scrabbled out of the hostile terrain. It was something of a surprise, then, to find a fairly civilized settlement at Puerto Ayora on Academy Bay, Santa Cruz Island, our first landfall, with a number of yachts and small trading vessels at anchor.

The birds and the beasts did not disappoint, however. They still lead their own life without fear of man, flourishing under the careful administration of the Ecuadorian government. There is a very real and active concern for the fragile ecology of the Galapagos. Tourism is controlled at a certain level, and it is very difficult for private yachts to get permission to cruise here. A great deal of paperwork is required far in advance and even this is not always enough. Cruise ships are limited, with no overlap allowed, and all visitors must be continually under the supervision of authorized government guides. This restrictive policy seems to be working despite the inevitable encroachments of the jet age.

Sea Cloud acquired two guides on arrival, who stayed with us for the entire visit. They were young, personable and very knowledgeable. Their information added immeasurably to our enjoyment. At Puerto Ayora, we were brought ashore in inflatables to the Charles Darwin Research Station a short way to the east of town on Academy

Bay, which was a real eye-opener. The launches weaved their way in through a maze of jagged lava rocks to the landing, where the short walk to the station was through an otherworldly stand of weirdly contorted cactus.

This was the only place where it is easy to see the creatures that gave the islands their name, the giant tortoises. In many sizes, and in age going back over a hundred years, they live in pens now. Those who want to can walk among them and meet them eye to beady eye. In the days of whaling and piracy, they were almost wiped out because of the ease of catching them and their great value as a source of fresh food on ships that were often at sea for several years. They are hard to find in natural habitats now, though the guides did point out their tracks on a beach we later visited. It was a good introduction to the Galapagan scene to meet them, even if it was in a controlled, protective situation.

The town that has only recently grown along the shores where the Angermeyer family used to hold sway has a few shops, beer joints, markets, a small park, and a boat landing for harbor traffic, and we browsed for a few hours. *Sea Cloud* then got underway for our next stop, a couple of rocky dots called the Plaza Islets on the east side of Santa Cruz. One of the confusions of cruising the Galapagos is that every island has names given by the British and Spaniards that are used interchangeably. Indefatigable is also Santa Cruz, James Island is Santiago, and Albemarle is Isabela, for example. Whatever their names, they each have an individuality.

Sea lions and tourist charter boat, Plaza Islets, Galapagos

Bartolome Island beach, Galapagos

The Plazas, which certainly have no relation to the New York hotel, are small rocky outcroppings that are a sanctuary for wildlife. Under guidance, we were taken ashore and requested to remain strictly on marked paths, indicated by small, black-topped yellow stakes. I strayed off of one to get a close-up photo of a basking sea lion and was politely called back in line by one of the guides.

The sea lions are everywhere, acting very much as if they own the joint, snoozing on the rocks, cavorting in the water, or sitting up and looking proudly over their domain. When they are in a nonrestricted area, it is possible to come right up to them for pictures and observation. They show no fear of humans at all. There were also land iguanas, yellowy-green and a foot or two long, who would stand stock-still even when someone poked a camera within inches of their baleful eyes.

Up a slope covered in gnarled bushes and twisted cactus, with wildflowers showing timid colors here and there, the designated path led to a clifftop overlooking a bird rookery. Here terns, gulls, boobies, and frigate birds swooped and swirled on the fresh trade. Nesting birds sat in the undergrowth with no concern for intruders. Looking down the face of the cliff several hundred feet to surf crashing on the rocks below, we could see hundreds of nests perched on ledges and in crevices, with birds constantly trading in and out of them.

There were several moderate-sized trawler-type cabin cruisers in the anchorage. The guides told us that they were charter cruises with guides aboard—one of the best ways for visitors to get around in the Galapagos. *Sea Cloud* stood offshore, outside the anchorage, and when we were all aboard in late afternoon she made a leisurely departure for an overnight passage of about forty miles to Bartholome Island, a small extinct volcano just off the east coast of mountainous James Island. We drifted quietly through the night to an after-breakfast excursion on a jewel of a beach in a spectacularly scenic anchorage called Sullivan Bay. The curve of the beach was punctuated at its western end by a pinnacle of red rock a couple of hundred feet high, with a snorkeling reef at its base. Those who tried it said it was fine. Others ambitiously climbed to the crater of the volcano for a 360-degree view of the island, and the beach itself was a pleasant attraction.

Rays slithered across the pale bottom a few feet from the shore and pelicans did a dive-bombing act around the perimeter. For a rest, they would land on the beach. It was possible to get within a few feet of them before they waddled huffily away. I had always heard a great deal about penguins in the Galapagos, but they evidently are not found on every island. Here, we finally saw one sitting on a rock ledge at the east end of the beach. I tried to get him on film but he jumped in just as I snapped and the pictured result was a white blur. He disappeared quickly, shooting away underwater like a small torpedo.

During lunch, *Sea Cloud* moved around the top of James Island, close enough for views of awesome cliffs, poking into a bay called Buccaneer Cove that was a pirate hangout of old. They would careen their vessels on the beach at the head of the cove, and evidently used the area in complete security. A few miles farther on, we came to anchor in the well-protected James Bay, which has a long beach on the inner end and an enormous black lava field off to port backed by three-thousand-foot-high mountains. I asked one of the guides if that was a recent flow of lava, as it glistened ominously in the sun, and the guide said that, yes, it was, about twenty thousand years ago.

James Bay was the climax of our encounters with Galapagan nature. Behind the beach, where there were a few deserted buildings of an abandoned salt mining operation at an inland crater lake, a trail led along the western shore, an amazing wasteland of lava rock in weird whorls and lumps, shot through with crevices and underground channels. There was a gentle surf sluicing in among the rocks, and the area was alive with sea lions and marine iguanas. The latter, in contrast to their yellow land cousins, are exactly the color of the rock, and they blend in so well in their wary immobility that it is hard to avoid stepping on them.

The sea lions are in complete charge, with mothers and pups napping on the rocks while the big males have a fine time riding the surf. They would slither off the lava and swim out to an offshore ledge, perching there till a wave caught their fancy, and then would ride it in. In one place, a large hole about thirty feet across was fed from underneath by the surf, and it would fill and empty with a great rush and swirl of foamy water. The guides told us it was called Darwin's Toilet.

It was as unusual a nature walk as could be imagined, and as a culmination to nature's show, as we rode the inflatables back to *Sea Cloud,* we spied a group of blue-footed booby birds perched on a lava ledge. We were used to boobies in many other cruising areas, but with their bright blue feet standing out starkly against the black, these seemed a symbol of all the strange things we had seen.

It was an all too brief experience, considering how much the Galapagos have to offer, but memorable in every way.

The cruise wound down quietly on the nine hundred-odd miles to Panama. For a while we were in the cool weather fostered by the Humboldt Current and the trade winds. The direct sun is always burning hot, but the general climate is well cooled, a strange phenomenon on the equator. However, our last few days were in the doldrums, soggy squalls and humid heat of the Gulf of Panama. I had experienced this twice before, so it was no surprise. The good sailing had ended. The squalid heat and messy atmosphere made a coda to a fascinating trip and heightened our sense of just how remarkable an experience it had been to sail a tall ship through the trades from Easter Island to the Galapagos.

18

▶ ▶ ▶ ▶ ▶ ▶ ▶ ▶ ▶ ▶ ▶ ▶ ▶

TO LEEWARD OF TAHITI
The Raiatea–Bora Bora Area

The wind was in the northwest, a rare occurrence in this region of southeast trades, but we welcomed it for the day's sail we had planned. In previous visits to Bora Bora, we had never seen its eastern side. With its lagoon waters completely enclosed by reef, Bora Bora only has one pass into its lagoon from the open Pacific, midway along the west side opposite the main town of Viatape, so the eastern side has very little traffic. This was a chance to get the feel of it as it must have been in the days before World War II brought military installations, and the jet age fostered tourism.

We were in the Beneteau 51 *Esperance,* a Moorings Company charter out of nearby Raiatea and we started from an anchorage off Viatape's Bora Bora Yacht Club. Martha and Dan Bliss joined Jane and me, and our French captain, Jean-Pierre Deval. *Esperance* slipped easily through the satin-smooth, dark blue lagoon water, in the deep area off Viatape, which paled to a translucent green as we rounded the north end into much shallower going. The airstrip, a legacy from the U.S. Army in World War II, was on its own *motu* (small islet) against the reef at the northeast corner. We went for a few miles through a channel

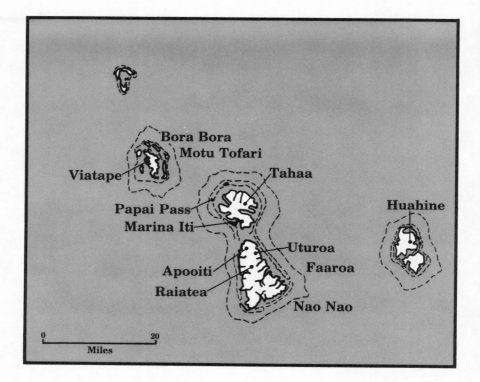

Bora Bora
Motu Tofari
Viatape
Tahaa
Papai Pass
Marina Iti
Huahine
Uturoa
Apooiti
Faaroa
Raiatea
Nao Nao

0   20
Miles

Bora Bora's striking peaks

with frequent turns, well marked on the chart and easy to eyeball. Still, we concentrated carefully while slacking sail for a run.

Bora Bora's major feature is a massive twin peak, an impressive landfall after twenty-three days at sea, which I first saw from my subchaser in 1943 on a convoy from Panama. Its changing perspectives were a continual magnet for eyes and cameras. In contrast to the deep lagoon off Viatape, the east side lagoon water is shallow, reflecting a rather eerie green glow against the dark green, topped by granite gray, of the mountains. A reminder of tourism plans gone awry was an abandoned resort complex on the coast here, with its elaborate white buildings sprawled up a hillside gradually succumbing to tropical growth.

Freed of the intricacies of the channel, we squared away for a broad reach south, seeming to float through air in the strange light. The reef to port, the windward one in normal trades, still showed a fringe of white where the open sea rollers self-destructed, with the dark cobalt of open Pacific beyond. Small motus were dotted along it, and Jean-Pierre recommended a luncheon anchorage off one of the larger ones, Motu Tofari. Martha and Dan took the dinghy to scout the dense stand of palms on the motu and came back proudly displaying delicate shell earrings they had bought from a Polynesian woman who lived there.

A big sailing catamaran loaded with hotel guests charged in to share the anchorage, dimming the isolated charm of the area a bit, but there was still relatively unspoiled South Sea island atmosphere. We made our way back to Viatape in the afternoon.

Bora Bora has to be the highlight of a cruise in Iles sous le Vent (Leeward Islands in relation to Tahiti) of French Polynesia. But Raiatea and Tahaa, circled by a common reef, have many attractions, and Huahine, twenty-five miles east of Raiatea is less touristed than the other islands. We did not have a chance to get to it on this cruise, but its landlocked inner lagoon, Port Bourayne, had been a high-light of an earlier charter.

The Moorings base on Raiatea is at a modern marina called Apooiti. We joined *Esperance* there after the one-hundred-mile connecting flight from Tahiti. It is an eight-hour overnight flight from California, and the best thing about it is the dawn view of golden sunglow on its peaks. Papeete, its city, has deteriorated into a sleazy, and very expensive, tourist trap, with a sad array of beat-up long-voyaging boats stern-to its quay. It is best to keep on going *sous le vent* as soon as possible. Raiatea and Tahaa have maintained their charm under modern pressures, but the glamor image that the name Tahiti used to evoke through the writings of Melville, Nordhoff and Hall, W. A. Robinson, Erling Tambs, Alain Gerbault (who is buried at the waterfront in Viatape), and others has been transferred to the other islands.

However, one advantage of modern developments is that this marvelous cruising area is available in the course of a normal vacation rather than at the end of a passage of almost five thousand miles from Panama or the West Coast. Many long-voyagers do come through, but many more sail-ors can now enjoy it through either bareboat or crewed chartering. South Pacific Yacht Charters was the pioneer firm in French Polynesia and Tonga, and The Moorings bought out the operation in the mid-1980s. They intro-duced their own familiar charter types, mostly Beneteaus, and we found *Esperance* ideal for the purpose.

The 51s are laid out expressly for chartering. There are three absolutely even double cabins with head, so there is no protocol problem over who gets the bridal suite. They are not big, but they are comfortable. As the only possible criticism of the layout, Dan, who is a sizable young man, found that operations in the head were more comfortable after lifting the door off its fittings.

The saloon is efficient and comfortable with the galley next to it and handy from the cockpit. We actually ate almost all our meals in the cockpit under the Bimini, a compulsory fitting in tropical climates. A pleasant feature there is a built-in swimming platform and ladder in the transom, with a shower head right there for rinsing off. There is a separate crew's quarters forward.

The 51 is an able sailer with easily handled rig, and she can be bareboated, but I like to have local experts along for added information in writing up an area, just as Basil Hazell made such a fine addition to our Grenadines cruise, and it was good to have Jean-Pierre with us. A compact, muscular middle-aged man with a ready smile and a twinkle in the eye, he had full command of delightfully accented English and he single-handedly wiped out my prejudices, based on long experience in the Lesser Antilles, against French sailors.

One advantage of Apooiti Marina as a base is that there are many good anchorages close by, and the first day does not have to be a long thrash, tough to take after jet lag and the routine of checking in. A complete guide to them is provided by The Moorings with good notes, and the anchorages are numbered for ready reference. On our first day, once we were squared away to leave, it was simple to make a quick reach the five miles northward in smooth lagoon waters to Marina Iti at the southern tip of Tahaa. This small resort and restaurant, a base for a French-operated charter fleet, was a new addition since our previous cruise. Another very welcome addition was some mooring buoys in the anchorage—at one hundred feet, it is one of the deepest in all the islands.

Tahaa is the least developed of these islands, with no airport, and no big resorts. They use private generators for electricity, and only recently added telephones. The natives live by fishing, farming, and harvesting copra, and the island is a good example of the timeless elements of

South Sea life. It has a choice of good anchorages and is worth several days of exploring, but our destination this time was Bora Bora.

An early, jet-lagged sack time prepared us for the morning departure on the twenty-five-mile open-sea crossing westward to Bora Bora, which stood highlighted in the early slant of sun, a tempting lure on the horizon. On our way out through Papai Pass, we saw natives standing on the reef, fishing and Jean-Pierre decided that he would too. The deep-sea ground swell was rearing and crashing on the reef, with spume from the crests blowing off to leeward in a delicate tracery, and, as we began to feel their rise and fall under the keel, he ran a line out astern.

He was hoping for a school tuna or *mahi-mahi* (dolphin) when there was a sudden screaming explosion on the reel and the line zinged out madly. Far astern a whopper of a fish broke the surface in a great burst of spray and started heading in the direction of Samoa in a series of wild leaps. Jean-Pierre let out an agonized cry and tried to tend the reel, but the rig was not set up for major game, and the excitement soon ended when the line went limp, just before stripping completely off the reel. It had looked like a marlin to my nonfisherman's eye, but Jean-Pierre thought that it was more likely a sailfish. Whatever it was, it provided an exciting start to the passage, which was a tame one, motorsailing over the long Pacific swells in a light north wind.

Inside the entrance through that one break in Bora Bora's reef, Teavanui Pass, there were moorings off Club Med and the Oa Oa Hotel, and Martha and Dan set off looking for the best price for a *pareu,* the colorful local cloth worn as a wraparound. Jean-Pierre put together a dish of *poisson cru,* raw tuna marinated in lime juice and spices, for an appropriately Polynesian dinner, and afterward we joined the crowd at Club Med, which was having some sort of weekly jump-up. I got the impression that absolutely everyone on the island, native and tourist, was there enjoying the music. It combined modern American with Polynesian, and the dancing was vigorous.

Our excursion to the east side took up the next day, and

Martha and Dan preparing for snorkeling via the transom ladder

that was followed by a windless one where the focus was snorkeling. Jean-Pierre piloted us to a sixteen-foot spot in the southern part of the lagoon off the Bora Bora Hotel, in among reefs and heads that provided fine diving for Martha and Dan. They reported swarms of fish of every description but some dead patches of coral.

On this kind of a charter, with food provided to order by The Moorings, it is fairly standard to allow for a couple of meals ashore, and since it happened to be a date when both couples became engaged (some forty-odd years apart), we celebrated at the Bora Bora Yacht Club. We had gone to pick up a mooring there since there was something of a surge through Teavanui Pass at Club Med. The yacht club is really a commercial restaurant, and a gathering place for sailors from all over the world. We had a fine dinner with all the French trimmings from the maître d's language to the brandy. The main course was a native fish baked in foil with vegetables. Called *paru,* it is pink with goggly eyes and its habitat is three hundred feet deep outside the reef. It is considered a great treat locally, and we agreed.

The breeze came back the next day, albeit from the northeast. This meant a close reach back to Tahaa after a smooth run down the west coast in the lee of the reef to the bend at the bottom. There, we hardened up to port. It was the best sail of the cruise for most of the way, with flying fish providing a continuing entertainment and booby birds (not blue-footed) swooping low around us. Before we made Papai Pass, however, a squadron of squalls marched in from all points of the horizon, and one finally settled in over us. It killed the good breeze with light zephyrs on the nose and a dousing of rain that followed us through the pass and down the lagoon to a mooring at Marina Iti.

By general consensus, having enjoyed the night before, we decided to eat ashore here as well. It was another success. The restaurant right on the beach, run by a young French couple, provided a fine "no menu" meal of a delicate soufflé as appetizer, *mahi-mahi, en brochette,* as main course, and dessert of a sherbert of local fruit. With the lagoon waters whispering on the beach outside and palms rustling overhead, frangipani and hibiscus on the table and Polynesian music faintly in the background, there was what might be called, in restaurant critics' terms, suitable ambience. The rain held off until we were back aboard. Then it came down in a thundering tattoo for most of the night, a disturbance to sleepers, but there was no wind or wave motion.

It was not quite so rainy in the morning, but there was still a light spatter and overcast, and we thought the best thing to do was to visit Uturoa, Raiatea's capital. This bustling little city is the center of activity for the whole area. We powered over in the wet and were able to tie up alongside. Martha and Dan, with five children to bring presents to, were more intent on shopping, and Jane and I turned them loose in the odd jumble of native stores to amble along the waterfront. Yachts and interisland freighters tie up along the quay, and we were interested in seeing a bright red freighter we had become familiar with on our previous visit. She runs a regular route through the four islands as one of their main sources of supply, and we had been told that her skipper was known as Captain Hernani, after the local brand of beer. It seems he was a great user of it and occasionally slipped into nautical error, like hitting reefs or running aground, but we were glad to see that she was still operating.

The skies cleared as the morning wore on, and we powered out to do some more motu exploring. Little Optimist sailing prams with bright green-and-red-striped sails were heading out for sailing lessons, evidently part of the school curriculum here. We made sail and had a lazy reach south inside the reef to Faaroa Bay, a deep indentation between mountains. Far up it, we had a quiet anchorage all to ourselves with the cool night air drifting down from the heights laden with deliciously mysterious tropical scents.

Schoolchildren in Optimist Prams, Uturoa

A special treat at Faaroa is a dinghy trip up the Faaroa River at the head of the bay. We had first done this on a 1967 visit when we were staying at the Bali Hai Hotel in Uturoa—it was a hotel specialty to take guests up the river by Boston Whaler. It was an exciting, exotic expedition, penetrating the jungle amid strange sights, sounds and smells as far as the Whaler could go and still turn around to return. Out of the breeze, the atmosphere was oppressively hot, and when we got to the pool the young man running the Whaler informed us that anyone who wanted to could take a swim. We all leaped in and cooled off nicely except the wife of the other couple with us, who was from Cincinnati. She looked down at the water from the safety of the Whaler and said, "It looks like the Ohio River to me. I'm not going swimming in it!"

This time, Jean-Pierre took us in the cool of the morning before breakfast, sliding over green-glass water where little schools of fish skittered across the surface. The jungle growth was dense, almost smothering, and strange birds flitted through the treetops. Two native women in a crude dugout canoe paddled past, saluting us silently by raising their paddles, and again we had the feeling of stepping back in time. When we stopped the motor to drift for a while, there was an overpowering silence, broken only by the occasional cries of the birds.

The rest of the day was a circumnavigation of Raiatea, threading through motus inside the reef, under the shadow of the great green peaks. Their steep flanks were slashed by dozens of pencil-thin waterfalls cascading down in eccentric patterns. It was a day of alternate clouds and sun, with cumuli clustering around the peaks and an occasional splash of rain swooping down. The breeze was fitful, playing tricks around the squalls. We were able to keep sailing most of the time though we stopped for lunch off a palm-lined beach on Ile Nao Nao, a large motu isolated on the reef, which, strangely, had an airstrip. There was no indication why one would be there, and Jean-Pierre had no explanation.

Reaching fast in a gusty wind sweeping down from the mountains, we rounded the bottom of the island and ran

Wind Song *at Uturoa*

into a bank of squalls that closed in quickly along the west coast. From there it was on with foul-weather gear and a wet slug in the open sea to get back north. Offshore, glimpsed through breaks in the squalls, we saw the four-masted schooner *Wind Song,* a 440-foot cruise ship with automated sails, making her way south, and I was especially interested to see that she had her sails "out" (not "up"; they unfurl off a stay at a computer's bidding). We were to cruise in her the following week. As it turned out, the cruise was very interesting, but not a sailing success, since there was seldom any wind. Being aboard her was a fascinating contrast to *Sea Cloud,* as computers did the work of *Sea Cloud*'s sixteen-person deck crew.

We took her from Tahiti to Huahine, Bora Bora, Raiatea, and Moorea. To demonstrate to me how the sails worked, the captain set the computer to unfurl the sails at 8 knots of wind, with about three hundred sensors all over the ship providing the information the computer needed. A one-cloud squall was a bit off our course, but the captain headed into it to find wind, the computer got the message, and the sails rolled out. Once through the squall, the wind went calm again and the sails rolled up with a screeching of the mammoth sheet blocks. No one had touched anything but the computer.

That would be next week, however. Now, she was disappearing in the gloom of the squalls, while *Esperance* powered on through a sloppy surface chop into calm waters for a last night's anchorage at one of those convenient moorings at Apooiti, with rain again drumming on the deck. We went ashore for a last nightcap with the friendly French couple at the restaurant, where I was able to grasp about one quarter of their banter with Jean-Pierre.

To turn *Esperance* in at Apooiti we had an easy reach down the lagoon, drinking in the play of clouds over Tahaa and Raiatea as the weather cleared, and taking a last look at Bora Bora's bold bulk off to the west, still and always the "trademark" of a very special area.

19

▶▶▶▶▶▶▶▶▶▶▶▶▶▶

IN CAPTAIN COOK'S WAKE
New Zealand's Bay of Islands

In November 1769, Captain James Cook, in my opinion one of the greatest sea captains and explorers in history, was ranging the east coast of New Zealand in his converted Whitby collier *Endeavour,* passed a high promontory and discovered on the west side "a large and pretty deep bay lying in Southwest by West, in which there appeared to be several islands." Encountering a head wind offshore, he decided to bear away to port and explore the bay, anchoring off an island fairly well into it, which the native Maoris called Motuarohia.

Endeavour's crew discovered that the natives were more elaborately tattooed and used more intricately carved canoes than any they had seen. In a week-long visit, Cook, who had ninety-six souls to feed aboard the 106-foot ship, traded with the natives for fish and vegetables, and filled his water casks. Joseph Banks, the naturalist who accompanied Cook, climbed the highest hill on Motuarohia for an overall view of the area and called it a "most spacious and well-sheltered harbor," and went on to describe it more fully in his journal. "The bay was indeed a most surprising place: it was full of innumerable islands forming as many harbours which must be as smooth as millponds as they

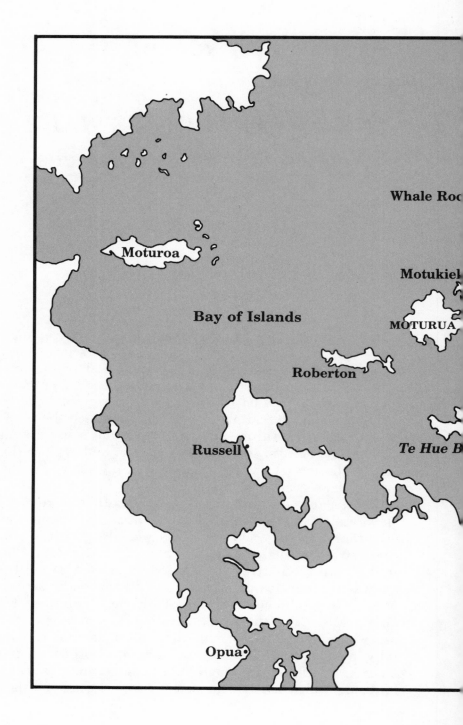

PACIFIC OCEAN

Piercy
Rock

Cape Brett

ahu

Waewaetorea

Deep
Water
Cove

Urupukapuka

Oke
Bay

Whangamumu

NEW ZEALAND

NORTH ISLAND

0 _____ 5
Nautical Miles

landlock one another numberless times. Everywhere around us we could see large Indian towns. Certainly we had seen no place as populous as this one."

In his voyages of exploration, which covered, over the years, almost the entire Pacific world from Antarctica to the Arctic and from both American shores to the Antipodes, Cook had the pleasure and privilege of naming most of the places he discovered, and this area he simply called Bay of Islands.

Ever since then, this lovely enclave at latitude 35° south has been a magnet and mecca for seafarers: first for other explorers, then whalers and traders, and today, despite its remote location, for sailors who appreciate a very special cruising grounds. Zane Grey brought it fame in the 1930s with his fabled sportfishing feats, and world voyagers like Eric and Susan Hiscock and John Guzzwell wrote glowingly of their visits. The Hiscocks liked it so much that they settled there, and Susan even remained when widowed and retired from voyaging.

The description by Banks was an accurate one, pointing out the abundance of close-together anchorages in a graceful setting. It is an extremely compact area that can be covered end to end in one day's sailing, but there are eighty-six islands within it and the deeply indented bays, coves, and river mouths make five hundred miles of coastline. The latitude, comparable to the north latitude of southern California or North Carolina, with special influence from the midocean location, means an equable climate with a sailing season that can last from October to May, and even the southern winter is mild enough for some good sailing conditions. Summer, however, December to April, is the high season, and Kiwis, as New Zealanders are affectionately called, flock there in their boats. New Zealand has the highest boat-per-capita ratio of any country, and the wonderful sailing opportunities that abound in most areas of its two big islands are widely enjoyed.

Our visit was in late February-early March for two weeks of flotilla cruises, one group per week, for readers of *Cruising World* magazine. Jane and I were the magazine's hosts, and the boats were arranged through New Zealand's biggest charter firm, Rainbow Yacht Charters. Each week we had a Rainbow employee with us as guide and general factotum. It was our first experience with flotilla cruising, and we found that it worked well for exploring strange waters, even though these could easily be handled solo by a newcomer. In them, we were reminded most, in the lay of the land, of the British Virgins and Australia's Whitsunday Islands inside the Great Barrier Reef. Our late (southern) summer weather was ideal. Kiwis had been moaning about a wet, windy summer, and in fact we had experienced a heavy storm in the week we spent on land before taking off.

That must have cleared the atmosphere, because we had brilliant skies with a sun that burned with unbelievable intensity in the pure air. I have not experienced a brighter sun in any other area worldwide. The breezes were gentle for the most part, with a day or two of very light stuff. Each day a parade of fair-weather cumulus clouds would march in from midmorning on, magically disappearing from evening twilight until the next midmorning. This made for great stargazing in the clear evening skies, and everyone soon became familiar with the local trademark, the Southern Cross.

The Bay of Islands is 150 miles north of Auckland, two thirds of the way up the North Island. Our group gathered in Auckland, which, in itself, is a teeming yachting center, loaded with major marinas and several active yacht clubs on its big harbor. Just outside, islands in the Huaraki Gulf form another fine cruising grounds. There are good harbors all the way up the coast to the Bay of Islands, but passaging is in the open Pacific. I had a fine time poking around the marinas and clubs of Auckland for a few days, looking at boats and talking to sailors. Kiwis are not quite as outgoing and bucko as Aussies, but in a quieter way, they are friendly, hospitable, and enthusiastic and very accomplished sailors.

Our trip north was by bus, three and a half scenic hours up and down in hilly country, with some great views across beaches to the open sea, field after field full of sheep, and a few small towns. Opua, where Rainbow Charters bases,

The charter base at Opua

is a very small town, with one general store, a restaurant, and a car ferry across Waikara Inlet to the Russell Peninsula across the way. It is a busy harbor, with many boats on permanent moorings, and it gives right onto the Bay of Islands. The bus drove onto the pier where our eleven boats were rafted, and there was a general transference of duffels and other gear for a busy half hour or so, followed by a briefing in the Rainbow office at the head of the pier.

The boats were a mixed bag from twenty-eight-foot Davidsons for couples, with Farr 34s and Chieftain 38s for larger groups. We were aboard a new Farr 42 that was being prepared for Rainbow's new charter service in Fiji's Yasawa Islands. She had been built in Australia, but the others were local products, well laid out and equipped for bareboating, though the roomy, high-freeboard Chieftains were not as good sailers as the rest. The Farr 42 was a fine performer and comfortably roomy. We had the Rainbow skipper-guide, Brian Douglas, with us, and a retired Greek-American bachelor, Nick Prokos. They were both excellent shipmates; Brian had a vast knowledge of the area, as well as a great interest in and awareness of yachting activities worldwide. Trim and wiry, he was a fine seaman: quick and skilled at taking care of the few problems that developed on the boats.

Nick, a Long Islander who had done a lot of sailing, was so good at galley slave chores and other helpful activities that he was awarded the Golden Dish Towel at a mock prize ceremony we had at Opua's restaurant at the end of the cruise. We got a kick out of using our minute knowledge of Greek, picked up in Aegean cruising, with him, especially the corruption of the toast *"Stinea sas"* (phonetic spelling), taught to us by our Greek sailing friend George Legakis. Instead of trying to say it with proper Greek accent, George's version for Americans is simply to say, "Skinny asses," and that became our nightly start of happy hour, much to Nick's amusement.

After all the tohubohu of boarding, there was still time for the flotilla to move out Veronica River the five miles to Russell for a change of scenery for the night. There was a gentle southeaster blowing, and it was a smooth reach between the gradually widening banks. Russell, well out on a long, skinny peninsula that juts into the bay, was the only real town on our itinerary. It is a popular resort with an interesting history. For a few months it was the site of New Zealand's first capital in 1841, and it was also the scene of a Maori attack in 1845 that wiped out most of the people and buildings. It was a rough, brawling "liberty port" for whalers breaking their long voyages. Some of that old aura remains in the buildings along the waterfront, the oldest church in New Zealand (now a police station), and the Captain Cook Museum. It is well worth a visit for a review of his remarkable career, as well as background on Maori legends and traditions. The Duke of Marlborough Hotel on the waterfronts, in its third reincarnation after fires, still has the feel of what it must have been like when it was the holder of the first liquor license in New Zealand. It must have witnessed some wild doings then but it is properly staid now, and we had an excellent dinner there.

There are three good anchorages in the Russell area: Kororareka Bay off the main town, and Matauwhi and Pomare around points to the south. We had originally planned to use Matauwhi, but it was full of boats, and Brian thought it would make more sense to be right off the town. Several crews wanted to eat ashore, and shopping for extra food supplies and liquor would be easier in the morning. Kororareka comes from the Maori name for the peculiar local denizens known as blue penguins, whose shy little eyes, beak, and top of head could sometimes be seen popping up in the harbors. Anchor we did in a good crowd of boats, and the constant coming and going of car ferries and tourist boats, but it was the place to be.

The business of Maori and English names is one of the puzzlements and fascinations of the area where Maori culture still has a strong influence. While we were there, a Maori child drowned in a river on the west side of the bay, and the local mariners' VHF radio station, a husband-and-wife affair privately operated as a message service for boats in the area, broadcast that there should be no swimming or boating in the river for three days, honoring a Maori custom. This radio station was most informal and folksy

and seemed to be a great help to all marine operations in
the area. It is supported by private subscription.

Morning was spent stocking up with extra supplies and
catching the liquor store when it opened just before noon,
plus buying dark glasses for me. I had not brought any,
and I had immediately been impressed by the brilliance of
the sunshine. The flotilla departed at midday for the first
rendezvous, Cook's anchorage, and we soon ran into confusion with the English-Maori name dichotomy. Cook had
found it called Motuarohia, but it is also known as Roberton,
named for a family that settled it early in the nineteenth
century with tragic results. They started farming and fishing, living off the land and sea, but the husband was
drowned in a boating accident soon afterward. Trying to
keep the place going, Mrs. Roberton, who was left with
two children, had two helpers, a white man named Bull
and a young Maori named Maketa, who was son of a chief.
Bull was noted for brutality, and Maketa reacted by kill-
ing him with an ax while he slept. When he told Mrs. Roberton what he had done, she said he would have to be tried
for murder under English law, so he killed her and the
children, the last one by chasing the Robertons' young son
up a cliff and throwing him off it. (Maketa was eventually
hanged.)

Despite this dark background, Roberton-Motuarohia has
a very attractive anchorage. Called Lagoon Bay, it faces a
long curve of white sand on a narrow neck of land between
two much hillier ends of the island. Our group explored
ashore, and swam off the beach. We found tidal pools among
the rocks on the other side, teeming with marine life.

Typical of the ease of finding new anchorages here, it
took less than an hour to move on in late afternoon, where
the fleet split up between Army Bay on Motorua and a
cove at the north end of Motukiekie, less than half a mile
across the way. To continue the confusion over names, Army
Bay, with a beautiful beach, is also called Waiwhapuku
Bay, and farther north in the Bay of Islands there is a
Moturua Island. Even the guidebook was confused, as the
northern one appears on the chart, but not in the text, as
Motorua.

Anchorage at Motukiekie

The beach was the main attraction at Army Bay. Our anchorage off Motukiekie was in a tight little cove with dramatic rock pillars to the north, a small beach for dinghy landing just inside the point, and high cliffs down the rest of the island's western shore. Starting at the dinghy beach, there is a walking track ascending in a steep climb and then following the island's highest ridge for its full length. The view from the path makes it well worth the climb, with an almost perpendicular look down on the boats in the anchorage and across the islands to the west, and then, farther up, a gorgeous panorama of the rest of the islands out to Cape Brett, where Cook turned in to make his discovery.

After a quiet night in the perfectly protected coves, most of the morning was spent in this kind of exploring. Then it was on to the next rendezvous at Oke Bay.

Oke Bay is a deep indentation in the Cape Brett Peninsula with perfect protection from every direction but northeast. It has the obligatory strip of white sand at the inner end, and high cliffs towering over the water on both sides. To get to it, we had the only tricky piloting of the week, threading our way through rocky islets in a narrow cut called Albert Channel between Urupukapuka Island and the Hauai Peninsula. Oddly enough, the best water was right along the shore inside the rocks, and I was glad that Brian knew the way. Most of the other boats were following us, but some were proceeding on their own, choosing to go outside the islands, and when we assembled in Oke Bay, the two Davidsons, the smallest boats in the fleet, had yet to show up.

One lack in the generally excellent flotilla organization was VHF communication for all boats. There was also no chase boat, and we watched anxiously when the two small boats finally appeared and began to take the wrong approach into Oke. There was a misleading wrong route inside an islet called Moturahurahu on the west side of the entrance, and we sat there helpless as both boats started through it. We saw the first one fetch up, while the other turned off. But the first one soon could be seen moving back out again and they finally came in the right way to the cheers of the assemblage. Fortunately, no damage had been done.

The plan for the next day was for a highly informal race around Cape Brett in the open Pacific to a harbor called Whangamumu on the seaward side, a course of about twelve miles. The wind was very light for most of the day, and we came upon some dramatic landmarks along the way. Cape Brett is a bold promontory over a thousand feet high, backed by more mountains on the peninsula. Cook followed his usual practice of naming prominent landmarks for members of his sponsoring organization, the Royal Society. It was Sir Piercy Brett in this case. A white lighthouse stands 450 feet up the slope in an area that can be reached only by boat or a hiking trail, as the road along the peninsula peters out at Oke Bay. Cook had a real inspiration in choosing a name for a unique island just off the point. This sheer pinnacle of rock, several hundred feet high, has a large hole right through it, and Cook had the whimsical notion of calling it Piercy Island. How appropriate can you get?

It is an area teeming with bird life, with excellent diving when the sea is calm enough, and a big cave to be explored on the western side of Piercy. A powered tourist catamaran routinely goes through the Hole in the Rock on its daily trips, at least when sea conditions permit, and we heard tales of someone having once gone through it in a helicopter—hard to believe. On this day, while we followed the race boats, a kayak would have been in danger in the hole, as great long Pacific swells were rolling in from a disturbance offshore that we later heard had damaged the *QE2* on her way into Auckland. In the open sea, their rise and fall was not terribly noticeable, as there was a long period between each swell, but when they came into shallow water or hit a bold cliff, like Piercy or Cape Brett, the results were impressive.

Great curtains of white would shoot far up the cliffs, with the reverse runoff a turbulent counterpoint, and it was a memorable scene as the boats inched their way along in the light going. I began to wonder what Whangamumu would be like in this granddaddy of all surges, as its entrance looked fairly open on the chart. We went on ahead of the racers to set up a finish line just inside the entrance, and we were surprised to find the round dollar of a harbor calm and serene. At the entrance, the swells were bashing themselves to foamy bits on the cliffs and rocks, but the points on both sides seemed to have just enough of an angle to break up the swells, and the harbor had perfect protection.

Aptly named Piercy Rock off Cape Brett

It was a place reeking of the past, as the ruins of a whaling try works that had been abandoned just before World War II made a monumental pile behind a pebbly beach, with a little stream running past. This made a haven for our dinghies. A short way up, at the beginning of some steep hills, there was a graceful little waterfall. We had a bring-your-own barbecue here, where everyone relaxed and enjoyed that special glow of having been offshore in unusual conditions before finding a colorful haven. The only shore access at Whangamumu is a hiking trail, and, with only one or two nonflotilla boats in the roomy anchorage, there was a marvelous feeling of escape.

It was the turnaround point for the cruise, and the sail back around Cape Brett was in diminished swells and a pleasant reaching breeze to a lunch stop at another isolated harbor with a past. This was Deep Water Cove, on the western side of Cape Brett's peninsula, and deep it was, but we were able to find good anchorage by forming a couple of rafts well into it. Its past fame comes from the fact that this was Zane Grey's base for his sportfishing exploits that amazed the angling world in the 1930s. But time and

vandalism had wiped out all traces of the thriving camp
that had covered the steep slopes at the head of the harbor. We had already seen that sportfishing still thrives here
during our stop at Russell, where a couple of hefty marlin
were being weighed in at the town dock when we arrived.

We used harbors on the "mainland" (North Island as op-
posed to the islands in the bay) for our last two nights
headed back to Opua. Te Hue Bay, tucked inside the last
point before Russell, had several local boats on moorings
and a camp on shore with a small pier. There was a water
hose on the pier, with an "honesty box" on a post next to
it for paying for any water used. The alternative name for
Te Hue is Assassination Cove, as it was here that an early
French explorer, DuFresne, and his men were ambushed
and slain by Maoris. We had a final raft-up here, with much
visiting between boats and exchanging of sea stories. Here,
Brian admitted that he was fascinated by the accents of
some of our group from places like Oklahoma, Massachusetts, and Cape Breton Island. We refrained from com-
menting how fascinated they were by his.

As we were leaving in the morning, we went close in to
Orokawa Beach, just outside Te Hue, and Brian took the
dinghy in and gathered some *pipis,* soft-shelled steamer
clams that grow just at the tide line and are a favorite
local delicacy. From here, we made a last night of it at
Russell, where almost everyone ate ashore, and Brian did
his final Good Samaritan act by diving to clear the propeller fouled by a line on one of the boats.

There was a smaller group for the second week, only four
boats, and we felt like old veterans repeating the basic
routine with them. Brian had been away from his family
long enough and so took some leave, and our guide this
week was a husky, sunburned seaman/fisherman named
Kevin Hirst. Kevin spent every moment that he could fishing, with considerable success. The major local type is a
bottom feeder called snapper, and we had a few meals from
his catches of these—good eating. We tried a couple of new
harbors, such as Pipi Bay on the southeast side of Motorua, and an island with a great arc of beach, Waewaetorea, where the diving was very good, and a graceful, open,

grass-covered hill just begged to be climbed for the view. Just north of its companion island, Okahu, is a barely submerged menace to navigation called Whale Rock. This was another of Cook's discoveries, rather inadvertently, as he hit it on his way out of the bay, but without damage, and, taken with following in Cook's wake as we were in this unique area, we were glad that no one followed him that closely.

Additional Information

The South Pacific

Of all the areas covered, this is, of course, much the widest in scope, stretching for about seven thousand miles from the Galapagos to Australia. There are interminable stretches of ocean, but there are also innumerable island groups along the way that offer the most tantalizing kind of challenge to the cruising sailor. As I have mentioned, West Coast sailors, with few good areas at home, tend to take off across this great expanse in search of adventure. Long-voyaging is the norm in the Pacific. Lately, however, charter bases have been established in several areas, allowing vacationers with limited time to sample the fabled South Sea island delights.

Again, my introduction to this area was via subchaser duty, and I will never forget my reaction when reporting to the operations officer in Panama. All we knew was that we were headed for Pacific duty, and the officer told me that our first leg on assignment to New Guinea, over eight thousand miles away, would be a passage of forty-eight hundred miles to Bora Bora.

"Bora who?" was my reaction, followed by the statement that our operating range was twelve hundred miles.

He assured me we would be in convoy, fueling from an LST, and he took me to a wall chart and showed me Bora Bora.

I think my most coherent reaction was "Wow!"

That was a great introduction to Pacific distances, and

the rugged peak of Bora Bora looming over the blue Pacific horizon was a never to be forgotten thrill after twenty-three days of nothing but empty horizon. Ever since then, it has symbolized the glamor and lure of the South Pacific for me.

The previous chapters have told of some of the interesting cruising targets, such as the Galapagos, Iles sous le Vent, and New Zealand's Bay of Islands. I have also sampled Tonga, Fiji, and the Whitsunday Islands of Australia's Great Barrier Reef, and all of them are very much worth the time and effort. A look at a world map will show how many more island groups there are to be explored, each covering hundreds of miles of ocean, and each with its own fascinating history and culture. Not many of them are set up to provide charters for fly-in visitors, and it is up to the individual long-voyager to do his own explorations. To name just a few, the Marshalls, Gilberts, Ellice, and Carolines, suddenly thrust in the limelight in World War II, are again relatively isolated, and it takes a well-equipped and self-sufficient boat to negotiate them.

A big difference that North Americans tend to forget is that the seasons are reversed south of the Equator. While the climate is tropical, with balmy breezes all year, the Southern summer during the Northern winter is the rainy season, with lighter breezes and the threat of hurricanes in some areas. Another factor is the weird El Niño Current, named because it usually appears at Christmas, the time of the Christ Child. This changes the direction of ocean currents and the temperature of the water, causing major climate variations, and droughts and floods as far away as Australia and Africa. It is an unpredictable occasional factor.

Many long-voyagers hole up in places like American Samoa or down in New Zealand to avoid the hurricane season. When we were in Pago Pago, Samoa, on our way to Tonga, there were a great many boats in layup at the very inner end of that rain-plagued harbor.

Most of our South Pacific visits happen to have been in the Northern winter. In three trips to the Tahiti area, the weather has varied from ideal to rainy and light winds. As noted, the New Zealand cruise was at the end of their summer and was delightful. In the Whitsundays it was September, early spring, with perfect weather and good breezes, but I understand that operations cease there in January and February because of heat and the danger of cyclones (hurricanes).

So the South Pacific is arbitrarily in the Northern winter section of the book, but the variations in season should be taken into account in planning a cruise or a long voyage in its waters.

Yachting centers Charter yachts and long-voyagers tend to assemble at Papeete; Raiatea; Pago Pago; Vavau; Tonga; Suva; Auckland; Bay of Islands; Sydney, Brisbane, and Shute Harbour. There are, of course, many more ports with some form of yachting facilities.

Chartering Papeete; Raiatea; Tonga; Yasawa, Fiji; Auckland; Bay of Islands; Sydney; Pitt Water; and Shute Harbour are bases for organized fleets. Crewed charters operate in the Iles sous le Vent, New Zealand, and the Great Barrier Reef, and there are flotilla cruises in the Yasawa group of Fiji.

Weather It is tropical throughout the South Pacific, with prevailing winds mostly trade winds from the easterly quadrant. Hurricanes a threat in the western regions in the Southern late summer.

Cruising grounds The whole Pacific is one vast cruising ground, but the charter centers of Iles sous le Vent, Tonga, Fiji, New Zealand, and the Great Barrier Reef are best set up for visitors. The Marquesas and Tuamotus are fascinating challenges for long-voyagers.

Special attractions Those include primitive, undeveloped areas; native cultures; diving; beaches; nature studies; scenery; and World War II history.

References Robinson, *Where to Cruise,* pp. 143–180; Hinz, *Landfalls of Paradise;* Davock, *Cruising Guide to Tahiti and the French Society Islands;* Thomas, *The Last Navigator;* Jones, *New Zealand's Bay of Islands.*

20

▶ ▶ ▶ ▶ ▶ ▶ ▶ ▶ ▶ ▶ ▶ ▶ ▶ ▶

THE MYSTERIOUS (SOUTH)
EAST
Cruising Out of Phuket, Thailand

Every other cruising area we have ever visited was somewhat familiar in advance from having read about it over the years or talked to sailors who had been there, but Phuket was completely unknown. I had heard about it for the first time just months before and did not even know how to pronounce it. In the Thai language, the *h* is silent and Phuket, an island on the Andaman Sea coast of Thailand, an hour's flight from Bangkok, is pronounced Poo-ket.

We were already headed for Southeast Asia in one of my stints of lecturing on a cruise ship, and I happened to see an article in a British boating magazine about Phuket cruising. A brokerage agency, Graham and Judy Millar's South Seas Yachts, was listed as having information and it was through their worldwide connections that arrangements were made for our Phuket adventure.

And an adventure it was, an experience in an area unlike any other in which we have cruised. Phuket is an island, thirty-two miles long, connected to the mainland by a causeway and enclosing island-filled Phang Na Bay, where there are anchorages enough for a week or more of exploring. Offshore in the Andaman Sea, an arm of the Indian

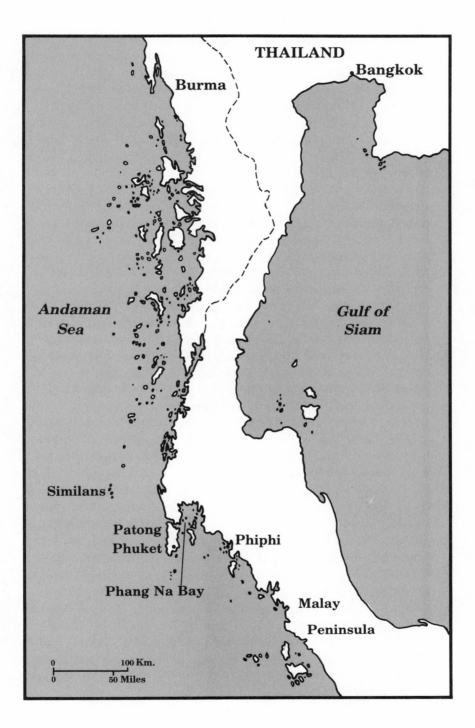

Ocean, there are strings of islands, with the closest, the Similans, sixty miles out. Phuket is oblong, with many coves and bays along both shores, and a succession of top-grade beaches that have become a major jet-age winter attraction for Europeans, who are about ten hours' flying time away. Some of the hotels are world-class luxury resorts, like Amanpuri, and there are also areas of honky-tonk sleaze. At 8° north, the climate is decidedly tropical, and there are two distinct seasons.

We were there in February, the height of the northeast monsoon. This is supposed to be the rainy season, but that only means passing showers, and we had ten days of warm, hazy weather, with no rain. From April to October, the southwest monsoon takes over, exposing Phuket's west coast to deep-sea surf rolling in from the Indian Ocean. When we were there, there were thirty crewed charter boats operating, and most of them would leave for the Gulf of Siam, Bali, or Singapore during the southwest season. A few would hole up in Ao Chalong, the best bay on Phuket's east coast. Now a bareboat service has been added, and chartering is on the increase. There are no marinas. All boarding is by dinghy off the beach.

We had lined up three boats to get a comparison of what was available, and the first was *Singa* (which incidentally means "lion" as in Singapore "the Lion Port"), a Sparkman & Stephens Hylas 47. We boarded her from the beach at a luxury resort catering especially to yachtsmen called the Phuket Yacht Club, which is at Nai Harn, a beach-lined bay at the southern tip of Phuket. Aboard were her owner, Tony Kozad, a transplanted Californian, and his Malaysian wife, Tulimah, with whom he operates Asia Islands Yacht Charters out of Singapore. Pascal Trouvier, a French sailor with many long voyages behind him, was breaking in as captain.

The Hylas 47 is a top-grade charter boat, center cockpit with a roomy layout, and an able sailer. A special feature, handy in this climate of almost perpetual sun, was a pair of solar panels for heating water and charging batteries. We had an introductory sail of about five miles in a fading northeast monsoon to the first island in the entrance to

Phang Na, anchoring in a long cove. A light sea breeze took over for the rest of the day. We were picking up local lore, such as this standard wind behavior, of the north-easter blowing at its freshest during the night and early morning. We learned that *Ko* means "island" and *Ao* means "bay," and we had our first glimpses of the distinctive local craft. Big fishing boats with live-aboard crews have pago-dalike aft deckhouses and great booms lined with light bulbs that are extended out at night to attract squid, the major local catch, to their nets. Phang Na Bay looks like a sea-going city at night with the lights of these vessels strung out across the horizon. There are smaller boats, called longtails, that we had already seen racing along as water taxis on the *klongs* (canals) of Bangkok. Here, these open, slender-hulled canoes of about thirty feet are fishing boats. They get their name from their peculiar outboard motors, which sit on the transom at an angle of about 70 degrees and have shafts sticking out astern for ten feet or more. Their cooling water intake is simply a scoop next to the

Thai squid-fishing boats with their long light booms

propeller on the shaft, from which the water is forced to the engine by the forward motion of the boat. They are ubiquitous, the noise they make is horrendous, and they shoot a great rooster tail in their wake as they speed along. Their crews follow the fish, squid, and prawns, camping on beaches at night in a nomadic life-style.

Our cove had both types but no other yachts, and the late-afternoon quiet was racked by the approach of long-tails coming in to the beach for the night. After sunset, the northeast monsoon came in freshly, and the rigging hummed with it through the dark hours. It was still there, blowing at 25 knots, when we headed into the bay in the morning. The water around us was a deep blue as we came out of the harbor. We put a reef in the main and set the working jib, and *Singa* put her rail down and made good work of it to windward. Soon we had left the blue behind and were slashing across pale green in a lively chop moving toward a seascape that looked like the illustration for a Gothic fairy tale or the work of a mad sculptor.

The weird island shapes of Phang Na Bay

Nowhere else have I seen anything like the spread of islands stretching off in the heat haze, sheer limestone cliffs rising to rounded peaks and eaten away at the base, looking oddly top-heavy. Where the water has surged against the lower section for untold centuries, jagged stalactites hang down. Scrubby vegetation clings to their cliffs, and here and there we could see catwalks and primitive ladders used by the longtail seamen going after bird's nests to be made into soup.

By noon the monsoon was fading, and we shook out the reef and glided over the pale water, which gradually changed from lime to tan as we moved northward. Rivers at Phang Na's head, opposite the north end of Phuket Island, feed mud into the water, discoloring it progressively. By the time the gentle sea breeze had replaced the monsoon, we were off an island called Ko Hyai, whose awesome cliffs towered hundreds of feet high. We anchored off its west side and took the dinghy along its rocky shores, ducking under the fantastic stalactites, until we found a tunnel, sea-scoured and exposed only below half-tide, that led into a lagoon in the island's heart. We entered its silent, secret world, perfectly circular, where scrubby trees hung improbably from crannies in the sheer walls. In a frenzy at our approach, schools of tiny fish skittered over the sheen of the water, with some landing in the boat. On one of the cliffs, a monkey scavenging along a rocky ledge shot up the wall in a panic at the sight of us, and a kingfisher eyed us suspiciously from a tree.

Through mauve twilight we went back to *Singa,* where Tulimah, a charming sprite of a hostess and a good cook, had a dinner of curried chicken, rice, and prawns ready. Afterward we sat in the cockpit in the soft air and felt the gradual return of the monsoon. We were in the lee of Ko Hyai's cliffs, but it found its way around the island in uneven gusts, and *Singa* swung around and rode to it as the night air freshened.

Before we took off in the morning, there was another exploration by dinghy to another nearby Ko, known to Westerners if not the natives as Paradise Island. Surrounded by this island and its neighbors, a small sloop was

A typical Phang Na Bay anchorage

tied in a lagoon in a Scandinavian moor, with lines fore-and-aft to trees on two of the cliffs that seemed to tower out of sight above her. Shafts of sunlight made their way down to her through whatever openings there were above. We poked into more caves and examined a small beach where someone had recently done some sand sculpture.

Sailing eastward toward the mainland, we stopped for lunch as the noonday calm descended at an isolated island called Ko Hong. We did some more lagoon exploring after poking along under the stalactites on the way in.

The noonday calm persisted, and we powered southeastward while long, slithery gar fish, a Phang Na parody of oceanic flying fish, skipped across the water ahead of us. As we moved away from the head of the bay, the water grew clearer and greener, and the monsoon came back earlier than usual—just as we anchored off another Ko, Dain Hok, far out in the middle of the bay. In addition to dinghy exploration here, there was also a chance to park our gar-

bage at a camp settlement on the beach. We enjoyed Tulimah's dinner in the cockpit while the monsoon sent cooling
backdrafts down the cliffs and the horizon to the westward came alive with the lights of the squid fishing boats.

Our session with *Singa* ended with a fine spinnaker run
back toward Phuket in the morning monsoon. We fueled
at a boat anchored in Ao Chalong and then powered in the
afternoon calm around the southern end of Phuket to Patong, a harbor on the west coast. Here we anchored in a
wide bay, perfectly protected from the northeast monsoon,
but wide open to the west, all the way to Africa. I didn't
know it at the time, but this is the center of what used to
be a tin mining operation. We dinghied ashore for dinner
to wind up the first of our three boat sessions, but it was
not the end of our adventures with *Singa*. More about
that later.

From her we transferred to the famous veteran ocean
racing maxi, *Stormvogel,* a seventy-one-foot ketch well
known around the world as a race participant in all the
major events, and now in charter service here. It was a
thrill to be aboard her, and I remembered sailing against
her in Bermuda Races back in the 1960s. She was manned
by two young New Zealanders, Graeme as skipper and Andy
as mate, and by Françoise, a French cook of charm and
ability.

Tulimah Kozad at Singa's *wheel*

In her we went the opposite way from our *Singa* cruise, reaching offshore to the Similan Islands from a predawn start, making the best of the morning monsoon. We had "all five" up—two jibs, main, mizzen staysail, and mizzen, and it was a fine ride. With a bone in her teeth, she surged across a smooth sea, arriving at the islands just as the monsoon did its noonday fade. We anchored in a lovely little bay for lunch, then moved on to a larger anchorage on the next island for the night. Here there were a couple of dive boats, with a small diving camp on the stretch of beach, and the clear pale water over white sand was alive with all sorts of small fish schooling under our shade. The beach was backed by a tumble of oddly shaped rocks, including one that looked like the head of Charlie Brown's Snoopy. They reminded us of The Baths in the British Virgin Islands.

Francoise had been busy in the galley for most of the afternoon, and the result was a memorable dinner of snapper, calamari (those things attracted by the lights on the fishing boats), salad, and fruit, and we finished the evening in a sea-story session in the saloon with the wide-voyaging New Zealanders.

The sail back to Phuket was not as successful, as the monsoon petered out in midmorning, and the rest of the passage was under power all the way down to Nai Harn. We had dinner of lamb Bretagne, salad, and chocolate mousse and finished the trip under a waxing moon after dark. This was where we were to board our final boat, a handsome fifty-nine-foot British-built motorsailer *Raden Mas* (Golden Prince) for a look at some areas of Phang Na Bay we hadn't touched in *Singa*. Another wandering Californian, Charles Daley, was the skipper of *Raden Mas,* with a crew of two Thai lads and a Malay, who took care of us with ever-present, smiling service.

Unfortunately, the monsoon was still absent, and we never got a chance to see the red sails of *Raden Mas* hoisted. We did the whole tour under power, starting with a lunch stop at isolated Ko Maithon halfway across Phang Na Bay to the eastward, where longtails buzzed about us in busy cacophony. Our target was Phiphidon (remember the silent *h*) out in the bay on its eastern side, and it was a strong contrast to the Similans and the lonely islands we had visited in *Singa*. Phi Phi is a major tourist attraction, famous for fine beaches and spectacular cliffs, caves, and rock formations. Its harbor was alive with boats, longtails, "pagoda" boats, a small cruise ship, and a few yachts. The beach at the head of the harbor was a hive of longtails lined up along the sand, backed by a fence that had a big sign saying PEE PEE CABINS—no silent *h* here. A central town dock saw steady traffic of tourist launches.

It was warm enough here for us to sleep on deck on the wide coach roof of the after cabin of *Raden Mas,* waking early to a bright, clear morning. Daley took us on a tour of the surrounding sights, little beaches tucked away between high cliffs with stalactites galore hanging down to the eroded bases and pinnacles of rock making eccentric patterns. On an offlying satellite island named Phraya Nak there was a tower of rock with a knob on top that looked, from a certain angle, just like ET—an appropriate symbol for this out-of-this-world area.

Raden Mas took us back to a final visit to Phuket Yacht Club before our flight back, but our story is not finished without an account of what happened with *Singa* the night we dinghied ashore for dinner at Patong. We anchored several hundred yards offshore, with Pascal handling the anchor, and he was such a good sailor that I must admit I had none of my usual misgivings about the anchoring habits of French sailors.

The inflatable was hauled well up on a wide beach, and we walked to a launderette several blocks inland on a street that ran at right angles to the waterfront. I have mentioned that Phuket has some sleazy areas, and this turned out to be the capital of sleaze. The neon-lit street was lined with bars advertising "girls" and "hostesses," and it looked like some of the rougher Navy liberty neighborhoods I had seen in years past. In case there was any doubt about the local activities, there was a prominently labeled VD treatment center right in among the bars.

We left the laundry to be picked up in the morning and walked back to the more sedate waterfront boulevard, where there were several restaurants, and the Kozads chose one they were familiar with. It was big and busy, but we had good seafood and then wandered back to the inflatable in midevening to go back to *Singa*.

The night was dark, and the monsoon had gained considerably in strength since we had gone ashore. Spray was flying, and there was a noticeable heft to it as we headed for the spot where *Singa* had been anchored.

No boat!

Right where she should have been, surrounded by boats we knew had been close to her, there was a black, empty spot.

There is nothing quite like the feeling of knowing that something is supposed to be in a certain place, but is not. We took a couple of quick turns around the other boats in hopes that we had somehow lost our bearings, but the truth finally struck home. She was gone.

Raden Mas, which Jane and I of course did not yet know, was right in the vicinity. Her cabin lights were on, and we came alongside and hailed Charlie Daley. When he came on deck, Tony quickly explained the situation and asked him if, by any chance, he had seen anything to do with *Singa,* but the answer was negative. He asked us aboard to use his radar, and immediately offered to take up a search. Quickly we got underway and headed over toward the southern point of the harbor to see if she had possibly gone aground there. There was no sign of her, and it could be seen that the wind was not quite right for driving her there. Its direction was directly out to the open sea from where *Singa* had been anchored.

My first reaction was that it must be a theft, an act of piracy of some sort, but Tony and Charlie both said that it was unlikely. No such incidents had happened here for a long time, the drug trade was being carried on farther down the coast, and it would really be surprising if she had been stolen. Tony quietly quizzed Pascal about the anchoring, and Pascal admitted that he had not checked the hold too carefully, as it seemed to have taken up properly.

We headed dead downwind into the Andaman, and the darkness ahead looked as though Patong was out there, not astern of us, as the lights of a few dozen squid boats blinked across the whole area. The radar had the measles with the multitude of targets these boats made, and it looked like a very long shot to be able to pick *Singa* out of the profusion of little green blips. We ranged back and forth, closing with target after target, only to find that it was a fishing boat, and, after a couple of hours, the decision was made that it was a futile prospect. We were a glum company as *Raden Mas* dropped the hook back at Patong.

Tony's main hope was that someone had picked *Singa* up and taken her into one of the many harbors along the coast, but there was no way to check that in a slow-moving boat at night. Charlie offered us bunks, and we had a fitful sleep of a couple of hours, but he had to get under way at 0430 to pick up his next charter, and we ferried ashore into the teeth of the monsoon that now felt cold, damp, and unfriendly. Fortunately, a not very fancy hotel on the beach had a couple of empty rooms, and a sad bunch of refugees checked in for a very short sleep.

Tony and Pascal were off on hired motorbikes at first light to make a tour of the harbors, and we had breakfast with Tulimah, trying to decide what was the best course of action. I had my wallet and a couple of shirts at the launderette but our luggage, passports, plane tickets, traveler's checks, checkbook, and cameras, and Jane's eyeglasses and medication, were all on *Singa*. Despite the fact that her potential loss was tremendous in terms of our inconvenience, Tulimah was most helpful about our predicament, and we started making a plan of action. She had a family connection with a doctor at the hospital, and he managed to fill most of the several blood-pressure medications Jane has to take, though he'd only had a few moments' sleep after a tough operating session. I bought tooth brushes, shaving gear and a pair of magnifying eyeglasses that Jane could use, and a long session at a branch of the Bank of Bangkok finally produced $1,000 worth of *bahts* against my American Express card, via a clerk who was extremely upset at such an unusual situation. His biggest problem was that I did not have a picture of myself (my driver's license didn't require it when I got it several years ago). That many *bahts* practically needs a wheelbarrow to handle, but I felt a little more secure.

Tony and Pascal came back at lunchtime with nothing to report, but Tony had been able to persuade the police to take a helicopter offshore that afternoon. Eight members of the force came along for the joyride, while the rest of us made our way to *Stormvogel,* just arrived in the harbor for our rendezvous. What to do about tickets, passports, etc., remained a knotty problem, but we decided to give it a little more time before facing up to it. It was a tense time of waiting.

Stormvogel's crew was shocked and most sympathetic over the situation, and we gathered in her cockpit in subdued silence waiting for a report from the helicopter, with the VHF on standby. Suddenly, about 1600, the radio boomed to life with Tony's voice loud and clear saying *"Stormvogel, Stormvogel;* this is *Singa.* Do you read?" That we did with whoops of joy, and he followed this up by reporting that he was aboard and on his way into Patong and would join us shortly. Pascal came back dejectedly from his search to hear the good news with a cry of relief. He had felt responsible, naturally, having set the anchor, and the explanation for dragging, after discussion with the *Stormvogel* hands, was that the holding ground at Patong is very hard because of the deposits of tin in the harbor bed, and that it slopes out rather quickly from shallow water in the anchorage to much deeper water. When the monsoon increased, she just slid off into the deep.

When *Singa* came in and the joyous reunion was complete, Tony told us how the helicopter had gone about forty miles downwind offshore, sighting nothing, and was circling back on a slightly more northerly route, just about to give up, when a little white dot was sighted off to port. All of them holding their breath, they swept down to circle it, and there was *Singa,* peacefully bobbing on the swells. She had her big cockpit awning up, and the ground tackle was handing over the bow, so she had forereached northward in the monsoon instead of drifting straight downwind, and had covered about twenty-five miles.

The swimming ladder was still over the stern from our

having gone ashore, so the helicopter dropped down to about thirty feet, Tony jumped out with hands over nose and private parts, climbed the ladder, and was safely aboard. The overhead light was still on in the cockpit, and our empty glasses from cocktail hour were still on the table.

And so one of the most unusual and adventurous cruises we have ever taken anywhere in the wide world of sailing, had an extra fillip of drama and excitement, fortunately with a happy ending.

Additional Information

Southeast Asia and the Islands

As I have said, this was a completely new area to me, and it is still a strange one to most North American sailors. Phuket has become an "in" place in the resort world and is fast building up as a sailing center too. World voyagers have discovered it as a landfall when eastbound in the Indian Ocean, a place for recovering from the long passage and regrouping for the areas ahead. Conversely, it has caught on with westbound voyagers as a place to stock up and do all necessary before heading out into the Andaman Sea and the Indian Ocean beyond.

It is a limited area, and the rest of that coast of Thailand, Malaya, and what used to be Burma is not set up for cruising at all, although the islands along Thailand look challenging on the map. Security, which is evidently not a problem in the Phuket area, is something to think about along the rest of the coast.

As explained, this is a seasonal area, with pleasant operating in the northeast monsoon, and a place to be away from in the southwest monsoon, which corresponds to the northern summer. During that time the Phuket-based boats either tie up on the east side of the island or head east for the Gulf of Siam and the Bali area, farther down the Java Sea. Singapore, an independent city-state on its own island at the southern tip of the Malay Peninsula, is also a base. Boats moving from Phuket to the Gulf of Siam or down to Bali all check through here on the way, and some stay.

Bali does not have particularly good harbors, but it is heavily touristed and developed, and customers are there for charter boats. It is a beautifully scenic island in itself, and the nearby islands of Lombok and Flores are interesting targets for a cruise. Above here, in the maze of islands west of New Guinea, it looks as though there would be some excellent, exciting cruising, but security is a problem, as it is in the Philippines as well. Long-voyagers who venture through here are somewhat at risk. Western Australia sailors are now coming up to the Bali area for winter cruising.

New Guinea has developed some cruising facilities along its north coast, and there is a wide choice of harbors. Security in them is reportedly a problem, with considerable thievery. I can attest, from World War II experience when our subchaser finally made it all the way out there, that the scenery is magnificent, but I cannot describe the ports or the natives, as the latter were mostly in hiding, and the harbors were in military use.

Someday, perhaps, these islands off Southeast Asia could become a new cruising mecca for those who have had their fill of the more familiar areas, but the time has not come yet.

Yachting centers Phuket; Singapore; Bali.

Chartering In those three areas.

Weather It is mild and pleasant in the northeast monsoon of winter, with exposed conditions at Phuket in the southwest monsoon; tropical throughout with rain frequent.

Cruising grounds Phuket; Similan Islands; Singapore area, and Bali area.

Special attractions Scenery, beaches, diving, native cultures.

References None available.

PART
IV

///

AFTERTHOUGHTS

There are many books providing compre-
hensive advice on cruising. In the preceding
chapters, only general advice on where to
cruise has been offered, but here follow some
thoughts that should be considered in
connection with the foregoing tour of great
cruising areas.

21

▶ ▶ ▶ ▶ ▶ ▶ ▶ ▶ ▶ ▶ ▶ ▶ ▶

LONG-VOYAGE ROUTES

Most of the cruises covered in the previous chapters were in areas reached by air, using locally based boats, which, as I have said, has meant so much in the expansion of worldwide cruising opportunities. Along with this increase in charter operations in a wide range of areas, there has also been great growth in long-voyaging. Ambitious sailors lucky enough to be able to sever home ties and take off over the horizon have followed in Slocum's wake in ever-larger numbers, and for them a guide to worldwide cruising must include the best sea routes to get to the favored areas. The success of long-voyaging depends on the best use of those routes. Many a starry-eyed start has had its hopes dashed in an unhappy experience on an imprac-tical route.

Even around home waters, it is obviously important to make the right choice in moving from one area to another. When we take our eighteen-foot catboat downriver from home base in Rumson on the Shrewsbury River to the open waters of Sandy Hook Bay and the Atlantic, we must play the tides, which flow swiftly in the Shrewsbury. The only way to go is with ebb tide in the morning and flood in the afternoon for a day of good open-water sailing. In the same way, over the years when we have headed from home to Long Island and New England in one of our cruising boats, a choice had to be made. Unless the tides were favorable on our scheduled departure day for a trip through New York Harbor, we would have to take the offshore route south of Long Island in the Atlantic to Montauk Point, and this meant being staffed and prepared for an overnight passage. If the tides are right, and we are able to pick up the flood at the Narrows between Staten Island and Brooklyn and carry it up the Upper Bay and into the East River, hitting the notorious race at Hell Gate at slack water and then carry the ebb out to the sound, we could make Norwalk, Connecticut in one long day.

To the Caribbean

Many local areas require that choices like the above be made, and the same philosophy with expanded horizons, should apply to offshore passage making. The most frequently used, and abused, offshore passage is from the northeast states to the Caribbean. It is a popular dream to take your own boat south, and a great many sailors have done it. Unfortunately, not all have done it correctly, and there have been difficulties each year, ranging from discomfort and disrupted schedules to outright tragedy.

The most obvious method is just to take off and go by direct route in the open ocean; this choice often includes a stop in Bermuda on the way. Unfortunately, it involves negotiating one of the most rugged stretches of ocean in the temperate zones, and I am not referring to the nonsense about the "Bermuda Triangle." That is a whole-cloth ghost story that somehow has caught the public fancy. There is no mystery about it; it is a rough, tricky oceanic area, especially in the crossing of the Gulf Stream between the States and Bermuda. I have been connected with the Bermuda Race since 1956 in covering it for the press, sailing in it, and serving on the Race Committee, and there have been very few of the biennial events that were "a piece of cake." In the first one I sailed in, in 1960, we ran into a suddenly developing disturbance that buzzsawed along a front hovering over the Gulf Stream and had wildly shifting winds with gusts up to 80 knots. One year we had to postpone the start because an out-of-season hurricane was tracking right across the rhumb line; and there have been several years with heavy going, resulting in dismastings and disablings of very well equipped and crewed boats.

And this is always in June, supposedly the tamest month for being offshore in the area. Most people naturally want to head south in the autumn, and this is a tricky time. The hurricane season lasts from July to October, with some maverick storms extending it on both ends on occasion, and soon after the threat of hurricanes subsides, winter storms become a factor. Many of these form very quickly in the turbulent area off Cape Hatteras, where continental fronts hit the warm, moist air around the Gulf Stream, generating all sorts of possibilities for rough weather.

Even though hurricanes are extensively tracked and reported, giving a warning of from several days to more than a week, it is important for a slow auxiliary to have an absolutely clear forecast on hurricane activity before heading for Bermuda. Even then, the actual crossing of the Gulf Stream can be a challenging affair, with rough conditions almost guaranteed.

From Bermuda south to the Virgins, through that nonexistent Bermuda Triangle, conditions should generally be much easier, though there is never a guarantee in any offshore passage. The unexpected should always be expected. The time allowed on the route via Bermuda, not counting waiting in port for a good forecast, should be at least three weeks.

An alternative to the direct offshore route, and one that is recommended as a better choice on the average, is to take the coastal route via Chesapeake Bay and the Intracoastal Waterway to Morehead City, North Carolina. From there wait for the forecast of a cold-front northwester to make a swift passage out across the Gulf Stream, and there is only a narrow time period, mid-October to early November, when this procedure is recommended.

It is not a good idea to start an offshore passage from anywhere south of Morehead on the ICW, as the coastline recedes off to the southwest so much that distances are greatly increased. Once south of Morehead, it is better to go all the way down to Florida and take one of the routes from there. This also involves a choice. A frequently used method, one that most professional delivery crews take in bringing new boats down for the Caribbean charter fleets or transferring private boats, is to head out from a southern Florida port, preferably on the wings of a cold front westerly, sailing via the Northwest and Northeast Providence channels through the Bahamas as quickly as possible and making easting offshore. If the normally expected southeast trade is blowing, this means thrashing into it on starboard tack out into the Atlantic until coming over onto port tack will allow laying the islands. If there is a northeast variant in the trade, the route can be adjusted.

In talking with professional crews who have made this passage often, I find that the abnormal and the unexpected are really what should be called normal. Delivery crews consider twelve days a successful passage for the average-sized auxiliary on this route.

The alternate to the offshore route, which requires a passage crew, is the island-hopping one that Carleton Mitchell originally dubbed "the Thorny Path." I can speak from experience on this one, as it was the way we took *Brunelle* from Florida to the Virgins in her maiden season, 1979. It had this prickly moniker because it is so often a succession of tough beats to windward on the passages between the islands. This is especially so if an attempt is being made to keep to a schedule. It is much better if time can be taken to wait out the heaviest periods of southeast trade on the nose. We took from January to May to wend our way through the Bahamas and on to the Caicos, Hispaniola, Puerto Rico, and the Virgins. Actually, the winter months were spent enjoying the Bahamas, after slugging our way across the Gulf Stream from Miami to Bimini, and we didn't start on south from Nassau in earnest until April. We had easy sailing down to Clarence Town, Long Island, a challenging but not really difficult close reach from Clarence Town to the Caicos, and a real break from there to Hispaniola. We waited out a week of strong trades while effecting a crew change and ended up powering overnight in a calm across what had been expected to be the ruggedest 150 miles of the itinerary. A few more days of waiting out strong easterlies gave us another calm night to power along the exposed north coast of Hispaniola, an area where the expected is to have strong winds on the nose and great seas sweeping in all the way from Africa. We did have it dead to windward across Mona Passage to Puerto Rico, but not in heavy going. If we had tried to go in the face of the wind that was blowing during the alternate weeks, it would have been a rough experience, tough on our sixty-plus bodies. Springtime gives more breaks in the heavy trades.

Another advantage of this route is that it can be handled with a small crew. We had one young man with us to spell the wheel watches and it worked out very well. Jane and I had passed the age where we could make overnight passages by ourselves, at least with any comfort.

From Europe

From Europe to the Caribbean, the trade wind route is known as the "milk run"; and hundreds of boats do it every year, including one big group that takes part in a cruising race. There is a problem from northern Europe in getting from the English Channel across the turbulent Bay of Biscay to the Spanish coast, especially in autumn. It should be done in summer if possible, but once the Gibraltar area is reached, the question becomes a choice of which island group to use for making the final departure. Most northerly are the Azores, then come the Canaries, and the Cape Verdes are far down off the African coast at 18° north. It is advisable to get an advance reading of how the trade wind is blowing at the moment, as its latitude can vary. It is probably most reliable down by the Cape Verdes, but it is out of the way to get there, and the facilities are somewhat primitive. The most usual compromise is the Canaries, where there is a good likelihood of picking up the trades fairly quickly and where the port facilities on some of the islands are adapted to visiting yachts.

We crossed from the Canaries to Martinique in *Sea Cloud* in November, and the first few days we headed southwest to get down to the trade wind belt were in a moderate wind on the nose, as there was a disturbance up by the Azores and this was part of the circulation around the bottom of it. There were also large ground swells moving out from the storm center. Access to a weather fax can be a big help in avoiding situations like this. Once in the trade, it is usually an easy slide to the islands, and some fast boats have made it in as little as two weeks, but a third week is more likely for the average boat. What "average" is on this run is a moot point, as everything from orange crates up seem to make it!

To Europe

As Columbus discovered after his first couple of voyages, and as the Spanish galleons practiced for years afterward, the return from the Caribbean to Europe should avoid the easterly trades by taking a great circle northward, benefiting from the Gulf Stream if starting far enough west, and not circling toward the east until somewhere in the latitude of Bermuda. It is then a help to know where the semipermanent Azores High is in mid-Atlantic, as it is much better to go in the circulation around its top rather than through the calm center. In a transatlantic race from Bermuda to Spain a few years ago, a fifty-footer that went around the top of the Azores High beat, boat for boat, a maxi that tried to take a straight rhumb line through the center of it.

North Atlantic

Crossing the North Atlantic from North America to Europe is relatively easy eastbound, with June the most popular month for doing it. The prevailing westerlies help, the Gulf Stream can be used, and the main problems are fog and, if going far enough north, icebergs. To sail westbound across the North Atlantic at these same latitudes is folly and is not done very often except in some of the stunt events like single-handed races. The cruising sailor is much wiser to take the great circle south via the trade wind latitudes to the Caribbean, or at least the Bahamas.

Around the World

The really ambitious long-voyagers who set off around the world have quite a few decisions to make. There is a great variation in routes, and the basic one is whether to go via the canals (Panama and Suez) or the capes (Horn and Good Hope) or a combination. The cape route is a real challenge, dramatized by the various around-the-world races for both crewed boats and single-handers that are held every so often. The more sensible choice on the Cape route is east-about in the prevailing breezes, but there are those hardy souls who have done it the other way, where the Horn is a particularly thorny challenge: Just read accounts of the old clipper ship passages.

There are also drawbacks to the canal route, with Panama having been unsettled recently and not half as hospitable to passaging yachtsmen as it used to be, and the Red Sea is a real bugaboo on the Suez route. It is physically difficult with its wind patterns and reef-lined shores, and considering the instability in the Middle East and the lack of security for the lone yacht, it is definitely a hazardous area. I have seen it from the deck of a ship in February when the weather was absolutely perfect, but the tales of those who have managed to negotiate it are not confidence inspiring. The best advice seems to be to cruise in company with one or more other yachts.

In taking the longer route across the Indian Ocean to South Africa, there is an awful lot of lonely sailing to do, and the southeast coast of Africa approaching Good Hope is an area of treacherous strong currents and mammoth seas. There is also the political problem in South Africa, but visiting yachtsmen are usually greeted hospitably by kindred souls among South African yachtsmen. It is then a long, lonely passage up the South Atlantic to Brazil, with fighting through the doldrums a major problem. Still, there is a cachet to having sailed around the world that attracts the adventurous in considerable numbers, and the practice continues.

We once had a rendezvous in the Virgins with friends who had just completed a three-year passage around the world via Panama and Good Hope, in which they took their time, broke up the schedule with flying visits home, and alternated crews, and the skipper was still chuckling over the fact that the only hard-on-the-wind leg they had in the whole circumnavigation was from Antigua to the Virgins when the trade was blowing strongly from well up in the northeast.

The Pacific

The Pacific is a vast playground for the long-voyager, and one of the major magnets for the adventurous. While the Caribbean has similar charms in a comparatively compact area that has mostly become highly civilized, the Pacific still has unspoiled areas spread out over an immense seascape, and it takes a different approach and a different kind of planning from operating to and in the Caribbean.

From the Caribbean and Panama, the classic route into the Pacific goes out across the equator to the Marquesas, Tuamotus, and Society islands. It is about forty-eight hundred miles from Panama to Tahiti, and this is one of the loneliest stretches of ocean in the world. I made the passage in my subchaser in 1943, and it was a frustrating feeling to sit on the flying bridge and watch the neat procession of trade wind waves and clouds marching in from the southeast on a perfect angle for a broad reach and have the diesel exhaust blowing up on the breeze to where I sat. It would have been perfect sailing once out of the Gulf of Panama, which, as noted on the *Sea Cloud* cruise, is an area of doldrums and vagrant squalls. In a sailing yacht it is a trying area, difficult to fight through.

Also, when we developed a mysterious leak, which I thought was hull damage but turned out to be from a missing plug in the seawater cooling system, I began to wonder about haul-out facilities. Studying the chart, I realized, when halfway between the Galapagos and Marquesas, that this seemed to be a stretch of ocean that was farther from land of any description than anywhere else in the world.

Because of excessive red tape, as mentioned, not many yachts stop in the Galapagos anymore, so the Marquesas offer the first haven on the route. I have not been there, but from all reports they are beautiful, relatively unspoiled, but without really good anchorages or facilities. The Tuamotus are a severe challenge in navigation and piloting because of their low profiles and unpredictable currents, but they are well worth visiting.

Tahiti, as explained in Chapter 18, has become a sad excuse for a tropical paradise, but the surrounding islands still have great charm and provide delightful cruising. A problem here is a recent decision by the French government to limit foreign boats to a six-month stay in the territory. Many long-voyagers used to use Tahiti as a break point in a world cruise, laying up for a while, but that is not possible at present writing. To avoid being at sea in the hurricane season here, known as the cyclone season, American Samoa has become a favorite layover spot, although Pago Pago does not have much to recommend it in the way of South Sea island charm.

West of the Society Islands there is a vast choice of archipelagos for exploring, some completely primitive, some quite developed. Most popular, and offering charter possibilities, are Tonga and Fiji.

Into the Indian Ocean

For world voyagers, the passage out of the Pacific to the Indian Ocean calls for a choice. The classic route is via the Torres Strait across the top of Australia to the Arafura and Timor Seas and on to the idyllic Cocos Islands at longitude 100° east after a stop at Darwin at the northwest tip of Australia. Instead of heading out into the Indian Ocean from the Timor Sea, voyagers have gone into the Java Sea via Flores, or the Lombok Strait at Bali, and north of the big islands of Indonesia to Singapore and perhaps up to Phuket before heading across the Indian Ocean.

That gives more opportunity for visiting islands and ports of exotic reputation. The right monsoon season is important.

Another route taken by slow-moving explorers is to cruise the north coast of New Guinea westward into the Moluccas. It provides fascinating glimpses of a still-primitive world, with some legitimate concern for security as a drawback. I can attest, from wartime duty, that the north coast of New Guinea is spectacularly scenic.

East in the Pacific

For long-voyagers who get to the South Pacific but do not want to go on around the world and endure the long, lonely passages involved, the best route back to the Americas is a problem. I have friends in the Virgins who brought a schooner there from New Zealand directly into the trade winds, a long and arduous passage that they did mostly under power, with extra drums of fuel on deck keeping them going. The Swan 65 *Tangaroa,* which I mentioned in Chapter 17 as on her way from New Zealand to the Caribbean, was following a sailing route through Tonga to Tahiti and then southeastward down to Easter Island, where she would pick up the southeast trade and Humboldt Current for a favorable lift up to Panama.

The alternative is to sail northward in the Pacific in a great circle route back to Hawaii, but this ends up in cold weather and with many long passages between isolated islands. Hawaii is, of course, a favorite target for long-voyagers from the West Coast, who can get there easily on a trade wind slide, exemplified by the downwind conditions of the biennial Transpac Race. If they are heading south to the tropical islands below the equator, there is then a lot of windward work and a session with the doldrums. To get back to the States from Hawaii, the drill is to head northeast to get above the big Pacific High that is almost permanently in position between southern California and Hawaii, until its reverse circulation is reached, providing westerlies.

Perhaps Slocum's world has shrunk, and it is much more familiar, but there is still room for much passaging.

22

▶ ▶ ▶ ▶ ▶ ▶ ▶ ▶ ▶ ▶ ▶ ▶ ▶ ▶

HOW TO ARRANGE
CHARTERS

From the preceding chapters, it is certainly obvious that chartering has become a major factor in worldwide cruising. Almost every area covered has organized chartering of some sort, providing all sorts of opportunities for vacationing sailors who had previously been limited to home waters. We have done a great amount of sailing in charter yachts in covering these areas, the number-one means we have had for getting to know such a variety of cruising grounds, and some thoughts on the practice are in order.

There are three types of chartering. By far the most popular now, and the major one for opening up new areas, is the commercial bareboat fleet. There are variations in this that will be discussed. Another form of bareboating is the individual charter of privately owned boats. This is done most often in areas with a relatively short season, where it is not practical for a commercial fleet to set up shop. The third method is the crewed charter yacht, where the charterers are treated as "hotel guests," pampered in relative luxury.

Arranging a charter with a commercial bareboat fleet is done directly with the operating company, as yacht brokers do not handle this type of business. However, yacht brokers are the key to the individual bareboat charter and the crewed charter. It is their business to know the boats they are handling and to suit the customer to the proper boat.

Bareboat fleets are a relatively recent phenomenon. Our first bareboat charter was in the Virgin Islands in 1966, when there were eleven boats available out of St. Thomas. It was a group of "one-off" boats, with no standardization. We made our own travel arrangements and did our own provision shopping in St. Thomas markets, and when it came time to turn the boat in, the local agent was nowhere to be found. None of this stopped us from having a fine time, which I wrote up in *Yachting*. Soon afterward I got a call from a man who introduced himself as Dr. John Van Ost, a dentist from Tenafly, New Jersey. He said, having read my article, that he thought there was an opportunity for an organized, standardized commercially operated fleet, and I agreed with him. The upshot was his establishment of CSY, the pioneer in the business, soon followed by The Moorings, and then, over the years, by many more entrepreneurs.

There are pitfalls and perils in such an operation, with early mistakes inevitable. They found that it was impractical to move boats north and south by the season. There were some false starts in developing standardized boats, and in the methods to sell them to private owners and operate them. Changes in tax laws over the years also forced changes in this setup. It was found that operating in the Bahamas did not work because of local political problems and because of the lay of the land. For example, George Town at the bottom of the Exuma chain seemed like a logical base for Exuman operations, but a twenty-mile beat in the open waters of Exuma Sound made a rugged ordeal of getting the boat back to base, upset scheduling, and actually caused some accidents.

Through all the ups and downs, the concept of commercially operated bareboat fleets caught on rapidly. The Virgins, both American and British, became the bareboat capital of world sailing, and the idea spread all over the globe. It is now a major element of the yachting world, with practices that have become standardized and are now widely accepted. From an original emphasis on simplicity to avoid breakdowns, competition has brought promotion of added amenities like microwaves, TVs and VCRS, cellular phones, and all sorts of other electronic marvels.

Speaking of simplicity, it is important to keep luggage and clothing to a minimum. Everyone tends to bring too much.

When you book with a fleet operator, in most cases the only thing you do on your own is get to the airport of origination. Most companies have their own travel bureau, or an arrangement with one, and air transportation can be arranged to fit in with the cruising schedule, often at favorable rates. You are met on arrival and taxied to the charter base, and, if need be, a hotel room is arranged for the first night. Provisioning of food and liquor is arranged ahead of time with the company's own commissary department, and this has grown into one of the major selling points. The food is almost universally top quality, and of course a day is saved that would otherwise be spent in shopping in strange markets.

Most charterers order partial provisioning, as part of the fun of a cruise is eating ashore when the opportunity presents. This is both an adventure and a break for the cook, who is usually "Mom" and does not consider it a vacation if she spends all her time in the galley. The number of restaurants available to eat at when ashore varies from place to place. When we first sailed in the British Virgins in 1964 there was one restaurant open to visiting yachtsmen, Marina Cay. Now a couple of weeks could be spent with a different place to eat every night. In contrast, Desolation Sound has none, and in Tonga the only shore meal we had was a specially prepared "luau" held once a week for people from boats.

The bareboat cruise starts with a thorough briefing at the company's base, usually full of good advice, and the boat is then checked out with a staff member. Provisions are piled in the main cabin so that the charterer can stow them and know where everything is. This looks like a daunting chore, but it is a good practice. Guidebooks and charts are, of course, provided, as is snorkeling gear, and boardboats can be rented.

Some bareboat companies offer "cruise and learn" programs, which can be a good way for beginners to break in. Another variation on straight bareboating, where the crew is in complete command of its own destiny, is to have a professional aboard from the company staff. This is not the same as being on a crewed charter, as the charter party still is responsible for galley operations and must participate physically in running the boat. The pro is along for local knowledge and to help if seamanship or piloting is a problem. As mentioned, I have enjoyed having pros like Basil Hazell in the Grenadines or Jean-Pierre Deval in the Iles sous le Vent for their local knowledge (and, it must be admitted, to work the anchor!). This can be a very good solution for charterers who are not completely confident in their abilities, or who only have one experienced sailor in a group of four or six, without having to pay the extra costs of a fully crewed charter.

If a bareboat company does not follow all these outlined procedures they usually do not stay in business long, and many companies have come and gone over the years.

As I have said, the yacht broker is the key to the individual bareboat charter and the crewed operations. They do not handle the fleet boats, as the operators prefer to do their own booking, act as their own agents, and not give commissions. In cases where a yacht broker is involved, the boat owner pays the commission. It is not charged to the client.

Chartering a private boat on a bareboat basis can be a tricky business unless the broker is familiar with the boat and its owner, and has a good idea of the abilities of the charterer. Unless a boat is well maintained and equipped, it should not be placed on charter, and the checking-out process with the charterer, either by the owner (preferably) or the broker, should be done very carefully. An owner tends to react as though his daughter were being raped when his pride and joy goes out on charter, and the process must be done carefully and correctly. The charterer has an obligation, not so important in commercial bareboating where clean-up crews operate, to turn the boat back in clean, shipshape condition, making a report on any gear that needs to be attended to.

Crewed chartering, which should be equated in cost to staying in a first-rate resort hotel, can be a wonderfully relaxing vacation, and, if the crew is good at its business, a stimulating and rewarding sailing and travel experience. The charter party can choose its own degree of involvement. If the choice is to loll in deck chairs and not lift a finger, that is a prerogative, but the crew will usually welcome some degree of participation in sail handling and steering, according to the charterer's desires and abilities. The big plus is in the galley department, where the

Sailing on a crewed charter; Stormvogel *in the Andaman Sea*

well-organized charter crew will make every effort to excel, and the guests are not expected to do anything but eat.

Most charter yachts are now equipped with all sorts of extras and fancy goodies, like video cameras to film a day's activities and then view the results in the main cabin in the evening, as well as Windsurfers, snorkeling equipment, and sometimes even water skis. Usually arrangements for Scuba diving must be made specially. If a yacht does not have Scuba gear, most areas have dive-boat operations, and a day's activity can be arranged, with a pickup directly from the yacht.

Yacht brokers become familiar with the boats they handle at specially arranged shows, usually held in late fall. Boats in a given area, such as the Virgins, Antigua, the Aegean, or other popular grounds, collect at one marina for several days and brokers come in from all directions to visit the boats and get to know the crews. It has developed that almost every yacht broker specializing in chartering is female, and these women do a thorough, conscientious job of casing the fleet. I have been to several of the shows, and it is amazing to see the amount of legwork and research that the brokers do. I remember one earnest broker who had a long list of questions on her pad as she put crew members through a real catechism, not only on their nautical background and abilities, but on their personalities and preferences.

Talking to a French captain, whose command of English was perhaps less than complete, she asked, pencil poised, "What are your hobbies and special interests? Do you like books, tennis, music, skiing?"

Looking a bit confused, the captain hesitated for a moment and then said slowly, "I like boats; I like women . . ." finishing with a Gallic shrug.

The hard work of these shows pays off, to the customer's benefit, and a competent broker is able to use personal knowledge to recommend a yacht in most of the popular areas worldwide. In an area where language may be a difficulty, as in the Aegean, or where local conditions are very special, as in Phuket, it is a very smart idea to take advantage of the professional abilities of a charter crew.

23

▶ ▶ ▶ ▶ ▶ ▶ ▶ ▶ ▶ ▶ ▶ ▶ ▶ ▶

PERSONAL OPINIONS
Boats and Rigs

In the roughly sixty years that I have been cruising, there have naturally been a great many boats of all shapes and sizes, borrowed, chartered or as a guest aboard, plus the boats I have owned myself, and this experience has inevitably led to the formation of some opinions. What it has also taught me is that those opinions, which I consider very well taken and thought out, are often completely disagreed with by sailors of equal experience. To play on an old gag, one man's must is another man's Pearson, and there is certainly room for varying opinions. If there were not, we could all have exactly the same boat. Now wouldn't that be something? If the good Lord meant us to have it that way, he wouldn't have given us naval architects.

Just in the chapters in this book, it is evident what wide variations there are in boats that can provide a successful cruise. The key, to me, is to analyze what best suits an owner's personal needs: what conditions the boat is to be used in, in what way it will be used, and, oh yes—finances. So many sad stories have resulted from someone overstepping what they can afford, from Donald Trump's *Princess* right on down. Operating expenses as well as original cost have to be considered. We had a period, when all three offspring were college age, when we had to cut back from a small cruising boat to an eighteen-foot catboat. (By the way, we liked the catboat, a Sanderling, so much for day sailing at home and overnighting that we still have her a quarter century later.)

Over the years, there have been developments in materials and equipment that have had the effect of changing thinking on what a boat is capable of and how it can be used. From wood to fiberglass and aluminum, from cotton to synthetics, from gas to diesel, from simple battery-operated equipment to sophisticated electronics, from eyeballing and sextant to radar and satellite navigation, the world of cruising sailboats has gone through amazing developments that have helped to change thinking and operations.

One's own age is another factor. When I got my first cruising boat, a twenty-four-foot Amphibi-Ette light-displacement sloop in my late thirties, I wanted to race as well as cruise, and we spent a lot of time and effort at both. She was trailerable, which opened up all sorts of possibilities, and we took her to Florida (and on to the Bahamas), the Great Lakes, Maine, and southern New England by road. It would have taken weeks (which were not available) to get her there on her own bottom, so we had full time available for actually cruising in a variety of waters. Trailing was work, in preparation and execution, which was fine when I was young and eager, but something I would not want to take on in later years.

It was a step up to an Out Island 36 when college tuition was no longer a factor. And, incidentally, I financed her, *Tanagra,* by recasting the mortgage on our house in those days of increasing real estate values. This worked out well, but I have never been able to convince Jane that the boat didn't really cost us anything! No longer racing-oriented, we enjoyed her for comfortable coastal cruising between Cape Cod and the Bahamas, and she was a well set up boat for entertaining friends and a now-adult family.

When we decided to branch out to Caribbean operations in semi and then full retirement, we wanted something a bit roomier and more ruggedly built for living aboard and offshore operations, and the CSY 37 *Brunelle* was the answer. In nine seasons of living aboard for as long as five months a winter, ranging from Florida to Grenada and the islands in between, we came to know her very well, firming up certain opinions, and I will point them up later.

All these boats were for coastal or Caribbean cruising, not intended for long passages, and I recognize that there is a separate breed of sailor, which I have never been, who likes long offshore passages across wide oceans for days and weeks on end. This different breed of sailor calls for a different type of boat, where self-steering, ruggedness of equipment, and seakeeping qualities are of paramount importance. When I meet them in some distant glamor area where I am enjoying a pleasant day-by-day, anchorage-to-anchorage cruise, I admire their feats and enjoy talking to them and listening to their tales, but I am happy to have had my long voyages by subchaser, the Bermuda Race, and *Sea Cloud*.

Over the years, there has been an interesting metamorphosis in bareboats. As pointed out in the previous chapter, they now have much more sophisticated equipment. I have always been of the opinion that the more gear there is on a boat, the more there is to go wrong and to need maintenance; I have never been on anything bigger than a rowboat, that had any kind of mechanical or electrical equipment, where everything on board was in working condition. This has always been true on boats with fuel gauges—I have never seen a fuel gauge on an auxiliary that worked. However, the competition in the bareboat trade has produced these "improvements."

Early bareboats were built to be strong, simple, and easy to maintain, and their sails were usually cast-iron bedsheets with no shape and no battens. Competition has, again, done away with this concept, and there has been an increasing trend toward speed in the bareboat fleets. The price to be paid here is in ease of handling sails. More speed usually means bigger jibs, fine for racing, but a flogging nuisance in a charter boat when the wind begins to pipe up.

The question of rig is another one where opinions vary.

I am of the opinion that under the mid-forties in overall length, a divided rig is not worth it. There is increased cost in spar, rigging and sail inventory, crowding in the cockpit, and lessening performance, at least on the wind. The main advantage is in ease of reducing sail to "jib and jigger" if it breezes on, and in added sail area with a mizzen staysail downwind, but these are not worth the disadvantages and can be handled in other ways in a single-sticker. The above refers to the ketch rig. The schooner rig is seldom seen, especially in bareboats, and is a special case for traditionalists who get a kick out of being under it.

Hull form and displacement are other areas for argument. Fortunately, the type of light displacement, fin keel, blade rudder boats fostered by the IOR rule for measuring race boats, is pretty well disappearing and was never a favorite for cruising. Skittish and requiring careful concentration on the wheel every moment, they were everything a good sailboat should not be. To make cruising a pleasure, a boat should be sea kindly, easy of motion, and dry, and should track and steer well. A momentary lapse in steering to pick up the binoculars or look at the chart should not be cause for a 180 degree wipeout. A long keel with attached rudder, or rudder on a skeg, is the answer.

In a great variety of boats it is amazing how many little glitches and imperfections that seem obvious when you are shipmates with them have been allowed to exist. A few examples include the placing of the stove so that you have to reach across it to get to the galley sink, at peril of armpit; or locating the galley on a thwartships shelf right below the ladder from the cockpit (anyone using the ladder would be liable to kick the cook in the face or step in the salad bowl). And I have seen engine instruments located belowdecks, engine controls down at foot level in the cockpit, and separate clutch and throttle located so that the helmsman had to reach through a large steering wheel to handle them.

Bunk placement is often poorly thought out, and a major and frequent sin is the jamming of too many bunks into a boat for its size so that it can be sold as a "seven-sleeper" or whatever. Heads in which men cannot stand up facing the bowl, both heads on one side of a boat with two (*Brunelle*'s only real fault), and not enough turning-around room in a head are other lapses. Reading lights for bunks is an amenity I really miss.

A major mistake, especially in a boat that is to be used for charter, is to skimp on cockpit space to make more room below. While cruising, a large percentage of the crew's waking hours is spent in the cockpit, and it should be made as comfortable as possible, with leg room, good backrests, and a place to brace feet. A good cockpit table and easily handled night lighting are other important points. Operating in the Caribbean in *Brunelle,* we ate less than twenty meals below in all our years of sailing her, and cockpit living was the key to cruising pleasure.

Since it is impossible to please everyone's varying demands in one boat, there is no way of coming up with an ideal one, but there are some standards, especially in charter boats, that should be considered, and racing success is not a factor, though adequately satisfying sailing performance should be.

A good bareboat should have private cabins for the number of couples expected aboard (two, four, or six people) each with private head, and the cabins should be equal in space and comfort: no fighting for the royal suite. It should have a galley laid out so that more than one person can work in it at a time, and, if possible, a wet bar that does not compete with galley operations. The cockpit should be roomy and comfortable, with a good table setup, and, in almost all cruising areas, have good shade from a Bimini and drop curtains. It is a nice touch to have a swimming ladder with accompanying shower nozzle built into the transom (also a safety factor in case of man overboard). In my book, the fancy electronics are an unnecessary extra, but there seems to be a demand for them.

The rig should be easily handled, with jiffy reefing on the main, roller furling on the jib, and, to my mind, should have a divided headrig instead of one large genoa so that area can quickly be reduced to just a staysail. There has been a recent trend to full battened mains with lazy jacks, and it is handy when dousing sail. The sail settles easily onto the boom, held in place by the lazy jacks, and does not need immediate attention if there are other things to be done. A drawback is in hoisting the main, as the sail must be precisely into the wind, or the battens will foul on the lazy jacks. This is not a problem when the boat can be steered into the wind, but if it cannot be, and the boom has to be let out to get the right angle, it can be a tricky operation. Some boats are now being equipped with easy-furl attachments, lines rigged through the sail to the leech that bring it down to the boom under control.

There is divided thought on rear cockpit versus center cockpit, and good points can be made for both. To me, the main advantage of the center cockpit is increased privacy through separating the cabins, but I have seen some boats that ruin this advantage by having a walk-through between the cabins, badly reducing cockpit space. A boat must be good-sized, close to fifty feet and up, to have a walk-through that does not do this. A walk-through also often hampers access to the engine.

In crewed yachts, there is such a variety in size and function that it is impossible to have one set of standards, and it is actually the crew that makes the difference in most cases. Their ability to make the guests feel relaxed, to cater to their needs and desires without a fuss, and to do a good nautical job of seamanship and picking the right anchorages and routes, is all-important. We have never had an unpleasant experience in a crewed yacht, and when you have eager, active young sailors and an excellent cook, like those on *Singa, Stormvogel,* and *Raden Mas,* the rewards can be great. One factor that is important here, too, is equal cabins.

As for *Brunelle* and why she suited us well, here is a brief analysis. First of all, she was extremely well built, which gave a special feeling of confidence. She was small enough for Jane and me to handle her by ourselves in day-time cruising. She was a good sea boat, very dry and able, and sailed well on all points, though not at racing speeds. In other words, she inspired confidence.

Her layout, which had a cabin forward, made up as either

Brunelle *worked out very well for her intended purpose; under way off Great Caminoe, British Virgins*

twin bunks or a double, with head; a small saloon with upper and lower bunks and a dinette amidships; an enclosed double cabin and head aft to port; and the refrigerator and galley to starboard, was comfortable and private. We only had more than four aboard on rare occasions, though the bunk space was fine for six. The cockpit was extremely comfortable, as was the helmsman's seat, though a minor drawback was visibility forward due to her raised deck construction.

There was good engine access to the 40-horsepower Westerbeke under the cockpit due to V-drive gearing, locker space was ample in the cockpit, and the bow-chocked 35-pound plow anchor was easy to handle. We started with a windlass but it blew fuses more often than not, and I scrapped it.

The rig proved ideal for our purposes. The 365-foot main was easy to handle, with a gallows frame a great plus in lowering it, and I could put in a jiffy reef by myself in about a minute. A special joy was the double headrig, with a high-cut roller-farling Yankee jib and a boomed staysail. With the ease of jiffy reefing the main and the choice of headsail, we had multiple combinations for handling varying wind strengths. She was a very stiff boat and could take up to the mid-30-knot range easily under staysail and full main. For more fun downwind, we had a Flasher, a poleless spinnaker that added greatly to performance and enjoyment in winds up to 15 knots from abeam to broad on the quarter.

Every inch of her was a compromise of some sort, and what boat isn't, but, after all the boats we had sailed in over the years under so many different conditions in so many different areas, she seemed to combine the features we wanted in a boat that was suited to the area we wanted to be in, and she did well by us over many many miles.

I guess that's what successful cruising is all about.

BIBLIOGRAPHY

Caribbean Cruising Handbook. Bill Robinson. G. P. Putnam, 1986.

Compleat Guide to Nassau, The. Steve Dodge. White Sound, 1987.

Cruising Cape Breton. Spray Magazine, Suite 102, 1127 Barrington St., Halifax, Nova Scotia, Canada B3H 2P8.

Cruising Guide to the Bay Islands of Honduras. Julius M. Wilensky. Wescott Cove, 1979.

Cruising Guide to California's Channel Islands. Brian M. Fagan. Western Marine Ent., 1983.

Cruising Guide to the Chesapeake. William T. Stone. Dodd, Mead & Co., 1983.

Cruising Guide to Coastal North Carolina. Claiborne Young. Blair, 1983.

Cruising Guide to Coastal South Carolina. Claiborne Young. Blair, 1985.

Cruising Guide to the Florida Keys. Frank Papys. Cy de Cosse, 1983.

Cruising Guide to the Great Lakes and Their Connecting Waterways. Marjorie C. Brazer. Contemporary Books, 1985.

Cruising Guide to Lake Champlain. Alan and Susan McKibben. Lake Champlain Publishing Co., Vermont.

Cruising Guide to the Leeward Islands. Chris Doyle. Cruising Guides, 1989.

Cruising Guide to Maine, Volume I: Kittery to Rockland. Don Johnson. Wescott Cove, 1986.

Cruising Guide to Maine, Volume II: Rockport to Eastport. Don Johnson. Wescott Cove, 1987.

Cruising Guide to the New England Coast. Roger Duncan and John P. Ware. Dodd, Mead & Co., 1983.

Cruising Guide to the Sea of Cortez: From La Paz to Mulege. Simon and Nancy Scott. Cruising Guides, 1988.

Cruising Guide to the Turquoise Coast of Turkey. Marcia Davock. Wescott Cove, 1989.

Cruising Guide to the Virgin Islands. Nancy and Simon Scott. Cruising Guides, 1988.

Cruising the Pacific Coast. Carolyn and Jack West. Pacific Search, 1984.

Cruising Guide to Tahiti and the French Society Islands. Marcia Davock. Wescott Cove, 1985.

Department of Development and Tourism, Box 2016, St. John's, Newfoundland, Canada, A1C 5R8.

Inland Waterways of France. David Edwards-May. Imray, Laurie, Norie & Wilson, 1984.

The Intracoastal Waterway. Jan and Bill Moeller. Seven Seas, 1986.

Landfalls of Paradise: The Guide to Pacific Islands. Earl R. Hinz. Western Marine Ent., 1988.

The Last Navigator. Stephen D. Thomas. Ballantine, 1988.

Mediterranean Cruising Handbook. Rod Heikell. State Mutual Books, 1986.

New Zealand's Bay of Islands. Claire Jones. Port of Opua Trading Co. Ltd., Opua, New Zealand.

North Sea Harbors and Pilotage: Calais to Den Helder. Jack Coote. Sheridan.

Over the Horizon. Bill Robinson. Van Nostrand, 1966.

Pacific Boating Almanac 1989: Northern California & Nevada. Peter L. Griffes. Western Marine Ent., 1988.

Pacific Boating Almanac 1989: Pacific Northwest & Alaska. Peter L. Griffes. Western Marine Ent., 1988.

Pacific Yachting's Cruising Guide to British Columbia, Volume II: Desolation Sound to Discovery Island. Don Watmough. Pacific Yachting Publishers. Vancouver, Canada.

Pacific Yachting's Cruising Guide to British Columbia, Volume IV: The West Coast of Vancouver Island. Don Watmough. Pacific Yachting Publishers. Vancouver, Canada.

St. Maarten/St. Martin Area + St. Kitts and Nevis. William J. Eiman, editor. VIP Charters, Philadelphia, Pa.

St. Vincent and the Grenadines: A Plural Country. Jill Bobrow and Dana Jinkins. W. W. Norton & Co., 1985.

South to the Caribbean: How to Carry Out the Dream of Sailing Your Own Boat to the Caribbean. Bill Robinson. W. W. Norton & Co., 1982.

Street's Cruising Guide to the Eastern Caribbean, Volumes I–IV. Donald M. Street, Jr. W. W. Norton & Co.

Virgin Anchorages. Simon and Nancy Scott. Cruising Guides, 1988.

Waterway Guide: Great Lakes Edition. Judith Powers, editor. Commercial Channels, 1990.

Where to Cruise. Bill Robinson. W. W. Norton & Co., 1984.

Yachtsman's Guide to the Bahamas. Meredith Fields, editor. Tropic Isle Publishers, 1989.

Yachtsman's Guide to the Virgin Islands. Meredith Fields, editor. Tropic Isle Publishers, 1989.

INDEX

Abacos, 150, 154, 155, 157, 160
Academy Bay, 222–223
Aegean cruises, 91–102, 288
Aegean Rally, 92, 96, 139
Allan's Cay, 152, 153
Anclote Keys, 113
Andros, 150
Anegada Passage, 171, 180, 209
Angel Island, 128
Anguilla, 179
Anguillita, 179, 181, 182
Annapolis, 106, 110, 111–112, 123, 124
Anse d'Arlet, 191, 192
Antigua, 159, 186, 195–197, 208, 280, 288
Apooiti Marina, 230, 231, 238
Asia Islands Yacht Charters, 258

Baccalieu Island, 35
Back Bay, 108
Baddeck, 36
Bahamas, 147–160, 276, 290
Baja California, 134
Banks, Joseph, 239–242
Bartlett, Bob, 37
Bay of Biscay, 86, 87, 88, 277
Bay of Faleron, 91
Bay of Islands, 239–255
Beneteau, 51, 227, 230–231
Bequia, 188, 200, 206, 207
Bermuda, 274–275, 278
Bermuda Races, 263, 274–275, 291
Berry Islands, 150, 154–157
Bitter End Yacht Club, 169–171, 173
Bliss, Dan, 52, 55, 60, 161, 163, 166, 191,
    227, 229, 231, 232, 233, 234
Bliss, Martha, 52, 161, 191, 227, 229, 232,
    233, 234
Bobby's Marina, 175, 177, 185
Boll, Carl, 31, 33
Boll, Shirley, 31, 35
Bonavista Bay, 32
Bonavista Harbour, 29, 32
Bora Bora, 227–238, 253–254
Bras d'Or Lake, 51

British Columbia, 23, 27
British Harbour, 31, 32, 33
British Virgin Islands, 161–176, 189, 199,
    208, 216, 285
Brown, Warren, 96
Brunelle, 113–114, 118, 147, 148, 172, 175,
    177, 191, 193, 197, 208, 216, 276, 291,
    293, 294–295
Brun-Lie, Arne, 63, 67, 70, 71–72
Brun-Lie, Ellen, 63, 67, 70
Buccaneer Marina, 121
Buckley, Bill, 219
Burnham-on-Crouch, 85–86, 87
Buzzards Bay, 41, 42, 44, 50, 199

Cabot, John, 32
Caicos, 157, 276
Cape Bonavista, 29, 38
Cape Breton Island, 36
Cape Brett, 249–251
Cape Cod, 41–48, 290
Carbonear, 36, 37
Caribbean, 207–213
    see also specific islands
Cassel Lake, 24–25
Cassidy, Cas, 93, 220
Catalina, 125, 131–132, 133, 134, 135
Charles Darwin Research Station, 222
Chesapeake Bay, 103–112, 274
Chubb, Percy, 174
Clark, Henry, 52, 53
Cloud Room, 173
Coast Mountains, 17, 26
Columbia, 50, 108
Columbia River, 28
Commencement Bay, 28
Conception Bay, 35, 36, 37
Conyers, Jean, 186, 197
Conyers, Nev, 186, 197
Cook, James, 18, 218, 239–242, 246, 247,
    249, 252
Coronados, 130, 131
Cortes Island, 22
Crab Creek, 110

Cruising Club of America, 31, 32, 36, 111, 174, 206
Cruising Club of Australia, 137
Cruising World, 18, 242
CSY, 284
CSY 37, 113, 163, 291
CSY 42, 163, 199, 210
CSY 44, 115
Cuttyhunk, 43, 47

Daley, Charles, 264, 265, 266, 267
Dalmatian Coast, 101, 102
Deception Pass, 27
Delaware Canal, 108
Desolation Sound, 17, 18–26, 28, 79, 285
DeSoto Point, 120
Deval, Jean-Pierre, 227, 229, 232–233, 236, 238, 286
Dominica, 192–194
Doniger, Bill, 163, 164, 166, 171
Douglas, Brian, 245, 246, 252
Dutch Harbor, 42

East Bay Marina, 148
Easter Island, 93, 214–226, 282
Eastern Shore, 110–111
Edam, 85
Edgartown, 44, 50
Effie Morrisey, 37
Egmont Channel, 120
Eleuthera, 150, 152, 157
Elizabeth Islands, 43, 47
*Elizabeth*³, 52–54, 59
El Niño Current, 254
English Channel, 86, 277
English Harbour, 196–197
Ensenada Race, 125, 129–130
Erie Canal, 61
Esperance, 227, 230, 238
Exumas, 148, 150, 152–153, 155, 157, 198, 284
Eye-deans, 139–140, 144

Faaroa Bay, 235–236
Family Islands, 147, 150, 159
Ferner, Finn, 63, 67, 71
Ferner, Monk, 63, 67, 70
Ferron, Robbie, 175
Fidalgo Island, 27
Fidelity, 29, 31, 35, 36
Florida, 113–124, 154
Friday Harbor, 18, 28
Fyn Archipelago, 75

Gagnebin, Al, 200, 207
Gagnebin, Genevieve, 200, 207
Galapagos, 93, 214–226, 253, 254, 280–281
Galesville, 106, 110, 123
George Town, 160, 284
Gibson Island, 107
Gibsons, 26
God's Cove, 33–34
Grates Point, 35
Gray, Jim, 18, 20, 22, 25
Great Bahama Bank, 150, 153, 157
Great Barrier Reef, 140, 141, 243, 254
Great Lakes, 52, 61, 62
Green Cay, 184
Grenada, 189

Grenadines, 79, 148, 189, 191, 198–213, 231, 286
Gretel, 137–139
Guadeloupe, 194, 195
Gulf Islands, 28
Gulf of California, 131, 134
Gumbs, Emile, 180–181

Haight, Debbie, 18, 20, 22
Haight, Jack, 18, 20, 22
Hamburgsund, 67
Hampton Roads, 105, 106, 108, 111, 123
Hanga Roa, 217, 218
Hankø, 63
Harbour Grace, 37
Havre de Grace, 37, 105–106
Havstenssund, 67
Hawaii, 282
Hawkesbury River, 141
Hazelett, Bill, 55, 56, 57
Hazell, Basil, 200–202, 204, 205, 231, 286
Helios, 163, 165, 174, 199, 210
Heyerdahl, Thor, 217, 220
Highborne Cay, 152–153
Highland Lakes, 61
Hirst, Kevin, 252
Holland, 76–88, 128
Holman, Betsy, 188
Horizons, 106, 111
Howe Sound, 17, 26, 28
Howland's Cove, 133
Huaraki Gulf, 243
Hydra, 92, 96–98, 99, 101
Hylas, 47, 258

Ile Pinels, 184
Iles sous le Vent, 230, 254, 255, 286
Indian Ocean cruises, 281–282
Inland Waterway Guide, 108
Inside Passage to Alaska, 19, 28
Intracoastal Waterway (ICW), 25, 80, 105, 108, 111, 113, 115, 118, 121–124, 148, 154, 275–276
Intrepid, 59
Invictus IV, 18, 20, 22
Ireland, 87
Ireland's Eye, 33
Isla Margarita, 212
Isle of Wight, 87
Isselmeer, 83–85
Isthmus, The, 131

James Cove, 37
Japan Current, 27
Jervis Inlet, 17
Jervis Sound, 28
Job's Cove, 36
Juliana, 76, 81

Kaag, 81–83
Kozad, Tony, 258, 266–269
Kozad, Tulimah, 258, 261, 263, 266, 267
Kragerø, 70
Kristiansand, 68, 72
Kusadasi, 94, 101

Lake Champlain, 52–62
Lake Lanier, 62
Lake of the Ozarks, 62

Lake Texoma, 61
Lapworth, Bill, 132, 133, 134
Lapworth, Peg, 133
Legakis, George, 96, 245
Legendary Yachts (Robinson), 220
Lesser Antilles, 186–197
Leverick Bay, 169
Lewis Channel, 22–23
Lindeman, Connie, 206
Lindeman, Neil, 206
Lindos, 94, 95
Linge, Jan, 63
Little Harbor, 174
Little Wicomico River, 108
Long Island cruising, 274
Long Island Sound, 42, 50, 51
Long Pond, 36
Lovenskiold, Severin, 18, 19, 20, 22
Lyford Cay, 149, 154

Mallett's Bay, 57–58
Manatee River, 120, 121
Mandraki Harbor, 93, 95–96
Mara Maru, 18, 22, 23
Marble Island, 58, 59
Mar Claro, 43–44, 46, 147
Marigot, 178, 182
Marina Cay, 167–168
Marstrand, 67, 74
Martha's Vineyard, 41, 42, 43
Martinique, 191, 278
Massachusetts Bay, 41
Mayreau, 202
Mediterranean cruising, 99–102
Mexico, 125, 129–130, 134–135, 212
Middle Harbor, 141–142
Millar, Graham, 256
Millar, Judy, 256
Minchin Cove, 31, 32
Minis, Dolly, 175, 178, 181, 182, 191, 197
Minis, Phil, 175, 182, 191, 197
Misingen, 63, 65, 67, 71
Mission Bay, 130–131, 135
Mitchell, Carlton, 276
Mollihawk, 191, 198
Monkey Point, 166–167
Moorings Company, The, 134, 191, 227, 230, 231, 233, 284
Morgan Out Island, 36, 108, 113–114
Motu Tofari, 229
Mount Baker, 26
Mount Hood, 27
Mount Rainier, 27
Mustique, 205
Mykonos, 92

Nantucket, 41, 44, 46, 50
Narragansett Bay, 43, 48, 51
Nassau, 147, 160
Nassau Harbor, 148–149, 154
Naushon Island, 47
Neuse River, 122, 124
Newfoundland, 27, 29–38, 50
New Jersey, 20, 25
Newman Sound, 31
Newport, 42, 48, 50
Newport Harbor, 125, 129, 132, 133, 135
Newport Yachting Center, 48
New Zealand, 239–255

Norfolk Harbor, 105
Norman Island, 173
North Atlantic cruises, 278–279
North Carolina, 122–123
Northeast Providence Channel, 150, 276
Northern California, 125–135
North Sea, 68, 74, 80, 83, 85, 86, 87
North Sound, 168
Northwest Passage, 19
Northwest Providence Channel, 155, 157, 276

Oak Bluffs, 41, 46
Old Perlican, 34
Old Point Comfort, 108
Olympic Mountains, 27
Opua, 243
Orcas Island, 28
Orient Bay, 184
Oslofjord, 22, 63, 68
Our Virgin Island (White), 167
Out Island, 36, 290

Pacific Northwest, 17–28, 125
Packer, Frank, 137–138
Pain de Sucre, 194
Panama, 93, 279, 280
Papagapitos, Vasos, 216
Parramatta River, 141
Patmos, 93, 95
Pedersen, Ray, 18
Peter Island, 174
Petit St. Vincent, 204–205, 206, 209
Philipsburg Harbor, 175, 177
Phuket, 256–270, 281
Pipe Creek, 153
Piraeus, 92, 94, 96, 99, 101
Pitt Water, 141
Plaza Islets, 223–226
Poros, 92, 99, 101
Port of Call Marina, 120
Portsmouth, 192, 193, 194
Port Townsend, 28
Post, Marjorie, 18
Prickly Pear Island, 168–169
Prideaux Haven, 19–20, 22
Princess, 289
Princeton Club of New York, 216
Prokos, Nick, 245
Puerto Ayora, 222
Puget Sound, 18, 26, 27, 28, 134

Quarterdeck Club, 169, 170

Raccoon Strait, 128
Raden Mas, 264–265, 266, 267, 294
Raiatea, 227, 230, 234, 236, 238, 255
Rainbow Yacht Charters, 243
Refuge Cove, 20
Rhode River, 110
Rhodes, 92, 93, 94, 95–96, 101
Riviera, 100, 101, 102
Road Town, 165, 173, 177
Robinson, Alice, 42, 43, 48
Robinson, Bill, 28, 67
Robinson, Jane, 18, 35, 42, 52, 63, 67, 72, 85, 86, 93, 111, 116, 119, 121, 130, 178, 181, 191, 219, 220, 227, 234, 242, 266, 290
Robinson, Robby, 48

Robinson, Will, 48
Roche Harbor, 28
Rose Island, 149–150
Rotterdam, 81, 83
Royal Cork Yacht Club, 87
Royal Newfoundland Yacht Club, 31, 36, 38
Royal Norwegian Yacht Club, 63
Royal Sydney Yacht Squadron, 137
Russell Peninsula, 245–246

Sabre 38, 42, 43
Sabrina II, 42, 47, 48
Sacramento River, 128
St. Barts, 184, 186, 187
St. Croix, 173
St. Francis Yacht Club, 127
St. Kitts, 179
St. Lucia, 191
St. Martin, 175–185, 189, 191, 209
St. Petersburg Beach, 118, 120
San Diego Harbor, 130–131, 135
Sandpiper, 115, 116, 121
Sandy Cay, 149
San Francisco Bay, 125, 127, 134, 135
San Juan Islands, 18
Santa Barbaras, 131
Santorini, 94
Sapphire Star, 163, 165, 174
Sardinia-Corsica area, 100, 101
Savary Island, 26
Scala Harbor, 94
Scandinavia, 63–75
Scandinavian moor, 20, 22, 65
Scott, Walter, 115–116, 118
Sea Cloud, 93–94, 214, 219, 220, 222, 223, 225, 226, 238, 278, 290, 291
Seyfarth, Fritz, 168
Shroud Cay, 153
Similan Islands, 258, 264
Singa, 258, 260, 263, 264, 265, 266–268, 294
Sir Francis Drake Channel, 169, 172
Sitting Ducks (Holman), 188
Skagerrak, 63–75
Skarv VII, 63, 68
Sloop Cove, 60
Smith Island, 107
Smith Sound, 32, 33
Sounion, 91, 92, 102
Southeast Asia, 269–270
Southern California, 125–135
Southern New England, 39–51
Southern Ocean Racing Circuit, 147
South Pacific, 253–255, 280–281
South Sea Yachts, 256
South to the Caribbean (Robinson), 194
Sow and Pigs Reef, 43
Spanish Wells, 151–152
SP Metalcraft Company, 18
Squirrel Cove, 22
Stag Cruise, 128
Stage Harbor, 41
Staniel Cay, 153, 160
Stave Island, 55, 56–57
Stephens, Olin, 139
Stirrup Cay, 155
Stone, Bill, 110
Stone, Herb, 110
Stormvogel, 263, 266, 294
Strait of Georgia, 17, 19, 23, 25–26, 28

Strait of Juan de Fuca, 27
Sunshine Coast, 26
Sunshine Skyway, 119, 120
Susquehanna River, 105, 106
Sydney, 136–144

Tahaa, 230, 231, 238
Tahiti, 219, 230, 238, 254, 280, 281
Tales of the Caribbean (Seyfarth), 168
Tampa Bay, 113, 115, 116–121, 123
Tanagra, 108, 113–114, 122, 147, 148, 152, 154, 290
Tangaroa, 218–219, 282
Tartan, 30, 52
Teakerne Arm, 23
Teavanui Pass, 232
Tenedos Bay, 18, 22
Terra Nova National Park, 31
Texada Island, 26
Theodoracopoulos, John, 96
Thormanby Island, 26
Tilghman Creek, 112
Tinsley Island, 128
Tobago Cays, 198–199, 200, 202, 204, 205, 206
Trellis, 166
Trinity, 33–34
Trinity Bay, 29, 30, 32, 33
Trouvier, Pascal, 258, 265, 267, 268
Trump, Donald, 289
Turkey, 94
Two on an Isle (White), 167

Unwin Range, 22

Valcour Lodge, 59–60
Valiant 40, 29
Vancouver, 17, 18
Vancouver, George, 18–19
Vancouver Island, 26, 27, 28
Van Ost, John, 284
Vashon Island, 28
Viatape, 227, 229, 230
Viking, 42, 46
Village Cay Marina, 173
Vim, 137–139
Vineyard Haven, 43, 44, 46
Virgin Gorda, 165, 168
Virgin Islands, 148, 275, 276, 280, 284, 286
Volendam, 83–85

Weistender Plassen, 76–80
West Redonda Island, 20, 22–23
Whatley, Paul, 173
"Where Cruising Was Invented" (Robinson), 39
Whidbey Island, 27
White, Robb, 167
Whitsunday Islands, 140, 243, 254, 255
Wiley, Marcia, 63, 67
Woods Hole, 44, 46, 50

Xanthous Nomad, 199, 205, 207

Yacht Haven, 148
Yachting, 44, 63, 85, 110, 284
Yachtsman's Guide, 151

Zaimis, George, 96, 99
Zea Marina, 96, 99

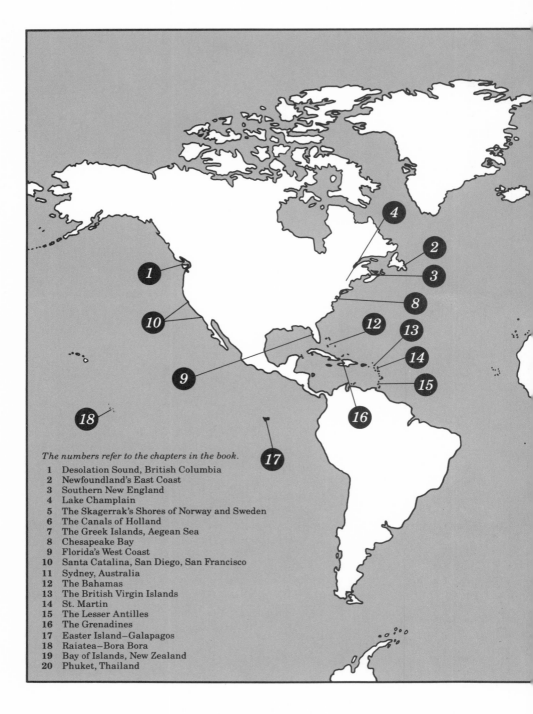

The numbers refer to the chapters in the book.

1   Desolation Sound, British Columbia
2   Newfoundland's East Coast
3   Southern New England
4   Lake Champlain
5   The Skagerrak's Shores of Norway and Sweden
6   The Canals of Holland
7   The Greek Islands, Aegean Sea
8   Chesapeake Bay
9   Florida's West Coast
10 Santa Catalina, San Diego, San Francisco
11 Sydney, Australia
12 The Bahamas
13 The British Virgin Islands
14 St. Martin
15 The Lesser Antilles
16 The Grenadines
17 Easter Island–Galapagos
18 Raiatea–Bora Bora
19 Bay of Islands, New Zealand
20 Phuket, Thailand